RAT LINE

Other Books by Robert McCurdy

Dog Robber

RAT
LINE

ROBERT MC CURDY

RED ANVIL PRESS
OAKLAND

RED ANVIL PRESS

1393 Old Homestead Drive, Second floor
Oakland, Oregon 97462—9506.
E-MAIL: editor@elderberrypress.com
TEL/FAX: 541.459.6043
http://elderberrypress.com

All Red Anvil books are available from your favorite bookstore, amazon.com,
or from our 24 hour order line: 1.800.431.1579

Library of Congress Control Number: 2007928459

Publisher's Catalog—in—Publication Data
Rat Line/Robert McCurdy
ISBN-13: 978-1-932762-80-8
ISBN-10: 1-932762809

1. WWII—fiction.
2. Military—fiction.
3. Occupation—fiction.
4. Post-war Germany—fiction.
5. Spy—fiction.
I. Title

This book was written, printed and bound in the United States of America.

Dedicated to my readers,
who communicated to me their favorable reviews of Dog Robber,
and who have been awaiting
the further adventures of Jim Colling;

And to my wife, Margie, who once again was my best critic.

PROLOGUE

JUNE, 1947

During his flight training on the B-29, Captain Bill Caldwell's instructors had repeatedly reminded him that the "Super Fort" was the biggest and best airplane in the world. It could fly faster, higher and farther than anything else in the air. Now, seated at the controls of his very own B-29, *The Sassy Lassie,* Caldwell found himself, as he often did, mentally comparing the larger bomber to the B-17's he had flown over Germany during the war. The huge plane was a bitch on take-off and landing, but a honey once it reached altitude. The four powerful Wright Cyclone engines seemed to Caldwell to be actually humming at 35,000 feet. The pressurized cabin meant that oxygen masks were for emergency use only, and the drafty cold of a B-17 was only an unpleasant memory. Caldwell had to admit that the lavish praise he had heard heaped on the '29 by pilots who had flown them in the Far East was not far off the mark.

Caldwell looked down at the expanse of water below them. The sky was cloudless, and the sun reflected from the Baltic in a dazzling play of light. It was a good day for flying, no one was shooting at them, and all-in-all, Caldwell was content. They were almost half-way through their flight plan, and his thoughts drifted to his wife and son waiting for him at the base in England. The Air Force had just recently allowed dependents to join lower-ranking officers who were stationed in Europe, and he and Doris were still becoming re-acquainted after months of separation. He found that getting to know his wife all over again was an experience that he enjoyed.

He calculated that after refueling in Norway, they would be home late the next day. He glanced over at Lieutenant Al Hammerslee, whom Caldwell still thought of as his co-pilot, even though the Air Force had decided that the lieutenant's official designation as part of the B-29 crew should be "pilot." Caldwell himself carried the title of "aircraft commander," but he continued to find it hard to think of himself as anything but the aircraft's pilot, and consequently felt it was his duty to spend the majority of their time in the air flying the bomber himself.

Hammerslee was obviously doing his best to keep from falling asleep. Out of the corner of his eye, Caldwell could see his co-pilot's chin first drop to his chest, then be jerked back upright as the lieutenant tried to remain awake. His lethargy was contagious, and Caldwell decided that he would let him take the controls on the return flight, and use one of the bunks to catch some sleep.

Their orders called for them to come within sight of the coast, then begin a long turn to the east and north, eventually circling so as to retrace their steps northwestward. They were instructed to stay well out over the water, beyond the three-mile limit. Radio silence was being observed, and so far, Caldwell had not heard any indication from his radar officer that the Russians had sent any interceptors to greet them. Caldwell had never flown this same pattern previously, and as he understood it, this kind of flight by an Air Force B-29 flight was unusual.

He and Hammerslee had been briefed on the mission in private, with the understanding that the rest of the aircraft's crew did not need to know about their destination and purpose. The two officers were told that the Navy had been conducting similar flights for some time, and that the Soviet response was consistent. As soon as they were a few miles from land, Soviet fighter planes would appear and shadow them, following the B-29 at the interceptors' lower maximum altitude, and breaking off only when the bomber turned back over the Baltic. The Navy commander who briefed them had remarked that so far, none of the Soviet fighters had fired on the American planes; but Caldwell could not dismiss the thought from his mind that one of the Russian pilots might decide to test whether it was possible to shoot down an American Super Fortress.

Relations between the U.S. and Russia had cooled significantly, and Caldwell concurred, from his perspective, with Churchill's assessment that an iron curtain had descended around Eastern Europe. Caldwell also admitted to himself that the U.S. was playing its own game with the Russians. Some were saying that certain American actions were "provocative," and that the Navy flights over the Baltic fell into that category. Officially, they were simply on a routine training flight; unofficially, they were a "ferret" intended to test the Russians' reaction to an aerial approach to their territory, and discover the nature, location and extent of their electronic warning systems.

When he had learned that his plane would be assigned to probing missions, Caldwell had speculated about the reasons why the Air Force had become involved. One reason might be inter-service rivalry with the Navy; as well as because the Air Force was in sole possession of America's long-range bombing capability. Equally likely, Caldwell thought, someone at the Pentagon had deemed it necessary that heavy bomber crews have the kind of practical experience that would be needed if war with the USSR became a reality.

The bomber's machine-guns, as well as the men required to man them, had been left behind to reduce the plane's normal weight and increase speed and altitude. This made Caldwell particularly apprehensive that they would be defenseless should they encounter Soviet interceptors superior to the ones they had seen so far. It was true that the Russian fighters described by the Navy commander who briefed them would probably not be able to match their altitude, but Caldwell believed that it would only be a matter of time before the Soviets had jet fighters, or they figured out how to outfit the older Yak or MIG propeller-driven types with improved engines.

He had heard his flight engineer, a veteran master sergeant named Buscombe, routinely insist, when the abilities of Soviet planes came up for discussion, that the American-made Lend-Lease P-39's could easily be up-graded to fly at 35,000 feet. That on-going argument would not be a feature of today's mission, however, since Buscombe had come down with some unspecified illness prior to their taking off, and had been replaced by a young sergeant with whom Caldwell had not flown before.

The electronics aspect of their mission was handled by three men Caldwell thought of as "the technicians." While they were classified as members of the B-29's flight crew, they were considered, to some extent, to be outsiders. The *Sassy Lassie* had made three practice flights over the North Sea before this mission, and the

bomber crew had been repeatedly reminded that what the technicians assigned to their plane were doing was classified as top secret,
and there was no off-duty social contact with them. The technicians
kept to themselves, and aside from friendly, but cursory, greetings
when boarding and disembarking, Caldwell had had no conversations with any of them, so that the details of what they actually did
remained a mystery.

Even though his immediate thoughts had been straying to other
subjects, Caldwell was continuously observing the instrument panel
in front of him. He leaned forward in disbelief when he saw the fuel
gauges for both tanks suddenly drop precipitously. He flipped the
switch for the reserves and saw the same result. He shouted for the
flight engineer, and the young sergeant who had replaced Buscombe
was suddenly crouched beside him.

"Jesus!" said Caldwell, "We're losing fuel. Get back there and
find out what's going on."

"Right, sir. I'm on my way."

Hammerslee was suddenly alert, scanning the instrument panel
himself, "Sir, everything else looks okay. Only thing that's a problem
is the fuel. Right now it looks like we're going to have to ditch in
the water."

"I know, Al. Get back there with that sergeant, whatever his name
is, and see what's going on. We're losing fuel somewhere."

Hammerslee unfastened his seat belt and clambered out of the
cockpit. Caldwell's mind was racing, watching the fuel gauges and
trying to simultaneously figure out how and why they would suddenly begin losing gasoline and whether they could make it to a
friendly airfield. The needles were resting on the empty mark, and
Caldwell calculated that he was not going to be able to keep the
bomber in the air much longer. The apparent choices were to crash
into the sea, or to land in what he believed was Poland. He delayed
their planned turn to parallel the coast, and held the bomber on
a course that would take them inland. At the same time, Caldwell
decided that a controlled descent was preferable to losing power at
35,000 feet, and began to reduce altitude.

He was suddenly aware that someone was beside him, and

glanced up to see the senior technician, a major.

"What's happening, Captain?"

"We're losing fuel, sir. Flight engineer's checking, but it doesn't look like we'll have enough to get us to Sweden, even if we can stop the loss."

"We have documents and equipment on board that can't fall into the hands of the Russians, Captain," said the major.

"You'd better jettison everything then, sir, as soon as you can."

The major pushed himself away to the rear of the plane, leaving Caldwell alone. The engines continued to hum, and he waited for the first signs of hesitancy and sputtering that would signal that the propellers would cease to turn. The altimeter showed they were below 25,000 feet.

There was a commotion as Hammerslee returned to the cockpit, the major close behind him. Hammerslee reported, "Bill, there's nothing we can see that accounts for the fuel loss. No sign of a spill outside, no spray, nothing."

The major did not wait for Hammerslee to finish before he said, "Captain, we're dumping our documents, but we can't find the wrench we need to undo the bolts holding our equipment in place. It's disappeared." Pointing through the forward windshield, he shouted, "You have to turn back over the sea and take her down there."

Still concentrating on the feel of the aircraft and the instrument panel, Caldwell suggested, "Why not just smash your gear up, sir?"

"We can't do that, Captain. It's rigged with an explosive that could tear the plane in two. In a few moments, we'll be well inland. You have to turn this plane around so it goes down in the sea."

"Sir, begging your pardon, but the Baltic is freezing even at this time of year. If we ditch, most or all of us could be dead within the hour, assuming we live through the crash."

"But the equipment can't fall into Russian hands," insisted the major.

Hammerslee interjected, "It doesn't look like we have a choice," pointing out the cockpit's windshield.

Two Russian fighters had taken up positions on either side of them, close enough that they could see the pilot on their right, the lower part of his face concealed by an oxygen mask, gesturing downward, towards the ground.

Caldwell heard a voice in his earphones, "Sir, there's some more Russkies above and behind us."

He looked out to see sand dunes and houses passing below, and heard the major excitedly demanding that he get the bomber back over the sea. He initiated the turn, knowing that doing so would burn more of their fast-diminishing supply of gasoline, but as soon as he began to alter course, a stream of tracers crossed his line of sight, causing him to reflexively turn back to his original course.

Caldwell cursed to himself that without the bomber's machine-guns, they had nothing with which to defend themselves. Another voice in his ear-phones reminded him that there were Russian inter-ceptors closing on them from above and behind, which would even-tually force him to further reduce altitude to avoid a collision.

The major was shouting at him to crash the plane into the ground, so that Caldwell had to raise his own voice to tell his radioman to signal their position and their situation. Despite the major's demands, he made up his mind. If it was to be land or crash, Caldwell chose to keep himself and his crew alive. He began his approach to the airfield towards which the Russian fighters were shepherding him.

Chapter 1

Three Months Earlier....
March, 1947

Almost immediately upon his arrival in Munich, Technician Fourth Class James T. Colling had been ordered by Major Vincent, the chief administrative officer of Colling's unit, the 511th General Hospital, to be arrested and transported to the military police stockade.

As Colling had been escorted past the booking desk, he had noticed the similarity of the MP facility to a Chicago police precinct house that he had once visited. Despite the many other thoughts swirling in his mind, Colling found himself surveying his surroundings and speculating whether he was correct in his observation that the former *Kriminalpolizei* station that the American Military Police had appropriated from the defeated Germans had been refurbished to comport with U.S. standards.

He had been placed in a large windowless holding cage that at first had held no inmates other than himself. The lower half of three brick walls of the cell were painted white, while the fourth side was taken up by a set of steel bars running from floor to ceiling, with the cell's door set in its center.

With little else to do, he had stretched out on one of the steel benches bolted to the walls and tried unsuccessfully to sleep. At some point, a guard had brought him a Bakelite plate containing a bologna sandwich and an aluminum canteen cup full of water. He had been required to turn over his wristwatch with the rest of his personal effects, so he could not be certain as to the time, but he had surmised that the evening was wearing on, when other prisoners were brought in to join him, and that it must be getting close to midnight.

He was now sharing the cell with five other American soldiers, all exhibiting signs of intoxication and having been engaged in various degrees of activity that Colling was aware policemen called "disorderly conduct." Fortunately, it was a week night, or the cell might have had more occupants.

Despite frequent predictions in the past that he would someday end up where he now found himself, this was, in fact, the first time that Colling had seen the inside of a prison cell, civilian or military. He did not count the few days he had spent in the British detention center in Lübeck just before returning to Munich. That had been a necessary result of having shown up suddenly, without proper identity papers, in the British Zone of occupation, following a harrowing four-day voyage across the Baltic from Poland in a battered fishing boat. The British had not charged him with anything, even though they had threatened that they might return him and his traveling companions to the Soviet authorities. His present situation was different. Major Vincent had ordered him jailed on charges of desertion.

While the MP's who had placed him under arrest had seemed sympathetic to his situation, regulations regarding prisoners had to be followed. Consequently, before they confined him, they had taken not only his watch, wallet and the other contents of his pockets, but his duffel bag as well. They also made him remove his uniform jacket. Apparently, they did not consider him a suicide candidate, and left him his belt and shoelaces. He was now seated on his bench, in his shirtsleeves, without the chevrons that denoted his rank, just another prisoner.

Colling had resigned himself to having to accept the consequences due him for being over five months late in returning from furlough. He had to admit that he had been fortunate that arrangements had been made for him to voluntarily report to the 511th, rather than allowing him to be picked up as a deserter. By letting him walk in on his own, it was possible that he would be deemed to have been AWOL, theoretically subject to a lesser degree of punishment.

What Colling had not anticipated was his having to answer to Major Vincent. The last time Colling had seen the major, the man had been the commanding officer of an infantry battalion in which

Colling was serving as a medic. That had been last fall, and Colling had been lead to believe that Vincent would be leaving active duty by the end of the year. Instead, he had turned up as a medical administrative officer assigned to the hospital to which Colling was now also assigned. Major Vincent had been unhappy with Colling from the time that they first met one another. The major was of the opinion that Colling had received special treatment when he had returned late from a previous furlough, and it was now apparent that the major intended to take the opportunity that had presented itself to settle the score.

In the morning, or perhaps the day after, he imagined he would be summoned before Vincent and would learn what the officer intended for him. Before leaving Lübeck, Colling had been promised that even though the 90-day limit that the Army deemed the demarcation between AWOL and desertion had been exceeded, that if he would return voluntarily, and then request and accept summary punishment, he would be able to avoid a prison sentence and a dishonorable discharge. Now with Vincent in the picture, he was concerned that things might not turn out as he had been told they would.

Despite the gloomy prospects facing him, Colling had no regrets about absenting himself from duty for such a protracted period of time. The reasons had been real and important to him from a personal standpoint. At the time, he would not have said that love was his motive for doing what he did, although he might have admitted to infatuation with a pretty face and figure.

Soon after his arrival in Germany at war's end, he had met and immediately fallen for Elizabeth Hamilton, an attractive blonde American Red Cross girl. In retrospect, he was not completely sure who had been the pursued and who the pursuer, but they had shared a passionate time together. She had convinced him, against Army regulations and his better judgment, to go with her to Poland, disguised as an American officer, in order to help a relative of hers come to the West. He later realized that she had chosen him for the task primarily because of his fluency in both German and Polish.

The Soviets occupying Poland had proven more difficult than

Elizabeth had predicted, and the escape from Poland; not with one relative, but with three men, had been a close-run affair. It was after the fact that Colling learned that Elizabeth was not acting out of familial loyalty. Rather, the three Polish men that they had rescued were not related to her, but were scientists whose specialties were deemed valuable to American atom bomb research. When Elizabeth failed to return his correspondence after their return to Germany, Colling had been disappointed, but had come to accept that she had no genuine affection for him.

Elizabeth had been acting on the orders of a military intelligence organization of which Colling still understood very little. He knew that a lieutenant colonel named Andrew Quarles was in charge, at least regarding its German and Eastern European operations; and that Quarles' office was in Heidelberg. It had been Quarles to whom Colling had gone when he read a newspaper item about Elizabeth's death in a jeep accident. He learned from Quarles that the accident was faked, and that Elizabeth was, in fact, confined in a Russian prison camp in Poland.

Quarles saw Elizabeth's situation as hopeless, but Colling decided to return to Poland on his own and attempt to find and free her. His first venture behind the Iron Curtain had taught him things about himself that he would not previously have imagined possible. He came to realize that he possessed a talent and ability to deceive, to react to danger, and to adapt to an unexpected or changing situation with success. He had, in addition, learned what it was like to kill another human being.

Those skills had been put to the test when he re-entered Poland to attempt to rescue Elizabeth. With some help from Quarles and Polish anti-Communists, he had managed to locate Elizabeth and spirit her out of the hands of the NKVD, the Soviet secret police. It had taken longer than he had anticipated...almost six months, far in excess of his allotted furlough. Because Lieutenant Colonel Quarles had received inaccurate information to the effect that both Elizabeth and he had been caught by the NKVD and killed before she could be rescued, the intelligence officer did not arrange for any cover story for his absence. Consequently, he had been listed by the

Army as a deserter. Their turning up in Lübeck had been a surprise to Quarles, and it had been impossible for the officer to use his influence to have the charges against Colling dropped. Now it remained to be seen whether the advice he had received from Quarles would remain valid with Major Vincent acting as Colling's judge and jury. The prospect of serving out his enlistment in an Army prison sent a chill down Colling's spine.

The other soldiers with Colling in the holding cage all exhibited signs of having drunk too much. One man was lying face down, asleep on the floor on the far side of the cage, near the channel in the floor that ran the length of one wall and served as a urinal. It appeared that he had attempted to throw up into the trough, but had missed, and his head was now surrounded by a puddle of vomit. His snores were audible, but not as loud as the combined cacophony emitted by two soldiers who were sleeping, slumped against each other on one of the other three steel benches attached to the cell's wall. A fourth man was stretched out on his back on one of the other benches, his eyes closed, apparently sleeping. The last of Colling's companions was a young soldier who would intermittently pace back and forth, then seat himself on the bench nearest to Colling's, all the time moaning and holding his head.

The man whom Colling had thought was sleeping suddenly shouted, "For Christ's sake, would you just shut the hell up!"

In response, the pacing soldier moaned and sat down, both hands pressed tightly to his temples. After a moment, he moaned again. Then he let out a peculiar cry that Colling remembered having heard before, and fell onto his back on the floor. Colling reacted quickly, lunging to try and keep the man's head from striking the concrete. He was unsure as to whether he had done so or not, but began bellowing for the guard, even as he slid his left arm under the young soldier's shoulders, holding him as he jerked violently, and his heels drummed the floor.

Except for the man lying in his own vomit, the other prisoners had been suddenly brought to life by the noise and confusion, and Colling shouted to them to call for the guard, causing all three of them to simultaneously rush to the bars and scream for help.

An MP came running, then froze as he saw Colling and the soldier on the floor.

"Get medical help!" shouted Colling, "He's having a seizure."

The MP hesitated, seeming to be considering whether he should follow the orders of a prisoner. He stepped closer to the bars, as if trying to make an assessment of his own before doing what Colling had asked. When he did, Colling saw that the MP had a pencil in one hand, and a folded section of newspaper in his other that could only mean that he had been working on a crossword puzzle. Colling shouted to the guard to give him the pencil, causing the MP to raise his hand and look at it. In an instant, one of the other prisoners snatched the pencil away and tossed it to Colling. Colling gave instructions to the nearest inmate about how to keep the writhing soldier's head from hitting the floor, and when the man followed Colling's directions, Colling pulled his own arm free and pried the seizing man's teeth apart, using his fingers to work the soldier's tongue up and forward and then shoved the pencil in between his teeth..

The spasms from the seizure ended suddenly, but Colling was still on his knees, helping to hold the young soldier's head when he heard the latch on the cell door clatter, and he turned his head, saying, "Would you please get some medical help?"

He looked up to see a man wearing a white coat over an Army uniform beside him. "Will I do for medical help, Soldier?"

"Yessir," said Colling, seeing the first lieutenant's bar on the collar of the man's shirt; and immediately recognizing that he was speaking to a physician. "Sorry, sir, but I didn't know the MPs had called the medics."

"That they did, for another guy who had his head laid open with a billy stick," said the doctor, as he knelt beside Colling and began examining the young soldier. "What happened?" he asked.

"Just a guess, sir, but I think it was an epileptic seizure."

"You a trained doctor, soldier?"

"No sir, but I have seen an epileptic fit before."

"Where was that?" asked the doctor, pulling up the unconscious soldier's eyelids and checked the dilation of his pupils.

"Back home, sir. In my dad's drug store. We had a customer who used to forget to take his Phenobarbital, and he had some seizures in the store. It scared hell out of the other customers."

"What's your name, Son?"

"James Colling, sir. Tech four, sir."

The doctor glanced at Colling's shirt, and seeing no insignia, asked, "You assigned to the medics?"

"Yessir, 511th."

Two men carrying a stretcher had arrived, and Colling and the lieutenant stood out of the way as the young soldier was lifted onto it.

"I'm Lieutenant Kenworth, Colling."

"Good to meet you, sir."

"I'm at the 511th, too. What are you doing in here?"

"AWOL, sir. I go up for my court in the morning, so I've been told."

"Well, I'll put in a good word for you with the hospital CO. 'Colling,' is it? I don't imagine it will save your stripes, but you did okay."

"Thanks, sir. And sir, could you tell me what your diagnosis is?"

"Yeah. Not epilepsy, per se, but I did feel a big lump on his right temple. My guess is these guys were in a fight, and the combination of too much to drink and a blow to the head triggered the seizure. When we get some x-rays, we may know more. But you did the right thing. A seizure is a seizure when it comes to first aid."

As Kenworth stepped through the door to the cell, his way was blocked by an MP wearing master sergeant's chevrons. The sergeant asked, a hint of concern in his voice, "Is he going to be all right, sir?"

The Lieutenant answered, pointing to Colling, "It could have been a lot worse if that man hadn't known what to do. You owe him. I'd suggest you might want to move him out of this piss-hole cage and into his own cell. And treat him right."

The NCO nodded his head and said, "Will do, sir. Thank you."

As soon as the doctor had departed, the MP master sergeant

pulled aside the door to the cell and motioned to Colling to come out. As they walked down the hall towards the booking area, the sergeant said, "My name is McNeese. I'm the non-commissioned officer in charge here. I'm going to do what the doctor asked, and we'll put you in your own cell. The bunk has a mattress, and you'll have your own sink and commode. I would appreciate it if you wouldn't mention it to that major over at the hospital. He told us to put you in with the drunks. He's a real horse's ass."

McNeese turned Colling over to a corporal, who retrieved Colling's duffel bag and uniform jacket from a locker, handed them to him, and led him to the building's cellar. The corporal commented, "Sarge's real nervous. The doc warned him that one more bad thing, and he'd take it up with the Provost Marshal."

"What for? Why would the lieutenant go to the Military Police commanding officer?" asked Colling.

"One guy tried to hang himself last week. Luckily we caught him just in time. We are told he ain't dead, but he is getting' a discharge and a ride to a VA hospital in the States. And night before last, some yo-yo rams his head into the drunk cage wall…fractured skull. And tonight the doc has to come over and sew up an obnoxious son-of-a-bitch that jumped Kelly, who had to tap him a few times with his stick to reason with him."

At the foot of the staircase leading to the station's basement, the corporal turned right and led Colling to the first cell in the hallway. As he opened its door, said, "Your home away from home."

Colling thanked him and dropped his duffel on the bunk. A minute later, the MP returned and handed Colling a stack of bed linens and a towel, then closed the door behind him. Colling unrolled the cot's mattress and used the sheets to make his bed. He knew the hour was late, but decided to write a letter to his parents back home in Bel Cors. Before he had left for Poland the previous fall, he had written to tell them that he was being assigned to the field on "maneuvers," and would have few opportunities to correspond.

Considering that over five months had passed without his writing, he was certain that they must be concerned. Quarles had informed Colling when they arrived in Lübeck that he had not communicated to Coling's parents his own belief that Coling was dead. As a result, Coling had wondered what they must be thinking about such a long stretch passing with no correspondence of any kind. He had penned a short note before flying out of Hamburg, telling them that he had been unexpectedly delayed in a remote training area, and had not had a chance to write more. Now he penned a longer letter, seeking to reassure them that he was in good health and having no problems with Army life. He debated whether to include any information about his pending court martial, but decided to defer discussion of that subject until he knew what was going to happen.

After Coling had finished addressing the letter to his parents, he decided that as he had his writing portfolio out, he might as well also write to Elizabeth. In his jacket pocket, he found the folded piece of paper with her U.S. address that she had given him when they said goodbye in Hamburg. He hesitated before beginning, unsure about what he should say. He avoided mentioning his incarceration, opting instead for a general statement that he was doing well, then going on to say how much he missed her, that he loved her, and expressing his anticipation that they might some day be married. When the missive was concluded, he re-read it, and decided he sounded silly. He was about to tear it up when he changed his mind. He folded the letter and inserted it into its envelope before dropping heavily into his cot.

Coling's cell had a small window near the ceiling, and when the sun shining on his face light woke him, he climbed out of the bunk. He stripped, and using a washcloth from his duffel bag, cleaned himself at the sink. Afterwards, he shaved; and then put on his uniform. He had placed his trousers between his mattress and the steel base of the cot when he made up his bed, and they were able to pass for having been pressed. His jacket still looked presentable, more so after he had touched up the shine on its brass collar insignia. When he had dressed, he was about to call for a guard when the cell door opened, revealing two MP's whom he did not recognize.

One of them, a sergeant, gestured for him to come out of the cell. "Come on," he said, "Sergeant McNeese says we're to take you to the mess hall for breakfast. If you promise not to try anything funny, we won't cuff you."

Colling readily agreed.

The two military policemen flanked him as they walked down the block and eventually turned into the arched tunnel-like entrance of a large gray-walled barracks. A sign beside the entrance proclaimed it to be "Spaulding Kaserne." They crossed the flag-stoned courtyard to a set of doors marked by a "Consolidated Mess" sign.

The MP's cleared Colling with the NCO checking meal tickets at the head of the serving line, and picked up trays themselves as Colling took his. He selected scrambled eggs, sausage, toast and oatmeal. At the end of the line, there were pitchers containing juice and coffee, and Colling helped himself.

The three of them sat together at a table. Aside from some brief comments regarding the food, the military policemen said little, and Colling decided that it was best not to attempt to converse. Neither MP said anything until they had finished and were retracing their steps across the quadrangle, when one of them asked, "What you expect they're gonna give you?"

Colling replied, "No idea. But at least I got a full stomach. Thanks, you guys; and tell Sergeant McNeese the same."

Both of his guards laughed. The one who had spoken first commented, "Don't be thankin' us too quick, Soldier. Condemned man always gets a great meal before the hangin'."

Colling smiled and nodded his head in agreement with the MP, but inside, he felt a twinge of unease as he pondered how pertinent the man's words might be.

CHAPTER 2

MARCH-APRIL, 1947

Colling was escorted by the two MP's to the administrative headquarters of the 511th General Hospital. As he was led through the outer office, he returned the nod of the tech-five at the reception desk whom he had seen when he was escorted to the stockade the day before. The man had signaled to Colling, as he was being taken away, that he had secreted Colling's suitcase under his desk. Now, as Colling was brought in, the only piece of luggage that Colling was carrying was his duffel bag, and he dropped it next to the clerk's desk. The suitcase that Colling had left with him contained Colling's money and his Luger, which had engendered some apprehension on Colling's part about the clerk's honesty. While Colling's mind was not completely at ease, he was comforted to some degree by the fact that the man had concealed the case. Colling speculated that the tech-five might be motivated by a personal dislike for Major Vincent.

The Major was behind his desk. Colling came to attention in front of him and saluted. He was aware that the military policemen had taken up positions behind him on either side of the door.

Before Colling could speak, Vincent, with an undisguised expression of distaste, said, "Well, Colling, despite my fervent desire to send you up for a general court martial, I've been told you intend to ask for a summary court and company punishment. Is that true?"

"Yessir. I request summary court martial, plead guilty, and request that you impose company punishment."

"You realize that I could deny your request, especially since you have been absent for 158 days. That qualifies as desertion."

Colling replied, "Yessir. I understand. But I did return to duty of my own accord."

Vincent had removed his glasses and was holding them in his right hand, looking back and forth from Colling to a file that lay open on the desk in front of him, seeming to be wrestling with his irritation. Colling thought that he could actually hear the officer gritting his teeth. There was a quiet cough behind Colling, which at first he thought had come from one of the MP's. Then Colling realized that the sound had come from further to his right. Vincent glanced up from the manila folder towards the source of the cough. Despite the urge to turn to see who might be behind him, Colling continued to stand rigidly at attention, his gaze fixed just above the major's balding head, concentrating on a picture of General Patton that was hanging on the wall behind the desk.

After more study of the file, Vincent spoke, "While I am not entirely happy to have to do so, Colling, I have been asked to accept your plea and determine that you have been absent without leave."

Colling breathed a silent sigh of relief as Vincent went on, "Since there is no dispute about your guilt, I intend to impose the maximum degree of punishment that I can, short of imprisonment in the stockade, which I have been told is not within my power."

As Colling listened to what Vincent was saying, it came to him that Quarles must have been at work behind the scenes. Someone had limited the major's authority. There was another cough from behind him, and Vincent went on, "You are hereby reduced to the rank of private. All pay and allowances for a period of 180 days are forfeited."

Having pronounced sentence, as it were, Vincent, seemingly less fractious, smiled thinly as he continued, "I would like to put you on permanent latrine and floor-scrubbing duty for an extended period, but I am informed that your medical skills are needed. I have given it some thought, and have decided that you will be assigned to regular duties, but that you will also serve guard duty for 60 days. Should you be found to be derelict in your duties while on guard, I will impose an additional day for each day you are found to have committed an infraction. Do you understand?"

Colling's mind was reeling. What Vincent was demanding was that he work all day as a medic, then again all night standing guard duty. Taken literally, there would be no time for sleep, and if Vincent found even an unpolished button or a smudged shoe, then he could add another day to his sentence. For a moment, he considered protesting, but then answered, "Yessir, I understand."

Vincent dismissed him, and Colling saluted and turned on his heel. As he did so, he observed a heavyset man with a touch of gray at his temples seated in a chair that had been positioned behind him. He was wearing an officer's shirt and trousers, but no jacket, and was turned in such a way that Colling could not make out the rank insignia on his right collar. Colling could see the officer's left shirt collar, however, and he was wearing the caduceus, consisting of a staff entwined by two serpents, indicating that he was a physician. The officer, a grim expression on his face, watched Colling as he strode out of Vincent's office.

Once they had ushered him out to the reception area, the MP's nodded a silent farewell to Colling, and departed. Colling stood in the middle of the room, uncertain about what to do next, when the clerk came from behind his desk and said, "I'm Joe Willoughby. I got your suitcase. When you get settled, you can pick it up, but right now's not a good time. Follow me and I'll show you where you bunk."

Colling picked up his duffel bag and trailed Willoughby out of the office. The 511th General Hospital consisted of a group of modern gray-painted stucco buildings that Colling guessed might have been constructed during the Nazi regime. Willoughby gave a running commentary as they traversed the building's corridors. The hospital's patient rooms and wards, clinics, offices and other components were contained in the largest, a four-story structure. The top two floors at one end of the building had been allocated as billets for enlisted personnel. Colling was later to learn that the two-story building behind the larger one housed the hospital's male officers and nurses on separate floors; and that there was a warehouse and garage behind the main structure. A black wrought-iron fence, its base bordered by a narrow strip of grass and shrubs, surrounded the entire complex.

Willoughby showed Colling to a squad bay containing twelve steel bunks, telling him that there were eleven other lower-ranking men assigned to the room. The tech-five pointed out Colling's bed, and the wall locker and foot locker that went with it. Before leaving, Willoughby informed Colling that he was to report to the outpatient dispensary on the first floor as soon as he had unpacked. The clerk's last words to him were a reminder to remove the tech-four chevrons from his uniforms as soon as possible.

Colling unpacked his belongings and made up his bunk. Fortunately it was not a double decker, so that he would not have anyone sleeping above or below him. A set of field equipment, including a helmet painted with Medical Corps red crosses in white circles, was already in the wall locker, and Colling assumed that he would, before long, be asked by a supply sergeant to sign for the gear.

The first floor hallway outside the outpatient dispensary was crowded with soldiers when Colling found his way to it. All the available chairs were occupied, and at least a dozen soldiers were standing or leaning against the corridor walls. They stared listlessly at Colling as he entered the treatment room.

A blonde nurse wearing major's insignia, and who Colling estimated to be in her middle thirties, was bandaging the hand of a soldier seated in a chair. She looked away from her task and at Colling and said, "Write your name on that clip-board, then wait outside."

Colling replied, "I'm Colling, ma'am. I'm assigned here as medic."

"Oh, good. There's a white jacket in that drawer over there. Put it on and take over here and finish dressing this. He's got a grease burn."

As Colling began wrapping the man's hand, the nurse said, "My name is Lucille Elliott. If you can do the work, you'll stay here. If you screw up, I'll see that you're re-assigned to one of the wards as an aide. Understand?"

"Yes ma'am."

Major Elliott picked up the clip-board and shouted a name into the hallway. A moment later, a PFC with a pronounced limp came in. As the man took a seat, the nurse opened a file cabinet and searched until she located a folder. She flipped it open and remarked that the soldier had been in two weeks earlier complaining of a pain in his wrist. She asked him today's reason for reporting on sick call, and he responded somewhat sheepishly that his ankle was hurting. She told him to remove the shoe and sock from his injured foot. When the PFC's foot was bare, she felt it, working up to his ankle, and asked whether the man was experiencing any pain. He yelped when she pushed upward on his toes. Some further probing, and the major asked if he had twisted his ankle. When the man replied that he thought he had, she told him he might have a mild sprain, but she was sending him to the doctor in the Casualty Ward for his opinion. If it was just a sprain, they would probably send him back to have his ankle taped.

While the major was conducting her examination, Colling had finished his bandaging. He confirmed the burned soldier's identity, and found the man's medical file folder on the table beside him. Colling made an appropriate entry as he had been trained to do, and after completing a release-from-duty form good for 24 hours, told the man he could return to his unit and take it easy for the rest of the day. Colling then found the next name on the list on the clip-board, and called it out.

Colling had pulled the new patient's medical folder from the file cabinet before the man had fully seated himself. While Major Elliott was finishing with the PFC with the twisted ankle, Colling listened as the soldier, a Sergeant Pullam, complained of a sore throat, and then, using a tongue depressor, Colling was able to see considerable inflammation. He handed the sergeant's folder to the major, asking if she thought an injection of penicillin was in order. She made her own examination of Pullam's throat, then told Colling to give him 600,000 units of the antibiotic. As Colling prepared the drug for administration, Major Elliott called in the next patient.

They continued working together in this fashion for the remainder of the morning. By noon, the line of soldiers reporting for sick call had disappeared, and Colling began cleaning up the dispensary as Major Elliott sat at her desk and completed the charts of the men seen that day, as well as other paperwork mandated by

Army regulations.

After the first couple of patients, it had become apparent to Colling that the hospital was holding sick call for a fairly large number of smaller Army units based in Munich that did not have their own medical detachments. While most of the problems for which the soldiers sought treatment were simple, he had been surprised at the freedom and authority that Major Elliott exercised in making decisions and prescribing medications. She had even asked him to suture three laceration cases, one of which Colling would have referred to a physician in his previous assignments. Nevertheless, he had put in the stitches, satisfied that there had been no damaged blood vessels needing repair, and making sure that the closure of the wound was neat and clean.

As if reading his thoughts, the major, while continuing to write entries on the forms in front of her, said, "We've got a shortage of doctors, Colling. That's why the CO gave me the authority to order drugs. I only send someone to Casualty if it looks like it's over my head."

"Yes, ma'am," replied Colling, "Captain Lewisohn was my CO at my last assignment, and he told me to go ahead and dispense on my own, except for penicillin and narcotics. I had to call him on the phone if I needed any of those."

"Did he ever turn you down?" asked the nurse.

Colling paused for a moment, thinking, and then replied, "You know, Ma'am, he never did."

The major asked, "Did he teach you how to handle sick call?"

"Not really, ma'am. I picked that up when I was a medic with the 40th Infantry, at Grabensheim. Then after that, I got assigned as the only medic at a DP camp near there, Camp 146...unless someone has given the place a name since I was there. I had to take care of most things myself. Dr. Lewisohn was at the regimental aid station in Kummersfeld, fifteen miles away. I called him with anything I couldn't handle by myself."

"I notice you sew a mean stitch. Where did you pick that up? Were you a combat medic?" asked the major.

"No ma'am. I came in too late for that. They signed the Japanese surrender while I was on my way to the 40th." Deciding further explanation was needed, Colling continued, "There were two Polish doctors at the DP camp. They were there to take care of the camp inmates.

"I speak a little Polish, so they took a liking to me and taught me a lot. They let me assist at surgery, and after awhile, they let me close incisions on surgical patients. I probably shouldn't admit it, but also I assisted at some deliveries, one was a C-section."

Major Elliott finished writing and as she recapped her fountain pen, said, "You know, Colling, the Colonel told me when he informed me you'd be assigned to me, that you were a pretty fair medic. So far, so good."

"Thanks, ma'am. But you should know that I'm under company punishment for being AWOL. I have to pull guard duty tonight and for the next 60 days. I'd appreciate it I could leave right on time this afternoon."

"Sixty days!" exclaimed the major. "How in Heaven's Name are you supposed to be able to be any good to me if you've been on guard duty all night?"

"I'll make it, ma'am. I can catch thirty winks when I can, and I can sleep some on weekends. I haven't got any choice."

The major looked at him for a moment, and said, "There's a holding room we use for observation that has two beds, in the back there. Afternoons are slow. Why don't you get some lunch, then after I've had a chance to eat, you can sack out for awhile. If it gets busy, I'll call you."

Colling hesitated, "Ma'am, I appreciate it, but if Major Vincent finds out, he won't like it."

"My experience with Major Vincent, Colling, is that he doesn't much like anything. If he has a problem, he can come see me."

When Major Elliott had released him to go eat lunch, he had sought out the 511th's guard-duty roster, which he discovered was posted beside the mess hall, and took the opportunity to find his own name among the twelve on the list. He saw that the daily guard mount started at 1700 and ended at 0700 the following morning. He had taken note that MP's were on duty at the hospital gate when he had arrived, and concluded that military policemen provided security during the day, with sentries drawn from the hospital's personnel assuming that responsibility overnight.

Under the heading "uniform" at the top of the guard roster it read, "Regulation Class A - Guard Mount," with a footnote that Eisenhower jackets were not permitted. Accordingly, as he prepared to report for duty later that afternoon, Colling put on his full-length Class A jacket, making sure to remove his tech-four chevrons before doing so. He also donned the leggings and web-belt that was among the field equipment in his wall locker. There was no rifle rack in the squad room, leading him to assume that weapons would be available at the guard post. He considered wearing the medic's helmet that had been part of the field gear, but decided against it. He surmised that helmet liners would be supplied when he reported to the NCO in charge of the guard detachment.

At 1630, Colling arrived at the small building beside the hospital's main gate that served as its guard barracks. The NCO wearing the "Sergeant of the Guard" brassard was a stocky staff sergeant whose broken nose and facial scars marked him as a boxer. Colling was the first to arrive, and the sergeant ordered him to attention, then conducted an inspection of Colling's uniform that Colling suspected had as its main purpose the discovery of some flaw blemish that could be blown out of proportion and serve as an excuse for verbal abuse or punishment, or both.

As he looked Colling up and down, the sergeant said, "My name is Bernie Wilson...Sergeant Wilson, to you. I think we'll get to know each other real good."

Several other soldiers had filed into the room while Wilson was occupied with Colling. Over the staff sergeant's shoulder, Colling could see them taking helmet liners from a shelf on the opposite wall. Each liner had been given a coat of shiny black enamel, and a red and white emblem consisting of a caduceus with "511th Gen. Hosp." in a scroll underneath it, had been painted on the sides of each. Based on his previous experience with Major Vincent, Colling guessed that the device had probably been personally designed by him.

Apparently unable to find anything amiss regarding Colling's appearance, Sergeant Wilson ordered everyone into formation. When Colling immediately fell into line with the others, Wilson shouted at him to get his headgear. As Colling retrieved a helmet liner and returned to his place in line, the staff sergeant was eyeing each man in turn, making critical comments about the state of each soldier's appearance. When Wilson reached Colling, he glanced at him, smiled and walked past without saying anything.

Wilson pulled keys from his pocket and unlocked a weapons rack set against the rear wall. It held only four M-1 rifles, which Wilson removed and handed in turn to four of the soldiers, calling each of them by name as he did so. Colling's name was not called, and he and the other seven men who had not been issued a weapon stood at ease, waiting for the sergeant to tell them what to do. Wilson paid them no attention as he ordered the men whom he had armed to clean their rifles, and there was a flurry of activity as the M-1's were disassembled and the task of bringing them up to the sergeant's standards begun.

As they heard the recorded bugle notes of Retreat coming over the outside loudspeakers, Wilson ordered the men with the rifles to fall in, and after ordering everyone to attention, began calling out names, indicating that there would be three squads of four men each. In rotation, each squad would take turns providing two sentries at the front gate, with one soldier each at the rear gate to the motor pool yard, and at the entry to the officer's barracks. The squad mounting guard would be at their posts for two hours, and when relieved, would return to the guard barracks for four hours. The process would then be repeated until the guard mount ended in the morning at 0700. There would be no formal changing of the guard, but Wilson reminded everyone that they were required to "conduct themselves in a military manner" in going to and from their assigned positions, where the man who was being relieved would hand over his weapon to the guard assuming the post.

Wilson reminded them that the men comprising the two squads who were not on duty were required to remain in the guard house while not walking their posts, in the unlikely event that it was necessary to "call out the guard."

One man from among them who would be assigned to the desk to answer the telephone and make sure that when each two-hour stint was concluded, that the men at their posts would be relieved by the next shift. Wilson himself would be in the separate room provided for the sergeant-of-the-guard, to be disturbed only if an emergency occurred.

Wilson concluded by informing Colling that he would have to man the desk whenever he was not standing guard. Colling realized that meant that he would not be afforded any opportunity to sleep. After Wilson ordered the first squad to take up their posts and dismissed the rest of the men, he disappeared into the sergeant-of-the-guard's quarters.

Colling sat down at the desk, and another guard, wearing the single chevron of a PFC, came over, and putting out his hand, said, "My name's Johnny Pennington. What the hell did you do to get on Wilson's shit-list?"

"I was AWOL, and took a summary court. I'm drawing guard duty for 60 days straight, and it doesn't look like the Sergeant is going to cut me any slack," answered Colling.

"Jeez," said Pennington. "I sure as hell don't envy you."

"As a word of advice, Johnny," said Colling, "It might not be a good idea to be seen talking to me. Wilson might decide to take it out on you if he thinks we're buddies."

Pennington agreed and went off to a poker game that four other soldiers had been calling to him to join.

Colling began examining the desk, opening its drawers, all of which were empty except the top center one, which contained pencils, a pad of paper for notes and messages and a supply of forms that appeared to be intended to be used to report unusual incidents that might happen during the guard mount.

Thumb-tacked to the wall above the desk were two lists of the names of officers, including their grades. One was labeled, "Officer-of-the-Day" and the other, "Medical Officer-of-the-Day." Colling did not recognize any of them, but assumed that the first must be made up of the hospital's non-physician officers, and the second, of physicians. He was unfamiliar with the regulations governing Army medical units, but he suspected that the MOD should be called if there were some kind of medical emergency, and the OD regarding any disorder or breach of hospital security.

Colling was in the third squad, so that his turn at standing sentry did not arrive until 2100. He was told that he was stationed at the motor pool post, and he marched off into the darkness with the soldier assigned to the officers' quarters, parting company when they reached the far end of the main hospital building. A circle of light led Colling to the rear entrance to the hospital grounds. The private whose place Colling was to take was leaning against the wrought iron fence next to the gate, smoking a cigarette, which he snuffed out as he spotted Colling approaching. He informed Colling that nothing was going on and after handing over his rifle, walked away into the darkness.

Colling was uncertain as to whether he should pace back and forth, or just stand in the "at ease" position next to the gate. Finally, he decided to combine the two, and would walk until he became tired, then stand for awhile. After an hour or so of this, he began to crave sleep, even though that afternoon he had been able to nap for almost three hours in the dispensary's observation ward. Suspecting that Wilson or Vincent might be watching and waiting to catch him in some infraction, however, he continued to follow Wilson's injunction about acting "in a military manner" as he stood guard.

Eventually, 2300 arrived, and he was relieved. On his arrival at the guardhouse, Colling was told by the Corporal who had temporarily taken his place at the desk that he could once again take over. In a few minutes, all the other guards were asleep, leaving Colling alone at the desk. The lights had been turned off, leaving the room in darkness, except for the circle of light provided by the small goose-neck lamp in front of Colling. The room became quiet, and in the darkness, Colling tried to remain awake by drawing geometric figures on the message pad in front of him.

Nevertheless, he found his head nodding as he fought his fatigue. He was thinking that it would be the most wonderful thing in the world to be able to lay his head down on the desk when he was jerked upright by Sergeant Wilson's shouting in his ear, "God damn it, Colling, wake up!'

Colling replied, "I am awake, Sergeant."

Another voice, that Colling immediately recognized belonged to Major Vincent, intruded, "Sleeping on sentry duty, heh, Colling? That's a court martial offense all by itself."

"I wasn't sleeping, sir," argued Colling, not bothering to argue that he was not on sentry duty.

Vincent was beside himself as he seemed to relish the thought of new charges against Colling. He asked, "If you're awake, Soldier, what time is it? And don't look at your watch."

Colling decided he had no choice but to take a guess, and replied, "11:35, sir. 2335 hours."

Vincent's face fell as he looked at his own wristwatch. "Well, you may not have been asleep, but sitting with your head in your arms is a violation of procedure." Turning to Wilson, Vincent said, "Sergeant, make a note that Private Colling will have an additional day of guard duty to perform."

"Will do, sir," said Wilson, a broad smile on his face.

The raised voices had roused the sleeping guards, who were sitting up, watching the encounter. As Vincent left, Wilson shouted at them to look to their own business, and get some sleep before the next shift.

The adrenalin rush produced by Vincent's visit kept Colling from nodding off for the rest of the night, but when the MPs arrived just before 0700, and he was permitted to leave the guard station, he was barely able to lift his feet to return to his billet. He wanted nothing more than to drop into his bunk, but instead he put on his white jacket and reported to Major Elliott. He was blinking his eyes when he walked into the dispensary.

The nurse looked at him and said, "Colling, you look like hell. Have you eaten yet?"

"No, ma'am."

"Well go over to the mess hall and get something. And drink lots of coffee. Sick call is starting to line up."

Colling ate as hurriedly as he could, given the amount of food that he loaded on his tray. He finished the meal by gulping down his third cup of coffee.

A full stomach and the caffeine brushed the cobwebs from his head, and he pitched in beside Major Elliott for the remainder of the morning. When the last patient had been seen, he obtained the major's permission to try and get some sleep.

He was awakened by being poked in the shoulder. The nurse was standing beside the bed, "Colling, get up. It's 1530. You need to eat before going on duty. Go ahead and get out of here."

The mess hall serving line was open early to all men assigned to guard duty, and Colling again loaded his tray, making sure to refill his coffee cup more than once. After eating, he went to his billet and changed into his service uniform, making sure that all of his brass and his shoes were polished. At 1645, he was in the sentry barracks. As soon as he had replaced his service cap with one of the helmet liners, Colling expected to have Sergeant Wilson ordering him to attention, but another NCO was assigned as sergeant of the guard. Colling had to remind himself that the assignment as sergeant of the guard would rotate through the roster of non-commissioned officers in the same way that it did with regard to the lower-ranking men serving sentry duty.

The new sergeant of the guard also assigned Colling to desk duty when not walking his post, and it was clear that Vincent had made that condition a permanent one. The night passed without any variation from the one before, except that Major Vincent arrived at just after midnight. He was visibly disappointed that Colling was wide awake, and left after only a few moments. An hour later, Vincent was back, obviously thinking Colling would relax after his first visit and fall asleep, but Colling remained alert, sitting at the desk.

Two more days passed before Saturday arrived. After morning inspection of their billets, the men not assigned to duty were free for the rest of the day. Colling, of course, was confined to the hospital grounds, but he welcomed the chance he would have to get some sleep. The dispensary was closed for the weekend, with all soldiers reporting for sick call diverted to the hospital's casualty ward.

Most of the soldiers were headed into the city, but many had chosen to eat their lunch at the hospital before leaving. Colling was working on a plate of C-ration franks and beans, groggily reading a copy of *Stars and Stripes*, when Willoughby, Major Vincent's clerk, sat down across from him.

"I see you've survived so far," said the tech-five.

"Just barely. I want to use the weekend to try and sleep some."

As he began to eat, Willoughby commented, "You know, the major has a German girl friend. A little Schatzie, you know?"

Wondering what interest Willoughby thought he might have in Vincent's love life, Colling replied, "So what?"

"So she works in the laundry. You haven't had the chance to check out the German broads who work here yet, but some of them are pretty nice."

"I thought I saw a notice posted that German female employees are off limits to hospital military personnel." said Colling.

"That's Vincent's rule. If he or Wilson catch you messing with any of the *Fräuleins,* there's all hell to pay, but it don't hurt to look. And there's a few guys take the chance anyway."

"But the major himself is getting a little on the side?" asked Colling.

"Yep. Not only that, but he made her foreman, or fore-lady, you could say, of the laundry women."

Colling's mind was working as he listened to Willoughby's description of Vincent's plump blonde paramour. He interrupted the tech-five to ask, "Is he shacked up with her some place?"

"Yeah. He had some family evicted from an apartment about six blocks from here so he could rent it. He's got her situated there, so he can visit her any time he likes."

Willoughby supplied the address of the place, and Colling wrote it down on one of the mess hall's paper napkins. That evening, while on guard duty, Colling thought over how he might use the information the clerk had given him to his advantage.

Sunday passed much like Saturday, except that Colling had more time to sleep. He was lying on his bunk after lunch when he was awakened by another soldier removing his belongings from his wall locker. When Colling looked up, the soldier explained that he was packing. His orders had finally come through to return to the States for reassignment, and he would be leaving in the morning. The man began tossing things onto his bunk, and Colling noticed a Thermos flask among them. When Colling asked, the soldier said that he was going to have to get rid of the articles he was sorting out. Two minutes later, Colling owned the Thermos.

Even after completing his guard shift on Sunday night, Colling was not as tired as he had been initially. Whether he was becoming accustomed to the long hours, or the several hours of uninterrupted sleep he had been able to enjoy over the weekend played a part, he decided to chance skipping his afternoon nap in the dispensary observation ward.

As soon as sick call was completed, he asked Major Elliott, "Ma'am, I was wondering whether I could get a pass from you to leave the post for an hour or so?"

"Why?" asked the nurse.

"It's kind of personal, ma'am."

"A girl?" said the major with a smile.

"Well, sort of, ma'am. It can wait if you can't do it."

"Okay, Colling," she replied. "I'll give you a chit that says you have to pick up something at the German apothecary down the street. But you better be back by 1400. If Major Vincent finds out, I'm going to have to think up some excuse why I let you go."

Colling agreed that he would return right away. The pass in his hand, he was allowed by the MP at the gate to exit the hospital grounds.

Fortunately, the address that Willoughby had provided was within easy walking distance from the 511th. The apartment was located in a dismal four-story building surrounding a central courtyard. Colling could see why Vincent had chosen the place. The major could park his jeep in the courtyard where it would be concealed from view while he was occupied with his girl friend.

Colling asked a woman who answered the door at one of the ground-floor apartments if she could direct him to the building superintendent. She pointed across the courtyard to a door, which Colling found was labeled with a card with the word *Wohnungsauf-seher* thumb-tacked to it at eye level.

The superintendent was an elderly man, thin and stooped with age. He seemed surprised when Colling spoke to him in German, and in fact, commented on Colling's command of the language. Colling explained that he had relatives of German descent back in America. When Colling mentioned Vincent, the man's mouth twisted with distaste, but as Colling explained what he wanted the man to do, and that he would pay him with a carton of cigarettes each week, his face brightened. He told Colling that not only was the major rude, but that he had not provided the usual gratuities or gifts due to the person who had the difficult task of overseeing the building.

The superintendent's name was Rudolf, but he asked Colling to call him "Rudi." He assured Colling that there was a telephone in his apartment, which was necessary because of the duties of his office. The little German was overjoyed when Colling gave him a carton of Lucky Strikes, and the man promised that he would do as Colling had asked.

Colling returned to the dispensary a few minutes before 1400. Major Elliott asked if he had accomplished his business, and he smiled broadly and told her that he had. She gave him a knowing look and grinned back at him.

It was just after 2300 when the guard room telephone rang. The ringing was muffled by Colling's having placed it in one of the drawers of the guard barracks desk. Colling had been resting his head in his arms when it rang, and he suddenly was alert as he picked up the receiver. Before Colling could say anything, he heard Rudi say, "He is leaving now," before abruptly hanging up.

Colling was sitting upright, sipping at a cup of coffee, when Vincent stuck his head in the door a few minutes later. Colling, trying not to smile, stood up, saluted and greeted him, "Good evening, sir. Everything seems to be quiet tonight."

The major only grunted and walked away. A moment later,

Colling heard a jeep engine starting and the vehicle being driven away.

As the weeks passed, Vincent came to look in with less and less frequency. Colling was able to get Willoughby to purchase his cigarette ration at the PX, and Major Elliott permitted him to "run errands" on a weekly basis so that Colling could deliver them to Rudi. Sergeant Wilson was assigned as sergeant of the guard on two more occasions, during which Colling sensed that the staff sergeant was watching him closely. Each time, Major Vincent put in an appearance, only to be greeted by an alert Colling manning the desk, standing to salute him when he entered the guard barracks.

Because he had been using the desk drawer to stifle the telephone's ring, it took several weeks before any of the guard NCOs noticed that Colling was receiving a brief call close to midnight every night. While Colling suspected that there might be curiosity about the messages, no one ever asked him about them, and apparently, no one mentioned them to Major Vincent or Sergeant Wilson.

CHAPTER 3

MAY, 1947

The first week of his assignment to guard duty, Colling had created a hand-made calendar for March through May, copying from the one hanging in the dispensary. He had crossed off each day that passed, anticipating ultimately reaching the little box representing the last day that he would be required to report to the guard barracks. At first, he drew an "X" through each day when he came off duty, but then as the days passed, he found himself forgetting to make a mark on the calendar for as long as a week. One Sunday, when he remembered to bring the chart up to date, he realized that he had only two days left, including the sixty-first day that Vincent had awarded him on his first night on duty. When he mentioned it to Major Elliott, she said, "Thank God. At least I'll be able to get a full day's work out of you, for a change."

His final night of standing sentry fell on a Tuesday. The weekly guard roster was posted each Monday morning, and on his way to breakfast, Colling stopped to check the bulletin board to make sure his name was no longer there. With a sigh of relief, he noted that the list of names did not have his on it for Wednesday and the remainder of the week. He wondered how long it would be before Vincent put his name on the regular rotation of guard duty. He fully expected to find himself scheduled for his turn in the week following.

When Colling was relieved from duty at 0700 on Wednesday, he had a sense of relief that he had not experienced since Quarles showed up at the British detention center in Lübeck. He was considering what he might do to celebrate when he walked into the dispensary. Major Elliott and Willoughby were waiting for him, and while the clerk shook his hand and clapped him on the back, the nurse handed him a plate containing a wedge of chocolate cake.

"Well, you said you'd make it, and you did," she said. "Congratulations. Vincent was certain he'd have you on permanent guard mount for the rest of your time here."

"Thank you, ma'am," said Colling, as he lifted a forkful of cake to his mouth. "Where'd you get this?"

"One of the German ladies that works in the mess hall made it for me. If I had the money, I'd set her up in her own bakery...for a cut of the profits, of course."

"Well, it's great. I really appreciate this, ma'am."

The nurse replied, "It's okay. Now eat up so we can get to work. And you, Willoughby, had better get back to your office before Major Vincent knows you're gone."

"You bet, Major," answered the clerk. "But it won't be long until I am really gone. I got my orders. I ship out, back to the States, in two weeks. That's fourteen days, to those of us who are counting."

"The only thing I'm counting, Willoughby, is the number of people in that line outside. Go on, get out of here," ordered the major.

Knowing that he would have time to himself when the dispensary closed left Colling with a pleasant feeling that did not leave him for the remainder of the day. When 1630 arrived, and Major Elliott locked the door behind them, he walked casually to the mess hall, planning, for a change, to take his time eating. He filled his tray and found a place with three men with whom he had shared guard duty. As they ate, they discussed the baseball season and how the return of most of the professional players from the service would affect things in the second year after the war had ended. When Colling was asked, he admitted that he was a Cubs fan; which produced a great deal of mirth, and effusive expressions of condolences from his companions.

Colling could have asked Major Elliott for a pass to go into Munich for the evening, but had deliberately not done so. Instead, he returned to his billet and took out his writing portfolio. During his ordeal, he had found a few moments to write to his parents two to three times a week, and he had had a monumental task in sorting through the pile of mail that had been forwarded from his previous assignment to the 40th Infantry, where it had accumulated during his absence in Poland. He had not bothered to try and peruse all the back issues of the Bel Cors weekly newspaper that his mother had arranged to be sent to him, but he had read his parents' letters. They were always started by his mother, and then his father would usually pen a few lines at the bottom of the last page.

As had been the case since he had started college in Madison in the fall of 1943, his mother was full of news about his sisters, his high school classmates, their neighbors and their other relatives, not only those of Polish descent on her side, but also those of German and Irish descent on her husband's. There also always seemed to be a concern about how hard Colling's father was working in his drug store. During the war, she had devoted much of her correspondence to the effects of shortages and rationing; and later, after he had joined the Army and arrived in Germany, she had filled her letters with news about who had returned from military service, and then later, about which girls they were marrying. She usually ended with a reminder that he should attend Mass and say Confession. His father always used his few lines to congratulate Colling regarding his promotions in rank, or to give advice about how to deal with NCOs, based on his experiences in the "First War." He sometimes conveyed news about the store, and indicated with some frequency how pleased he would be when Colling received his discharge, returned to college to finish his pharmacy studies, and would come home to help him run the place.

For the first four weeks after his arrival at the 511th, Colling had received a letter a week from Elizabeth. Each had been no more than three pages in length, and began with the words, "My Darling," which made Colling's heart leap the first two or three times he read them. She closed with "All my love, Liz;" but between these first and last phrases, there were no other words of affection. Invariably the remainder of the letter would consist of a rather matter-of-fact description of various people she was becoming reacquainted with, and places she was visiting. Much of her correspondence dealt with social events that seemed to be important to her.

Colling had written a short reply to each of her letters, explaining that he had little spare time to devote to composing longer responses.

He was certain that she had received the letter he had written from his cell in the Munich MP station, but she had made no comment regarding his suggestion of marriage. He was further discouraged by the decrease in frequency of Elizabeth's letters. Receiving her letters had recently widened to two-week intervals, and nearly a month had passed since her last letter.

Among the mail delivered to the dispensary that afternoon were four letters for him. Three were addressed in his mother's hand. The fourth bore Elizabeth's unmistakable neat script. Colling decided to read those from his parents first, and answer them, before opening the one from Elizabeth. Whether his choice of priorities was a case of saving the best for last, or putting off anticipated bad news, he could not say.

He wrote a long letter to his parents, continuing to avoid mentioning his court martial, but describing in more detail his work with Major Elliott in the dispensary. When he had finished, he turned to Elizabeth's letter. It was no different from those she had sent previously. She went on about some dance at a country club, listing the names of those who were present, so that her description of the affair read like a newspaper society column. Colling caught himself applying the word "snobbish" as he read what she had written. He penned his own letter, mentioning that he had completed his punishment, and discussing the work he was doing in the hospital dispensary. He had begun the letter with "My Darling," as Elizabeth had hers; and closed as she had, with "All my love," before signing his name.

Colling had a sinking feeling that this exchange of letters with Elizabeth would be a repetition of their course of correspondence after their first journey together into Poland; and that he would hear from her less and less, until she ceased writing altogether. Despite his misgivings, he decided that he would wait and see what developed. After all, he had to concede that there was really no other choice open to him.

At noon the next day, Colling found a seat at a table with Willoughby in the mess hall. Once seated, Colling inquired, "You still have my suitcase?"

The clerk assured him, "It's still under my desk. I shoved it as far back as I could. Nobody other than you and me know about it."

"When can I pick it up?" asked Colling.

"You can come with me to the office after we finish eating. Vincent's usually not around until later in the afternoon. He likes long lunches at the officers' club."

Willoughby proved to be correct, and Colling was able to secure his case and lock it in his wall locker before returning to the dispensary for the afternoon. That evening, when Colling had a moment alone in the barracks, he was able to check its contents. The civilian clothing that he had worn in Poland was rumpled and smelled stale, and he removed all of it to his laundry bag to take to be washed and dry cleaned at some German laundry.

More important was the concealed compartment containing his Luger pistol, false documents and money. He had estimated that there would be nearly $6,000 in U.S. currency in the suitcase, but now that he had the opportunity to count it, he discovered that he actually had several hundred dollars more than he had thought. He replaced the gun, identity papers and most of the money under the false bottom in the case, and shoved it far back to the rear of his wall locker. Colling held $100 out for future use, hiding the bills by folding them lengthwise and tucking them into the lining of his service cap.

The items concealed in the suitcase were all contraband. The Luger was an unauthorized personal weapon, the false identity papers with his picture on them could land him in the stockade, and possession of American currency had been forbidden to overseas U.S. military personnel since 1946.

American occupation forces were paid in military scrip called Military Payment Certificates, which were the only form of money that could be used to make purchases in the PX and other Army facilities. At the end of a soldier's overseas service, the amount of MPC that could be converted into American currency was limited, based on the man's pay rate. Holding excessive amounts of MPC was deemed evidence of involvement in the black market, so that those who possessed extra scrip usually disposed of it by purchases in the PX of goods that were then shipped home to spouses and other family members. MPC were periodically recalled and a new series issued that were of a different color and design; and only a short period of time to exchange old notes for new was allowed, after which the old series became non-exchangeable and worthless.

With Vincent's ruling that Colling would suffer six months' loss of pay and allowances, all back pay due to Colling had been cancelled. He was now a private, making $75 a month, twenty-five dollars a month less than he had as a tech-four. There had been two pay days since he had joined the hospital, but Colling had had only a limited need for money, and consequently he had drawn only twenty dollars in MPC each month, leaving the rest on deposit in his pay account.

After the weekly inspection on Saturday morning, Colling decided he would use his new-found freedom to explore Munich. With two of the other men from his squad bay, he caught a streetcar and rode into the heart of the city. They spent the afternoon wandering the streets; taking in the sights. While the devastation caused by the war was not as widespread as Colling had seen in Poland, they passed numerous areas where crews of Germans, both men and women, were laboring by hand to remove piles of broken debris while simultaneously salvaging anything useful that might remain.

They located the main American post exchange that had been established in a former German department store. As Colling browsed through the place, it was clear that the merchandise offered was of a greater variety than that which was available in the PX located in the hospital. One useful item that Colling picked up from stack marked, "free" was a mimeographed brochure and map of Munich showing the city's points of interest, and they set out to see each of them.

After reaching the fourth site shown on the map, however, he and his friends became discouraged at the run-down condition of what remained of the monuments celebrating the former Kingdom of Bavaria, and decided to look for somewhere that they could buy a beer that did not have an "Off Limits" sign outside.

Even before they had left their quarters at the 511th, Colling's fellow soldiers had been after him to use his ability to speak German to proposition the younger women they passed on the street. Tired of their pressuring, he finally stopped two girls who looked reasonably presentable. Colling asked their names, and then told them that the two men with him thought they were very attractive, and wanted to buy them something to eat and perhaps a beer or two. After expressing a possible interest in joining the Americans, especially if it would entail the opportunity for a meal, one of the women asked why Colling was not making the offer for himself. Putting on a forlorn expression, Colling told them that he was married and was being true to his wife.

When it was clear that the two girls had accepted the invitation, Colling translated the women's response for his companions, at the same time virtually pushing each of the girls to a male partner. He seemed to have made an appropriate selection, because they paired off and were soon strolling along, arm-in-arm. When he was asked to come with them, he used the expression, "fifth wheel" and sent them on their way.

A short time later, Colling had found a seat at an outdoor cafe and spent over an hour sipping beer and watching the passing crowd. He decided it was time to leave when dusk arrived and he was approached for the second time by a prostitute. He remembered passing an Army movie theater a few blocks from the hospital. Even though he could not recall the name of the film that was playing, Colling decided to take it in anyway.

On Monday, he found Willoughby sitting alone in the mess hall, reading *Stars and Stripes* while he worked on a breakfast of powdered eggs and Spam. The clerk put down his paper when Colling sat down with him.

"Everything okay with your luggage, Jim?" he asked.

"Right. And I want to thank you for keeping it safe for me," said Colling, as he reached across the table and slipped a twenty-dollar bill into Willoughby's hand.

"Jeez," said the clerk, when he recognized its denomination. "Thanks. First greenback I've seen in over a year."

"I'm the one who owes you thanks," replied Colling. "For keeping my stuff safe, and keeping your mouth shut about it."

As Colling began eating, Willoughby turned his attention back to his own breakfast, but then as he finished the last morsel of a slice of toast, Willoughby leaned forward and asked in a quiet voice, "You interested in having a way to go anywhere you want in the hospital?"

"What do you mean?" asked Colling.

"What if I was to tell you I got a passkey that can open every locked door in this place?" replied Willoughby.

Colling paused for a moment before saying, "I'd be interested. I'm guessing you might want to see some more green?"

"You're the first guy I've seen who has dollars. I been trying to figure out how to get myself a few bucks for after I'm discharged, but all's anyone's got is MPC, and I already got too much to cash in when I go home, nearly a hundred bucks' worth too much."

"Tell you what," offered Colling, "I'll give you dollars for the extra MPC, and something on top of that for the key. But first, tell me how you got it."

The clerk surveyed their surroundings to see who might be within earshot, then said, "When I took over as clerk, I was going through my desk, and I found a big ring of keys. Anyway, I told the exec at that time, Captain Cambridge, that I had these keys, left over from when the Kraut army was running the place. But he told me that the Kraut doctors who were here when our guys arrived had turned over the keys to the place. This ring was a bunch of extras. There ain't no code stamped on any of 'em, so he told me I had to go around and try and match up the keys with the different locks in the place.

"I spent over a month trying them damned keys in every damned door. I actually found a key to every one, and I put tags on all of 'em. But I did find four keys that fit *all* the locks. And I only told the Captain that I found two skeleton keys, which I gave to him. I kept quiet about the other two, figuring they might come in handy some day."

Colling asked, "You ever do a little 'breaking and entering' on your own?"

"A couple of times, after Vincent took over. He keeps a couple of bottles of whiskey in his office, and I tapped into them until I had nearly a fifth to celebrate with last Christmas. Far as I know, he never noticed."

"But nobody else knows about this?"

"Nope," replied Willoughby.

"How much you want?"

"I figure if you take the extra MPC off my hands, another fifty should do it."

"For both keys, right?" said Colling.

"Right.'

Colling agreed to have the money by noon, and told Willoughby he would see him at lunch as they exited the mess hall.

After picking up the keys from Willoughby, Colling did not run into him again for several days. When he failed to see the clerk in the mess hall for nearly a week running, he realized that he must have returned to the States. This was confirmed when a PFC named McIntyre, who bunked in the same squad bay as Colling, asked Colling if he had heard that Major Vincent had been relieved from his assignment and sent back Stateside.

Colling's curiosity was aroused, and he asked, "Why'd he have to leave?"

"His old lady caught him with that Schatzie he was shacked up with."

"I thought Vincent's wife was back in the States," said Colling.

"She was, but Willoughby cut orders and travel authorization papers so she and their two girls could come over," said McIntyre.

"How the hell did he pull that off?" asked Colling.

"I got to hand it to the guy. He knew the Major would just as soon not have the wifey come over, especially since he had a nice set-up going for himself. But Willoughby went ahead and drew up the request and forged Vincent's signature, and put it in front of the Colonel in a stack of papers to be signed. I think the Colonel had no idea he was approving the request."

"After the request was approved, Willoughby went ahead and cut the orders, and the travel vouchers and sends 'em up and gets 'em signed by the Colonel. Then he writes a letter from the Colonel, welcoming Mrs. Vincent to the unit, and telling her that it would be nice if she would surprise the Major when she arrives, and not to mention it to the Major in any of her letters. Willoughby then gets the Old Man to sign it the same way he did before."

"Then, and this is the good part, Willoughby has got the name of the transport ship that's bringing her and the kids over, and he checks with some buddy of his in Wilhelmshaven about when it's going to come in. So he gets the word, and knows she is coming to Munich on a train that arrives in the evening, and he meets her at the station with the staff car. He tells Mrs. Vincent that the Major has rented an apartment for them, and he'll drive her and the girls to it."

"Willoughby left on the 2200 train that night...nice timing for him, but he didn't have a chance to say anything to anybody about what happened when they got to Vincent's love nest. But one of the guys in the casualty ward says that the Major's wife came screaming into the hospital, and the officer of the day had to track down the Colonel at the officers' club to come talk to her. Apparently, she and the girls walked in on hubby while he was in the saddle, so to speak. I would imagine it was a sight to behold."

Colling was unable to conceal his amusement as the PFC told his tale, and both he and McIntyre were laughing as he finished. Colling then asked, "So the Colonel calls Vincent on the carpet?"

"Oh, yeah. The Old Man is pissed off. Everybody knows he hasn't been too happy with Vincent anyway, and this is the last straw. He tells Vincent he's relieved, and to pack his bags. Conduct unbecoming an officer, moral turpitude, or something like that," replied McIntyre.

Colling smiled as he thought, *Good old Willoughby. I couldn't have done better myself.*

Treating patients in the dispensary had become a routine. Colling and Major Elliott would work as a team, seeing those who reported for sick call in the morning, and then the major would spend the afternoon completing paperwork, while Colling cleaned the place thoroughly and replenished supplies. When he finished his own work, Colling would often volunteer to file records or to type documents that the nurse might need.

Major Elliott had given Colling the task of keeping up to date a special file of 3 by 5 cards that she had created. The index cards held the names of the more than 400 men and women assigned to the hospital, and their blood types. All new arrivals were required to have their blood re-typed, and the major was keeping a record of each individual's type and the date the test was performed.

One afternoon, as Colling was inserting the cards for new arrivals into the wooden file box, and removing the cards of those who had been reassigned elsewhere, he asked her, "Ma'am, would it be useful to have a duplicate card for everybody, only filed by blood type?"

The nurse looked up from the supply order form she was reviewing, thought for a moment, then said, "It might come in handy to be able to look up who has a particular type of blood. Sure, go ahead and do it."

As he reached into a drawer and took out a pack of blank three-by-five cards, Colling wondered whether he should have made the suggestion, considering that he would have to make a duplicate for every one of the cards in the file. He reminded himself to order another file box to hold them all.

It took him the rest of the week to complete the task he had taken upon himself. When he was done, he showed Major Elliott the second box of cards that he had labeled "Blood Types." When she voiced her approval, he asked her if he might use a jeep to go to Camp 146. He explained that he wanted to pick up some of his belongings that had been left there the previous fall, when he went on furlough.

The major told him that she could not approve a jeep, but she could authorize his taking an ambulance to the 151st Medical Dispensary at Kummersfeld, one of the hospital's satellite facilities. There was a load of medical supplies that were to be delivered there, and once that was done, she did not care if he drove the extra distance to Camp 146 before returning. She agreed to sign a vehicle authorization as well as a pass that he could use on Saturday.

When Saturday arrived, the chits that the major gave him allowed Colling to skip the morning's inspection, but he did have to work by himself to load the cartons of supplies into the ambulance. Staff Sergeant Wilson grudgingly signed the vehicle out to him, clearly annoyed that Major Elliott had picked Saturday to re-supply the Kummersfeld facility, then locked his office and left. Except for a private who was sweeping the floor of the motor pool garage, Colling was left on his own with the pile of cardboard boxes that he had to deliver, and it took him an extra half-hour to move all of them into the rear of the ambulance.

Colling had never driven from Munich to Kummersfeld, and had some concern about what the condition of the roads might be. Travel over such a long distance was usually by rail. When stationed at the kaserne in Grabensheim, however, he had frequently traveled by jeep and ambulance between the various small towns that were within the area of occupation assigned to his infantry regiment. He found that two years of repair work on the German roads had brought some improvement, and he enjoyed being at the wheel of the ambulance, negotiating the curving *Autobahn* past farms with their newly-planted fields, and through stands of pine forest.

He pulled up in front of the Kummersfeld dispensary a little over two hours after leaving the hospital. A corporal was on duty at the reception desk, and he agreed to assist Colling in unloading and transferring the supplies to a storage room. As they carried boxes into the building, Colling asked if Captain Lewisohn was still around. The corporal assured him, "Yeah, the doc is still here, but he's not on duty. Probably spending the weekend with his girlfriend."

Colling commented, "I didn't know he had a girlfriend. Is she German or one of the nurses?"

"Well, German, kind of. She's Jewish. One of them refugees. Showed up here right around Christmas. MPs brought her in."

"The MPs?" asked Colling.

"Yeah. They found her layin' alongside the road just outta town.

She'd passed out, and they brought her here. The doc took her in. Some said he should-a sent her back to where she came from, but he got a crush on her, and she stayed. Not exactly according to Hoy-lee, if you know what I mean.

"Anyway, the doc gave her a job in the dispensary when she got better, and found her a room in town. I understand it wasn't easy, her bein' Jewish, and all," added the corporal. "The Krauts still don't cotton to Jews. But I think the doc straightened 'em out."

When the ambulance was emptied, Colling climbed back into its cab and headed for Camp 146. As he drove, he thought about Captain Lewisohn. While serving under him, Colling had not really given any thought to his being Jewish. He had been vaguely aware of the doctor's religion, but it was something that Colling simply took as a matter of fact, and not something warranting any conscious consideration. Lewisohn had always been fair with Colling, and he was a first-rate physician; but Colling had felt that he displayed a serious cynicism that Colling had attributed to the man's having been a front-line surgeon during the war. Colling speculated as to whether this woman would prompt a change in the Captain's attitude. He hoped it would.

The gate at Camp 146 was manned by one American soldier, who waved Colling through without asking questions or to see papers. It was a big change from when Colling had been stationed at the camp's clinic the year before. There were always three guards on the gate at that time, and they stopped everyone, even Army personnel.

The wooden barracks were more weathered than they had been, and Colling noticed that some were missing sections of the tar paper that covered their roofs. It was clear that the place was being allowed to deteriorate, and since he saw only an occasional person out in the camp's dusty streets, he assumed that its population must have decreased considerably.

He was wondering whether the Polish physicians he had befriended would still be there as he pulled up in front of the building that housed the medical facility. He was heartened to see that the

"Medical Dispensary" sign with its red cross remained in place over its open double doors.

The same wooden bench was still situated just inside the entrance. In Colling's time, it had always held a line of male and female refugees waiting to be seen by a doctor. There was no one presently seated on it, but Colling could hear a conversation in Polish coming from the examination room, so he leaned around the door jamb to see who was speaking. As he did so, his old friend, Dr. Antonin Parnieskaya, looked up from the ophthalmoscope he was using to examine the eye of a man seated in a chair before him, and seeing Colling, smiled broadly as he said loudly in Polish, "Colling, it was told you had deserted and fled to America!"

Parnieskaya, his patient momentarily forgotten, came forward to embrace Colling. "Thank God, you still live!"

Colling, the familiar Polish words coming to him easily, replied, "A mere rumor, my friend. I have, as you see, returned in good health."

The doctor excused himself and turned to his patient informing him that his eyes would have to be washed with boric acid solution. Parnieskaya took a small bottle and an eye cup from one of the room's medicine cabinets, and after irrigating the man's eyes, handed him the container and cup, telling him to avoid rubbing his inflamed eyes, and to wash them three times a day as he had been shown.

When they were alone, the doctor looked at Colling and said, "I remain unable to believe that you are standing here."

"But I am. It is so good to see you once more, my friend. You must give me news of Cheska, Basia, and Maria. Do they remain here?"

"Neh, neh," replied Parnieskaya, "The doctor Cheska has married the nurse Basia at Christmas, and they have emigrated to some place in the wilds of Canada. Very fortunate, perhaps, I do not know whether they will encounter the white bears or not.

"More fortunate for certain was Maria, who hit it off with an American dentist, a lieutenant, who was sent by UN people for purposes of improving the health of the teeth of the inmates of this camp. A dismal task, I fear, given years of malnutrition and neglect.

But Maria offered to assist him...she did, after all, possess the skills of a surgical nurse, as you know; and to serve as interpreter for him. You remember that Maria made it her objective to learn English. I believe you provided her with some tutoring in that regard?"

"That is true. I was able to find a simple vocabulary text and a dictionary for her," said Colling, wondering whether the American dentist might have found Maria a challenge to his professional skill, as the young woman, though pretty enough, had suffered from bad teeth when Colling had last seen her.

Colling continued, "Did I understand you to say that the camp is now under the UN? Is it not that agency of the United Nations called 'UNRRA'?"

"It is so. The American Military Government detachment that was here has gone, as have most of the inhabitants of this place."

"But there was an Army guard at the gate as I entered."

"Just so. Not more than a squad remains. And that only to serve to quell any disagreements between the camp inmates and the Germans outside. In truth, things have been quiet for some time now. It could be that the camp will be closed at the end of the summer."

"And what are your plans?"

"I have a cousin who lives in Pittsburgh, Pennsylvania. She left Poland many years ago, but I have, with great fortune, located her, and she has agreed to serve as my...how do you say it in English, 'my sponsor.' And in addition, the American officers who were assigned here were kind enough to write letters on my behalf."

"I wish you good fortune, my friend," said Colling.

As Parnieskaya finished expressing his thanks, Colling went on to the purpose of his visit, asking if his wall locker remained where it had been. The doctor assured him that it was still in the next room.

The Polish doctor watched from the doorway as Colling inspected his locker. The uniforms and cartons of cigarettes he had left behind were gone, as were the Leica camera, Zeiss binoculars and radio that he had stored on its bottom shelf. The false panel at the rear of the top shelf had not been disturbed. Colling pulled out the thin sheet of wood and ran his hand around inside the concealed compartment. As he had expected, he found a handful of MPC, now valueless because of the change in the military currency that occurred in Colling's absence. Colling decided that rather than throw it away, he would send it to his relatives in the States as souvenirs.

"Did someone come and take my property?" asked Colling.

"Yes, my friend," replied Parnieskaya, "Months ago. An officer...a major, and a sergeant. They took everything. They were very amused by it all. The sergeant smashed your radio by stamping his foot upon it. Everything else they took. Because I believed you dead, and because I am in no position to interfere with an American officer, I said nothing."

"The officer," asked Colling, "Was he a small man, wearing glasses, and with his head going bald?"

"Just so," said the doctor, "And the sergeant was a hard-faced man with the same look that one sees in the SS...not to be trusted, but easily feared."

"I know these men," replied Colling. "I for certain, know these men."

Parnieskaya added, "I gave the pieces of your radio to a man in the camp who scavenges for such things, and who possesses the ability to rehabilitate them into something useful. I can attempt to find him and recover what remains, if you wish."

"Neh, my friend, that is not necessary," replied Colling, "I give you my thanks for preserving my belongings as long as you were able, and I wish you the best as you go to live in America. Perhaps some day we shall see one another again. Please, if you would, to write down the address of your cousin in Pittsburgh, Pennsylvania, so that I may correspond with you?"

There was one last embrace as they parted. The Polish doctor was standing on the steps of the dispensary, his hand raised in farewell, as Colling drove away.

Colling had controlled his anger while with Parnieskaya; but at the wheel of the ambulance, he found himself working into a rage as thought about Major Vincent and Sergeant Wilson stealing his things, and how they had been "amused" while they did so. Vincent was out of his reach, and perhaps had received his just deserts, but knowing what he now knew, Colling would have preferred to exact revenge on the little man personally. Wilson was another matter. By the time he reached the outskirts of Munich, Colling had convinced himself to keep his emotions in check, and to concentrate on finding a way to get even with the staff sergeant...perhaps a little more than even, in fact.

CHAPTER 4

MAY – JUNE, 1947

While Colling's desire to find a way to get back at Sergeant Wilson was a matter of priority, he was unable to devote a great deal of effort to conceiving a way of doing so. His responsibilities in the dispensary took up most of his weekdays, and he continued to find seeing patients and assisting Major Elliott to be interesting and fulfilling. At first, he used his free time to become better acquainted with his fellow Americans and the Germans employed at the hospital. Eventually, his off-duty hours with other soldiers were taken up to a fair extent with discussions about sports, griping about military life, and comparing opinions about movies and those who starred in them.

Other pass-times consisted of playing two or three games of baseball a week, drinking, and the occasional penny-ante poker game. Colling enjoyed the physical exertion involved in the first of these, finding he had was able to regain some of the skills he had possessed when he played short-stop in high school and college intramurals. As far as drinking was concerned, Colling joined in primarily for the purpose of sociality; limiting his consumption considerably more than many of his companions. In playing poker, Colling found that he was generally able to out-think his opponents, and by avoiding ill-advised moves, was a consistent but moderate winner. Over time, his gains were greater than those with whom he played.

On duty, his greatest satisfaction came when the occasional patient presented with unusual symptoms, or when what seemed to be a commonly-heard complaint was actually a life-threatening emergency. An example of the latter situation occurred one morning when a middle-aged master sergeant from an Engineer battalion was brought in by one of his men, perspiring heavily and complaining of severe back pain. Colling was the first to see the man, and was about to assign his symptoms to a strained back when the sergeant said it felt like something was "tearing loose inside."

Colling interrupted Major Elliott to relay the comment, speaking in a low voice, and said he had seen a ruptured aortic aneurysm while at Camp 146, and the signs were the same. Without any hesitation, the nurse agreed, ordering Colling to put the master sergeant on a wheeled stretcher and to push him to the operating room as quickly as he could. The major telephoned ahead, so that when Colling arrived, two nurses in gowns, masks and gloves were waiting to take the sergeant into the operating room.

Later that day, a surgeon dropped by the dispensary to thank Major Elliott and inform her that the sergeant remained in serious condition, but at least he was alive. Another few minutes, perhaps, and he would not have survived. As Colling stood listening to the discussion, he saw the nurse glance in his direction for an instant, then turn away. After the surgeon had gone, he had expected her to make some comment, but she simply returned to the paperwork on her desk.

While not performing his assigned responsibilities or engaged in leisurely pursuits, Colling had gradually resumed his previous interest in entrepreneurial activity. In the past, he had run a flourishing business buying items of uniform clothing from soldiers leaving his unit for discharge, and reselling them to newly-arrived replacements. He had also engaged in one instance of using Army vehicles and military travel and customs authorizations to smuggle alcoholic beverages into, and out of, Germany, and made a handsome profit in the bargain. There had also been the making of small loans to men requiring funds in the last week before the monthly payday, on the basis of seven dollars repaid for five loaned, or twelve for ten. The latter, at a lower rate of interest, had been the more popular.

But things had changed. There was not as much turn-over in personnel, rendering uniform sales less frequent. His current assignment did not lend itself to official travel across the borders of neighboring countries, so that smuggling was not possible. And with virtually all transactions between soldiers under a requirement to use military scrip, the prospect of profit from usury held no attraction for him.

Colling reconciled himself to operating on a smaller scale. He quickly located a half-dozen men and women attached to the 511th who were non-smokers like himself. He then offered them more money for the use of their monthly tobacco ration than others did. This gave Colling access to twenty-eight cartons of cigarettes each month, for which he paid one dollar a carton, plus what he had to pay for the use of the ration cards. He originally anticipated simply reselling them to the German civilians working for the hospital who had accumulated MPC, for three dollars a carton. As it turned out, he found it more advantageous to use the cigarettes in trade.

Because he spoke German fluently, and had made a serious effort to befriend the German hospital employees, Colling had an edge in locating and bartering for what he wanted. At first, based on his previous experience, Colling had attempted to arrange trades for precision merchandise, such as cameras or binoculars. He rapidly discovered that such items were in short supply, having been quickly snapped up in the early days of the occupation.

Colling learned, however, that the Germans did have a store of military accoutrements that could be resold to American soldiers as "war" souvenirs. Because most of the present occupying force was made up of men who had not seen combat, they jumped at the chance to take home genuine "captured" artifacts that they would presumably brag about to their friends and loved ones.

Colling had found that one of the more plentiful, and popular, items was the Nazi ceremonial dagger. A couple of cartons of ciga- rettes would get him one of the weapons, which he could resell to Army personnel for from $15 to $25. The problem, of course, was that soldiers could usually only pay in scrip. After some thought, however, Colling struck upon a solution.

He used the greater part of his profits to purchase nylon stockings in the PX, using MPC. He then mailed them home to his parents, to be sold in his father's drug store. A pair cost Colling a little over a dollar, which was less than his father paid at wholesale from his own suppliers, when and if they had them in stock. Colling's mother had written to let him know that the wholesale cost was being deposited into Colling's old savings account at the First National of Bel Cors, and the balance had quickly begun to mount up.

No one at any of the four PX's where Colling regularly went to buy stockings seemed to find it odd that Colling was buying so many pairs of nylons in assorted sizes, and no one at the post office questioned his frequent shipments home. At least for the moment, he found himself with plenty of MPC to spend, while only having to draw a minimum amount of his pay each month. Colling expected that it would only be a matter of time before someone in a position of authority took an interest in what he was doing.

Colling was sure that that time had arrived when Major Elliott informed him that he was to report to the hospital CO's office as soon as sick call was completed. While walking down the hallway towards the hospital headquarters, he tried to come up with a plausible story to explain why he would buy so many nylon stockings, but he remained unable to think of anything as he entered the outer office and announced to the PFC at the desk that he had been summoned to see the commanding officer. Colling stood waiting for only a few seconds before a heavy-set master sergeant appeared from Vincent's old office and told Colling to follow him.

The hospital commander turned out to be the same middle-aged officer who had been sitting behind him at his court martial. Colling had not seen him since, but now, as he came to attention in front of his desk and saluted, he saw the colonel's eagles, confirming his earlier impression that the officer was the hospital's commanding officer, Colonel Barrowsmith.

"Private James T. Colling reporting as ordered, sir," said Colling.

"At ease, Colling," said the colonel, returning Colling's salute and then dismissing the master sergeant. "I'm Colonel Barrowsmith. I think you've seen me before."

"Yessir," answered Colling.

"Colling, I understand that you speak German pretty well. I took Scientific German in college, but never did really learn to speak it very well."

"Yessir. I speak German," said Colling.

"And I hear you have a pretty good relationship with the locals we employ."

"Well, sir, I will say that I can talk to them, but I don't know how much of a relationship I have. I would guess that some of the men have German girl friends who are a lot closer," responded Colling, at the same time thinking how silly what he had just said must sound.

"I imagine yours is a somewhat different relationship, Colling. My understanding is that you know a few of them on more of a... how should I say this?...business basis. I've heard they've helped you find war souvenirs that you've sold to some of our men."

Thinking, *Oh-oh, here it comes!* Colling searched for a response, then said, "Sir, I admit it. I have been selling stuff, but..."

Barrowsmith interrupted, "Forget that, Colling. I don't care what you do on your own time, just as long as it's reasonably legal."

"Yessir," responded Colling, his initial anxiety somewhat allayed, but concerned about what the definition of "reasonably legal" might turn out to be.

The colonel continued, "I wanted to ask you, Colling, if you think it might be possible to find a place for me and my wife to live. She's due to arrive in a month or so, and since the Army lifted all the restrictions on officer's dependents, there aren't enough billets to take care of all the wives and kids coming over."

"Housing Office can't help, sir?"

"I've applied, and because of my rank, I get preference, but the places they showed me are just too small, and frankly, quite dismal. There's talk of constructing some of those plywood pre-fabs that they used for family housing during the war, and that may happen, but even then, that just wouldn't be suitable."

While the colonel was speaking, Colling was mulling over his chances of success, and the probable benefit to himself if he could do what the colonel was asking. When Barrowsmith finished talking, there was no hesitation on Colling's part. "I think I might be able to do something, sir. I'll have to ask some contacts I have among the Germans. Will this be for just you and Mrs. Barrowsmith, or are there children, as well"

"Just the wife, Colling," replied Barrowsmith, "My sons are grown."

"Very good, sir. And sir, it would be helpful if you could get me a jeep authorization and a general pass off the post. I'll want to inspect any real estate before I recommend it to you. Also, sir, I'll need an okay for a German civilian to ride with me."

"I understand completely, Colling. You can pick them up this afternoon. And if you need anything, ask Sergeant Gayle, he's the master sergeant who brought you in. He's doing Vincent's job since he left us."

"Thank you, sir. I'll get right on it," said Colling, as he came to attention and saluted.

Colling returned to the dispensary and informed Major Elliott of the colonel's request. He promised her that he would not let it interfere with sick call, but did add that on a few days, he might have to be away during the afternoon.

Reminding the major that his meeting with Colonel Barrowsmith had made him late for lunch, Colling headed for the hospital mess hall. Spam and reconstituted potatoes was the main dish, as it was several days a month. Colling wondered how much Spam the Army actually had in storage, and whether the popular GI joke that it would finally run out during World War Three might be true.

When he passed his used mess tray through the window to one of the German dishwashers, Colling asked in German if Fritz was around. The man shouted Fritz' name over his shoulder, and a moment later, Fritz Meltzer's face appeared at the window. He greeted Colling with a smile, which was to be expected, given that he had proven to be one of Colling's best sources for war souvenirs. Colling had once asked Fritz if he had a warehouse full of ceremonial daggers, and the little German had just smiled and shrugged his shoulders.

"What is it that I can do for you, Colling?" asked Meltzer.

"A moment of your time is required," replied Colling. "Are you able to speak with me at the rear door of this place?"

"For certain," said Meltzer, gesturing to Colling, "Come, come. I will be there in a moment."

It took Colling five minutes to reach the back steps of the mess hall. Meltzer was waiting for him, leaning against the wall and smoking a cigarette.

Colling spoke first, "I have an important thing that must be done for Colonel Barrowsmith."

The German's eyes widened, and he nodded knowingly as he said, "Truly, when the *Herr Oberst* Barrowsmith wants something, it must be of great importance, Colling. How may I be of service?"

"The Colonel's woman soon will come from the United States to join him, and they will need living quarters. Do you perhaps know where they might be found? And none of these cramped apartments, Fritz. A good, decent place is what is desired."

Meltzer rubbed his chin for a few seconds, then said, "I may know of such a place. It is near the Nymphenburg. Do you know that neighborhood?"

"I do not, but it is a good distance from the hospital, no?"

"Not so far, west of the city, in Pasing. The streetcars have been repaired in that district, and of course *Herr Oberst* has the use of a staff car, is this not true?"

"True enough. But you understand that I must inspect this place before I stake my reputation on a recommendation to my colonel?"

"Of course, Colling. I can take you there this very afternoon, if it is your wish."

"It is. I will pick you up at this place about 15 hours. *Herr Oberst* has provided me with a jeep."

Colling invited Meltzer to ride beside him in the jeep so that the German might more easily provide directions. Meltzer was obviously disconcerted at the stares he received from the American soldiers they passed as Colling drove through the city center. Even after two years, it was not common for German nationals to ride as passengers in Army vehicles, especially in the front seat.

Their surroundings gradually changed into a suburban environment of broad tree-lined streets. There was little obvious bomb damage in the Nymphenburg district. Colling speculated that the presence of the Nymphenburg Palace, a cultural and historical site, was the reason that the area had been spared destruction.

Meltzer directed him down a shaded street leading off the main thoroughfare, then pointed out a large house set back from the street behind a wrought-iron picket fence. Colling pulled into the circular flag-stoned driveway and parked. As Colling climbed out of the jeep and followed Meltzer up the steps to its front door, he glanced about, looking over the place.

It appeared that the house had three stories, with the gabled top floor perhaps containing servants' quarters. As with most buildings that had survived the war, it was long overdue to be painted, and some of the trim around the windows was conspicuously weathered. Despite its mild shabbiness, it could be of a size that might prove suitable to Colonel Barrowsmith, and Colling was confident that it would be possible for him to find the materials needed to make the necessary repairs and improvements.

The young woman who answered Meltzer's knock took Colling by surprise. He had expected a middle-aged or elderly householder; instead, a dark-haired woman in her twenties was standing before him. She was perhaps a bit too thin, as were most Germans without connections to the occupation, but it was not enough to detract from her attractiveness.

She was wearing a faded gray jumper worn over a light-colored blouse, as well as the usual white cotton Bavarian stockings. While the manner in which she was dressed would have made another woman seem ordinary, the way in which she carried herself suggested unusual strength and determination. Most startling to Colling was the violet color of her eyes.

Colling was aware that the teen-aged English actress, Elizabeth Taylor, was said to have violet eyes, even though he had never been able to verify that by her appearances on the motion picture screen. And until this moment, he had never really believed that that could be true. Moreover, she was staring straight at him, an expression on her face somewhere between indifference and contempt.

She turned and spoke in a level voice to Meltzer, who was standing cap in hand, "Who are you? Has this greedy dunderheaded foreign thief been brought by you to steal from us even more? We have little enough as it is."

Colling immediately realized that the woman believed that he could not understand German, and that he had brought Meltzer as an interpreter. Colling was impressed by her cleverness in avoiding the use of the German words for "American," or other obvious epithets that might be recognized by an English-speaker. She was clearly choosing her words to eliminate the possibility that the gist of what she was saying might be picked up by him, while at the same time suppressing any emotional inflection in her voice that might reveal that she was throwing insults in his direction.

Before Meltzer, who was twisting his cap and looking nervously at Colling, could say anything, Colling replied in German, using the courteous form of address, "*Meine gnädige Fräulein*, I wish to assure you that neither I nor *Herr* Meltzer, here, have any desire to steal anything from you. I am called James Colling, and while my poor aunt in Wisconsin, that is in America, often chided me as a dunderhead when I was a child, at no time have I been afforded the title of 'thief.' "

Colling smiled broadly at the disconcerted expression on the woman's face, then continued, "And whom am I having the pleasure of addressing?"

"Veronika Schönenberg is my name," she replied, quickly regaining her composure and, to Colling's dismay, some of her previous hostility.

"So this is the house of you and your man, *Herr* Schönenberg, I presume?"

"No. The house of my parents, Albert and Marie Schönenberg. What is it that you want?"

"Ah, yes," said Colling, continuing to smile, "My colonel is seeking quarters. Herr Meltzer here has directed me to you. Is your assistance possible?"

Colling watched Miss Schönenberg's lovely violet eyes snap at him as she replied, "Why not just requisition the place? There are only a few lowly Germans living here. You Americans can simply throw everyone into the street, is that not so? Everywhere else this has been done, has it not?"

Aware that his smile was undoubtedly irritating Miss Schönenberg, and somewhat enjoying the emotional effect he was eliciting, even if it were negative, Colling said, "If displacing refugees is the only means by which my colonel might find housing, then he will be opposed to such a course. He intends to pay any rent out of his own pocket, and not to seek requisition of your parents' home. Come, Fritz, we shall go elsewhere."

Colling had not fully turned to leave before Miss Schönenberg called him back, "Wait. It may be possible that something can be done. Please come in."

The foyer of the house into which the young woman led them was impressive, though bare of furnishings. A dark hardwood floor complimented richly paneled walls. The tall windows on either side of the entrance doorway that should have held heavy drapes were bare, and there were none of the usual touches Colling associated with such houses, such as paintings or sculpture. Straight ahead he could see into what he judged to be a large sitting room. Instead of sofas and easy chairs, the room was crisscrossed with ropes hung with sheets that subdivided it into cubicles. Cots and pallets littered the floor, making it clear that its occupants were likely the refugees of whom Miss Schönenberg had spoken.

Colling was unable to decide whether or not the young woman's attitude towards him had become less negative as she invited him and Meltzer to tour the house. Simple tables and chairs had been placed in a large dining room designed for formal occasions, which Miss Schönenberg explained was where meals were served. She led them along a short hallway and down a flight of steps into a kitchen that filled one end of the cellar. As they walked through, two women were preparing food while small children played on the brick floor.

Colling and Meltzer followed Miss Schönenberg back to the ground floor, where she conducted them through the library opposite the dining room. Its shelves were bare, and Colling wondered where the books might have gone. Seeming to read his thoughts, Miss Schönenberg mentioned that its contents were in storage. She pointed to a closed door and explained that behind it was a study that her father had used as an office, and which had been converted into living quarters for her parents. There was no effort on her part to introduce the elder Schönenbergs, and without further comment, the young woman asked them to follow her up the front staircase to the second floor, pointing out that all of its bedrooms were being shared by their tenants.

Colling was pleased to see that there was a large bathroom on the second floor, and when he asked whether there were other such facilities in the house, Miss Schönenberg informed him that there was a water closet off the entrance hall, and another located next to a shower room in the cellar.

Colling inquired whether she intended to show them the third floor, and Miss Schönenberg replied that the servants' quarters in the garret were presently occupied by herself and four other young unmarried females. Colling asked how many people the Schönenbergs were sheltering, and she responded that there were twenty-six at present.

Colling asked to view the grounds, and the young woman led them through a glassed-in sunroom where French doors opened onto a large open area behind the house. While Colling suspected that the space had been kept properly landscaped in the past, the shrubs and grass were not doing well. The look on Colling's face prompted Miss Schönenberg to apologize that the landscaping had been neglected for some time.

A separate two-story building with three sets of large double doors that Colling surmised must serve as a garage was situated directly behind the mansion. Miss Schönenberg explained that it had originally served as a carriage house, and Colling asked if there were any automobiles inside. The young woman replied that all of her parents' autos had been taken by the *Wehrmacht* long ago.

What appeared to be a vegetable garden was laid out beside the garage, and a man wearing a German army uniform was using a hoe between its rows. Colling pointed in the man's direction and asked, "Is this man a gardener?"

"He belonged to my brother's *Abteilung*. He and two of his *Kameraden* came to the American Zone to avoid capture by the

Russians. All is correct; he has been released by the Ami's. It is today his turn to work the garden."

"And his comrades?" asked Colling.

"They work clearing rubble, as do most of the others who live here. It is poor employment, but they gain a few marks and a ration of potatoes and flour. Sometimes some sauerkraut," she answered, then her eyes flashed again, and she asked, "I am sure you know in English that word 'Kraut,' is that not so?"

"Yes, *Fräulein*, I know that word. And while my comrades may use it freely, I do not. It is one of those words, like 'Ami' that I try not to speak."

She avoided his gaze, and Colling momentarily regretted having turned her own words back at her. Despite the young woman's evident hostility, he did find her attractive, and he had to admit that in the back of his mind, he had been trying to figure out how he could arrange to see her in the future. He had not received a letter from Elizabeth in well over a month, and making Miss Schönenberg's acquaintance was providing him with a reason to finally give up on any hope that he might have had regarding that relationship.

Because of its serving as home to more than two dozen refugees, it did not appear to Colling that the Schönenberg house would be available to Colonel Barrowsmith and his wife. Consequently, Colling's thoughts again turned to what excuses he could use to visit the place and have further contact with the violet-eyed young brunette.

It took Colling a moment to realize that Miss Schönenberg had said something to him, and he apologized, "Please excuse me, *Fräulein*, I was distracted. What did you say?"

"I said that your Colonel may be fortunate. The people here are all from five families. Just yesterday they have received travel vouchers to proceed to the British Zone. The men journeyed north some weeks ago. They had heard that factories were being revived there. This has proven true, and arrangements have been made by the UN relief agency that their women and children may rejoin them. They will go from here in the morning on Monday. We will miss the money the government pays us...twenty marks per person each month."

Colling's heart jumped, as much from the expectation that he would see this woman again as from the possibility of pleasing his commanding officer, and he said, "*Sehr, sehr, gut.* I will inform my Colonel immediately."

"Not so," said Miss Schönenberg, "The United Nations agency called the 'UNRRA' has a list of those to place in housing, and I fear that there will be twenty or thirty more to take the place of those who depart."

Colling gave this some thought before asking, "Are you certain that the UN makes these placements?"

He had begun to roll an idea around in his head as the young woman assured him that the United Nations agency was indeed charged with dealing with displaced persons.

Colling told her that he would return later in the afternoon, and with Meltzer at his heels, trotted back to the jeep. At its wheel, he asked Meltzer if he knew of a medical doctor, and the German replied that he did.

He drove to the 511th at breakneck speed, skidding to a halt in front of the entrance. Major Elliott was on the telephone when Colling entered the dispensary and began rummaging in a drawer in one of the counters. The nurse asked him what he was looking for just as he found it. While Colling was rolling the form he had pulled from the drawer into the typewriter and began tapping its keys, he informed her that this was part of finding quarters for Colonel Barrowsmith, and that he would need only a few minutes. Finished with his typing, he thanked the major and walked quickly out the door.

Colling next retrieved some items from his wall locker and stuffed them into a canvas carryall before returning to the jeep, where Meltzer was still seated, waiting for him. Colling threw the bag into the rear of the vehicle, and following the German's directions, only a little more than fifteen minutes later, they pulled up in front of the run-down apartment block where Meltzer said the physician kept an office.

Meltzer led him up two dark flights of stairs, and after squinting in the dim light to find the number of the flat he was seeking, the German knocked on its door. A stooped, balding older man answered, but seeing Colling's uniform, tried to slam the door in Meltzer's face. Meltzer pushed back, however, shouting the man's name, addressing him as "*Herr Artz*," and finally the old man relented.

Colling produced the form he had brought from the dispensary and handed it to the physician, saying, "*Herr Artz*, please. I wish you to sign this form."

"But this is a quarantine form," said the doctor.

"Correct. This is a matter of great importance. If you will affix your signature here, where I am pointing, I will give you these three cartons of American cigarettes, this sugar, and this coffee," said Colling, taking the items from his carryall and placing them in front of the old man.

The physician's eyes widened, causing Colling to be concerned that he would refuse to sign, but then the man took the fountain pen that Colling offered, and scratched his name in the place where he was shown.

Colling and Meltzer clattered down the stairs to the jeep and Colling asked the German if he knew where the UNRRA housing office was. Meltzer gave him the address, and Colling drove there, one eye on the street in front of him and the other alert for any MP jeeps that might be interested in his exceeding the speed limit.

The reception counter at the United Nations establishment was manned by a German civil servant who Colling surmised owed his position, to the fact that he could act as an interpreter for the Swedish official whom the German had to summon when Colling shoved the quarantine form across to him.

Recalling the name that he had heard the clerk use to summon the United Nations Relief and Rehabilitation Administration representative to the reception desk, Colling kept to English as he explained, "Mr. Lundquist, I'm under orders to deliver this quarantine form to you. There's a house at 42 Kleberstrasse where you've got a bunch of folks, and you have to stop sending anybody else over there until the medical officer can check things out."

Lundquist read the form, before looking up and saying, "It says there's meningitis there."

"Yes, that's right, sir. A case reported in at the 511th yesterday. Main thing now is, I'm supposed to tell you, is to not expose anyone else."

The Swede turned to his German clerk, "Take 42 Kleberstrasse off the housing list, Ludwig." He turned to Colling, "Tell your officer thank you very much, Private."

"I'll do that, sir. I got to go put up the warning signs now, sir, if you'll excuse me."

Back in the jeep, Colling wondered whether the travel office for UNRRA knew what the housing office for UNRRA was doing. He had wagered that the two, like all bureaucracies, did not, in which case, the five German families would be gone and Colonel Barrowsmith and his wife would be moving into the Schönenberg house.

If, on the other hand, he were proved wrong, his ploy would result in the refugees being caught in the quarantine that he had created, confined by United Nations health officials, and prevented from leaving for the north. It would then be necessary to come up with a way to have them medically cleared so that they could proceed. He thought about the Schönenberg woman and her violet eyes and decided he would cross that bridge when he came to it, if he came to it.

Chapter 5

June, 1947

Colling's intuition regarding lack of intra-agency communication within the United Nations Relief and Rehabilitation Administration proved correct. When he returned to the Schönenberg house three days later, the group of Germans that had been under UNRRA's care had departed to take up their new lives in the British Zone.

Miss Schönenberg had been concerned when he had tacked up one of the signs warning that the place was infected with meningitis, but he explained to her that the notice was intended only to forestall the assignment of any more tenants by United Nations. Colling assured her that there was no reason to fear the existence of any actual contagious disease.

Once Colling had confirmed that the refugees were gone, he let Miss Schönenberg know that he would be bringing his colonel to inspect the house the following afternoon. He took note of the fact that the ropes and drapes that had partitioned the larger rooms had been removed, and she said that she would have the house in presentable condition when Colonel Barrowsmith came to call. Colling reminded her to remove the quarantine notice prior to the officer's arrival.

Colling was about to go when he remembered to ask if there were a telephone in the house, explaining that his colonel would require one. Miss Schönenberg told him that the apparatus remained, but service had been shut off, and they had not been able to afford to pay for it to be restored. Colling made a note to notify Sergeant Gayle that he would have to contact the German post office or the Signal Corps and use the colonel's influence to have the phone reconnected.

As Colling was leaving, she told him that "*Fräulein* Schönenberg" was much too formal, and that he could use her Christian name,

"Veronika" Colling told her that if she wished, she might address him as "Jim," but suggested she use "Private Colling" when his colonel was present.

As he walked down the front steps, he thought, *It looks like I'm making progress*, but later, while driving to the hospital, he realized that she had not yet introduced him to her parents. Even so, he smiled as he contemplated the fact that he had never known a girl called "Veronika," and that Veronica Lake was the only person he had ever heard of with that name; but then, he thought, smiling to himself, *that* Veronica was a movie star in Hollywood.

Colonel Barrowsmith's staff car was one of the standard olive drab Army Plymouths. The colonel rode in the back, while Colling sat in front beside the driver. Colling was acquainted with the PFC who was driving, and knew his name was Bill, but he could not remember the man's last name. They exchanged a brief acknowledgement of each other's presence as Colling slid into his seat.

Colling positioned himself so that he was partially turned, his arm on the back of the front seat, in order that he could look at Colonel Barrowsmith as he conversed with him. The colonel commented on the pleasant appearance of the neighborhood, remarking that he and some other officers had taken a guided tour of the Nymphenburg Palace a few months earlier. Because a portion of the structure continued to be used for U.S. military purposes, he had been able to tour only a limited part of the interior, but he added that he had had the opportunity to take some snapshots of the exterior of the building and the gardens.

The colonel leaned forward as they turned into Kleberstrasse, apparently admiring the fine houses on either side, and when they pulled into the circular driveway of Number 42, Colonel Barrowsmith said to Colling, "It looks like you've hit the jackpot, son."

Colling replied, "It's a nice house, sir, but it needs some work. It's been used to house displaced persons, and the inside is a little bare."

Colling knocked at the door, and Veronika answered. She smiled pleasantly, gesturing them to enter while expressing a welcome on behalf of her family. As they walked through the entrance, Colling

introduced Colonel Barrowsmith, addressing Veronika as "*Fräulein
Schönenberg.*" Colling noticed that the young woman was wearing
a stylish black dress that he guessed had been brought out especially
for the occasion. It complimented her dark hair perfectly, and Colling
sensed that Colonel Barrowsmith was immediately taken with the
young woman.

A moment later, as he followed the colonel into the foyer,
Colling was astonished to see that that the interior of the house was
completely unrecognizable from when he last had seen it. Drapes
had been hung; there were stands holding marble sculptures placed
against the walls, which now held a quartet of oil portraits that
Colling gauged, from the costumes worn by their subjects, to date
from the eighteenth-century.

"Beautiful, beautiful," said Colonel Barrowsmith, as he scrutinized their surroundings. Veronika was nodding, seeming to
understand what the colonel was saying, when Colling, suddenly
recalling that he had to fill the role of interpreter, translated the
officer's compliments into German.

Colling continued to act as an intermediary between the two as
Veronika led them through the house. He repeated her comments
in English to his commanding officer, and rendered the colonel's
questions into German for Veronika to answer. As he accompanied
them through the ground floor, he observed that every room was
now provided with what looked to Colling to be expensive furnishings, and when Colling remarked to Veronika that they had not
been there when he had last visited, she replied with a smile that
everything had been taken out of storage.

From the library windows overlooking the grounds at the rear
of the house, Colonel Barrowsmith watched one of the *Wehrmacht*
men who lived in the garage pushing a wheelbarrow, and he asked
who he was. Without bothering to translate the officer's question
for Veronika, Colling explained that the man had been attached to
the same unit as one of Miss Schönenberg's brothers, and was being allowed to occupy a room on the second floor of the converted
carriage house. Colling added that the brother was missing on the
Eastern Front, and that there were two other former soldiers still

in residence. It was expected that they would move on as soon as they could locate their families or find regular employment. Colling mentioned that the men kept the grounds in some semblance of order, and also tended the vegetable garden, and suggested that Colonel Barrowsmith might want to defer asking that they be told to leave. The colonel responded by saying that a good officer looks after his men, and that he would do the same if he were in the Schönenbergs' place.

Eventually, they came to the study, and Veronika invited them to meet her parents. Colling explained to the colonel that the couple had taken up residence in the study when the rest of the house had been occupied by displaced persons.

Veronika led them into the room, and Colling found himself unprepared for what he encountered. Colling had created a mental impression of the elder Schönenbergs that rested in part on speculation that their station in life had made them chose to isolate themselves from the ragged group of refugees that had been foisted off on them. Instead, when he saw that *Herr* Schönenberg was seated in a wheelchair, he realized that their choice of the first floor study was no doubt based on the old man's inability to climb or be carried to the second floor bedrooms.

Herr Schönenberg shook Colonel Barrowsmith's hand first, then Colling's, greeting the two Americans politely. Colling translated the old man's words into English as he expressed his assurances that he and his wife were pleased that the colonel had selected their home as his personal quarters. He asked Colling to confirm to his colonel that they wanted their daughter, Veronika, to handle the details, such as the rent and what servants would be available as a condition of the lease. Colling did as he asked, but left out any mention of servants, telling the colonel only that Veronika would be acting for her parents.

Colonel Barrowsmith expressed his satisfaction to Colling when they returned to the foyer; and asked him to find out how much rent would be required, and when he might move in. Rather than posing the question to Veronika, Colling asked the officer to step out of earshot, and quietly said, "Sir, she and her parents spoke to me about this before, and her parents will be willing to accept your housing allowance. You can see that a place like this in the States would ordinarily rent for three or four hundred a month, and the Allied Authority has only been paying them 20 marks a person per month to house displaced persons. They had 26 of them in here last week, and that's only a little over 500 marks...fifty bucks a month."

The colonel gave a low whistle through his teeth at this information, then asked, "How the hell do they survive? Three of them on that kind of money?"

"Well, sir, they do have a garden out back, and I think the refugees shared some of their rations with them. And they probably get some rations of their own...I don't know. But anyway, sir, I understand a colonel's quarters allowance is about $120 a month, that's more than double what they're getting now. And when Mrs. Barrowsmith arrives, sir, you'll have commissary privileges, so you can get them some extra food. A little extra in the form of coffee or sugar, and some meat once in awhile, would be really appreciated. And I think I can arrange for you and your wife to get some servants in the bargain. Let me see what I can do."

"Of course, of course," said Colonel Barrowsmith.

Colling turned to Veronika and asked if he had heard her father correctly when he said that servants came with the house. She replied that they did. Two of the refugees had expressed their desire to serve in the house of a high-ranking American officer. An older woman had asked to remain as cook, and her daughter could serve as a maid. They were looking forward to the benefits of such an arrangement, and wanted only room and board in return.

Colling went to back to stand beside Colonel Barrowsmith, and said in a low voice, "Sir, I think I can talk them into keeping their cook and maid here, if you can see your way clear to pay another twenty dollars a month."

"My wife will be delighted, I'm sure," said Colonel Barrowsmith, "Tell Miss Schönenberg that we accept. I'll send you over with the money later today."

Colling informed Veronika that Colonel Barrowsmith would take the place, and was willing to pay 1400 marks a month in rent, ending with a warning to her that she should not allow herself to appear overly pleased with the news. She did not entirely conform to his advice, so that her face lit up in a smile directed at the colonel as she shook his hand. It was the first time that Colling had seen her smile openly, and he found himself even more taken with her.

As their staff car was pulling away, Colonel Barrowsmith enthusiastically thanked Colling for finding the Schönenberg house for him, describing it as a "mansion," and speculated about Mrs. Barrowsmith's reaction when she saw the place. Colling modestly told him that he was simply fortunate to have located it, and the colonel settled back in his seat, smiling. The officer did not initiate any additional conversation, leaving the two enlisted men to ride in silence for the remainder of the return to the 511th.

While Colonel Barrowsmith made arrangements to obtain 1400 marks in Allied Military Currency for Colling to deliver to his new German landlord, Colling went to the dispensary to report to Major Elliott that he had found lodging for their commanding officer.

After he had related the afternoon's events, the nurse said, "You will definitely be in the CO's good graces. He's been telling everyone how much he's missed his wife."

"Well, ma'am," said Colling, "It was good just to help out."

"Well, Colling," she replied, mildly mocking his deferential attitude, "It looks like the colonel wanted to help you out, too. He signed orders this morning bumping you up to PFC."

The promotion should have pleased him more than it did, but aside from a few more dollars in pay each month, the difference in status between a private and a private first class was not that great. His quarters would still be in the squad bay with eleven other men, and he would continue to stand inspections and draw guard duty. Nevertheless, Colling intended to thank the colonel when he went to pick up the rent money, but he did not have a chance to do so. Instead, Sergeant Gayle came out and handed him an envelope almost as soon as he entered the headquarters office, and told him it was from the colonel.

When Colling handed Veronika the envelope, she opened it and examined the sheaf of bills it contained. For the second time that day, she smiled, only this time directly at him, and he found himself grinning back at her, holding her gaze for as long as he was able. Out of either shyness, or her recollection of how irritating he had been when they first met, she looked away, and her expression changed as she seemed to him to remember that she should not be making such an obvious display. She extended her hand and when he took it, she simply thanked him, addressing him as "Jim."

Rather than let things end on this note, Colling asked her if he might call on her on the weekend. He was fully expecting her to decline when she surprised him by saying that Saturday afternoon would be acceptable.

During the days that remained until Saturday, Colling found it hard to keep his mind from wandering to Veronika and what their day together would be like, even as he saw patients in the dispensary. While he was applying a dressing to the hand of a soldier who had lacerated it while jumping from the back of a deuce-and-a-half truck, he was picturing how Veronika's violet eyes were set off by the dark hair framing her face; when his train of thought was interrupted by Major Elliott speaking excitedly on the telephone. Since Colling had not known the nurse to be anything other than composed when dealing with medical emergencies, he was instantly alert.

Colling was trying to figure out from the major's end of the conversation what the call was about while he was finishing pressing the last piece of adhesive into place. He dismissed the soldier, advising him to return for a re-check of his wound in a couple of days. As he did so, Major Elliott said, "Colling, they've got a bad one in the Casualty Ward. Jeep accident with internal bleeding. He's still alive, but they're sending one of those new planes, you know, like an autogyro....to get him to the airport so he can be flown to Augsberg."

"A helicopter?" said Colling.

"Right, that's it. They need us to check the blood type cards and get a couple of donors drawn right away. He's a type B, and the doctors want to use B donors if at all possible."

"Why not O's?" asked Colling, aware that type O was supposed to be compatible with all blood types.

"Doctor says he's been getting too many reactions lately. Wants to go with type B, only to try and avoid it."

Colling flipped to the "Type B" section of the blood-type card file. Among 400 men and women assigned to the hospital, there were only 31 with type B. Nearly half of them were assigned to the 511th's outlying dispensaries and clinics, and would not be immediately available. Colling took the remaining cards and ran to the switchboard room where the center for the hospital's loudspeakers was located. He burst in and after explaining the emergency, he picked up the microphone and began speaking into it. He could hear his voice echoing in the corridor outside, asking that the personnel whose names were being read to report to the Casualty Ward immediately to give blood.

Colling repeated the message three times, and then hurried to the Casualty Ward to see what results he had produced. He found Major Elliott in discussion with one of the surgeons, and saw that four men were on stretchers in the hallway, in various stages of having blood drawn from their arms.

When Colling was standing beside her and the physician, Major Elliott said to him, "We rousted four out of the bushes."

"Some are probably on furlough or off-post," replied Colling.

The surgeon, a captain whose name Colling remembered when Major Elliott addressed him as Doctor Jackson, remarked, "That helicopter will be here in a few minutes, and we won't have time to draw any more blood. These four pints are all that we can send with him."

At that moment, there was a commotion as a white-jacketed medic came through the ward's double doors from the parking lot, shouting "Let's go, people! The helicopter's here, and its engine is running, the pilot says he needs to get in the air! We got a C-47 waiting out at the air field."

Surgeon Jackson began giving orders, and there was what Colling would have termed "orderly confusion," as the patient was wheeled out, followed by medics and nurses carrying the four bottles that had just been filled with blood. Colling followed Major Elliott outside, and watched as the injured soldier was loaded onto another stretcher which was pushed through a door in the side of the strange-looking aircraft.

Colling happened to notice that two soldiers had come to stand behind him, and he turned and recognized them as men whose names were on the cards in Colling's hand. "Hey, Jim. Can we still give blood?" asked one of them.

Colling tugged at Major Elliott's shoulder, "Ma'am, these guys are two more donors."

"We don't have time to draw any more blood, Colling."

"Yes, ma'am, but maybe they could go in the helicopter, and give blood on the way."

Major Elliott shouted something at Dr. Jackson over the sound of the turning rotors, and the surgeon in turn shouted and waved at the aircraft's pilot, and after receiving the thumb's up sign from him, turned and motioned the two men forward. In a moment, one was seated in the cockpit, and the other had squeezed in beside the stretcher in its rear. Like those around him, Colling clasped his hands over his ears and squinted his eyes as the helicopter laboriously lifted off with a roar and a cloud of dust.

After he had brushed dirt and sand off his clothes and out of his hair, Colling thought nothing more of the incident, preferring instead to imagine how he would spend the day with Veronika when Saturday finally arrived.

On Friday arrived, he was experiencing even more acute anticipation concerning how his day with Veronika would go, when Major Elliott informed him that Colonel Barrowsmith wanted to speak to him. His immediate reaction was that his commanding officer was either formulating plans to ruin his weekend or had decided not to rent the Schönenberg house after all.

Colling was convinced that his concerns were well-placed when Colonel Barrowsmith asked him to sit down after the usual military formalities had been completed.

"Colling, I suppose you know that there are people around here who have a good opinion of you, don't you?"

"Well, sir, I hope so," said Colling, wondering where this was leading.

The colonel picked up a sheet of paper from his desk and said, "This is a letter from Colonel Jacobsen, commander of the 38th General Hospital in Augsberg. It commends the personnel of the 511th for their quick action and initiative in saving the life of Technical Sergeant Hubert Wells. Do you know who Sergeant Wells is?"

"No, sir. I don't"

"Sergeant Wells is the fellow that we air-lifted to Augsberg this week. If I had a more experienced orthopedist and a vascular man here, we wouldn't have had to do that, but doctors are in short supply in the Army right now. As it is, I've had to contract with a German neurosurgeon and an ophthalmologist until they get me some replacements from the States."

"Yessir," replied Colling, still not sure why he had been summoned, unless the colonel wanted him to go out and recruit German contract physicians.

"Anyway, Colling, the reason I asked to see you was that Colonel Jacobsen was particularly impressed with the fact that two compatible blood donors were sent with the patient. He called me on the phone and wanted to know how we were able to identify donors so quickly."

"Yessir," said Colling quizzically, but as he finally began to understand what the colonel was getting at, he added, "Major Elliott had me set up the cross-filing index, sir. I'm glad it did some good."

"Major Elliott disagrees, Colling. She says it was your idea. And she told me about that aneurysm case that you recognized. And Dr. Kenworth happened to mention your name to me before your court martial. Said you did the right thing when some drunk had a seizure in the stockade."

Colling was still not completely sure what the conversation was all about, and he began to be concerned that Colonel Barrowsmith was leading up to a re-enlistment speech, or an offer to send him to Officer's Candidate School or the like, something that could not be turned down without incurring the commanding officer's displeasure. He decided that it would be a bad move to be self-effacing, which would be his natural reaction in this sort of situation, and elected instead to treat things matter-of-factly.

"I just followed my training, sir. And begging your pardon, sir, but Major Elliott needs to take credit for the blood type card file. It was her idea, not mine."

"Be that as it may, Colling, I'm giving your back your stripes. As of today, you are a tech-four again. Sergeant Gayle will handle getting you moved into NCO's quarters."

"Thank you, sir. I really didn't expect this," replied Colling.

"You deserve it. And I want you to know I'm headed up to Wilhelmshaven this weekend to meet my wife at the boat. Sergeant Gayle will let you know when we arrive at the train station on Sunday. I want you to come with us when she sees the house. She says she's been taking a Berlitz course to learn German, but I still think you'd better be there to translate for us."

Colling indicated that he would be pleased to be of help, and recognizing that the interview had come to an end, he stood, saluted the colonel, turned on his heel and strode out of the room. In the outer office, he asked the clerk manning the desk for Sergeant Gayle, but before he could finish the sentence, he heard the master sergeant call out his name from his own office.

"Here's your promotion orders," said Gayle, handing him a mimeographed copy, "I put you in with Hardesty. You know him?"

"Sure, Sarge," said Colling, remembering Hardesty as a tech-four who was assigned to the x-ray department.

"Get your gear moved this afternoon after retreat. Have your stripes sewed on all your uniforms by Monday. Your work assignment will stay with Major Elliott. For some reason, she thinks you know what you're doing."

Major Elliott congratulated Colling when he returned to the dispensary, then told him to go ahead and take his uniform jackets and shirts over to the hospital laundry and see if he could get one of the German seamstresses to put his stripes on over the weekend.

That night, Colling had all of his belongings moved to his new quarters. He knew Hardesty only slightly, but while arranging his uniforms and equipment in the room that they would be sharing, he discovered him to be friendly without being intrusive, a combination that Colling found suited him just fine.

The elevation in rank brought additional responsibilities, which for Colling meant conducting a pre-inspection of a half-dozen of the lower-ranking enlisted men in the adjacent squad bay, prior to the customary Saturday morning inspection by one of the senior sergeants and the officer of the day. Colling looked over the equipment that had been spread out for review by his six charges, found a few small deficiencies, and offered advice on their correction. He was heartened to see that Sergeant Gayle and Lieutenant Bernstein, the pharmacy officer, were assigned to perform the inspection, and was pleased when they passed through the area with only a cursory look around.

Colling had sewn one set of his tech-four stripes on his Eisenhower jacket, anticipating that Veronika might notice that he had gained promotion. He took one last look in the mirror to make sure that he was presenting a soldierly appearance, brass polished and shoes shined, before leaving the hospital. He rode the *Strassenbahn* to the Nymphenburg district, and a half-hour later, alighted from the streetcar at the corner of Kleberstrasse and Nymphenburgerstrasse.

Veronica answered the door at Colling's knock and invited him in. She was wearing a blue calico dirndl that accented her eyes. More startling to Colling was the tantalizing view provided by the dress's low-cut bodice. Colling had to keep forcing his eyes in a less embarrassing direction, afraid that she would catch him staring. By way of distracting himself from where his thoughts were wandering, he suggested that they might take the streetcar to a restaurant he had passed on his way from the city center. She agreed, but asked first that he speak with her parents.

Her hand was on the handle of the door to the study when she said, "I see that you have received an elevation in rank, to *Unteroffizier*, is that not so?"

"No, in the American Army, it is *Techniker der Viertel Klasse*," said Colling, "But similar to sergeant, it is true."

Veronika once again introduced him to father and mother, pointing out that Colling had received a promotion. *Herr* Schönenberg congratulated him on his good fortune, adding that Colonel Barrowsmith must have a high opinion of him. The old man then asked Colling to be seated, and speaking in an unusually serious tone, said, "You understand, do you not, that Veronika is our only daughter, and that I and my wife have a concern for her well-being?"

"Yes, of these things I could not but be aware, sir," answered Colling, conscious that *Frau* Schönenberg was watching him intently. Veronika had seated herself to one side, presumably so as to appear neutral, thought Colling.

"We do not wish that you think that Veronika will be a passing fancy, easily forgotten once you have gone back across the ocean."

"Absolutely not, sir. I assure you that my intentions are honorable," said Colling, wondering what the next stage of his instructions might be. He wanted to tell the old man that all he wanted to do was to take his daughter to lunch, but thought better of it.

Afterwards, Colling surmised that it might have been the expression on his face that caused *Herr* Schönenberg to say, "*Gut*, I am satisfied. You may call on Veronika so long as she wishes you to do so. If you are not good to her, you will have to answer to me."

Colling responded by telling the couple that they would have nothing to worry about, at the same time thinking that it was more likely that he was the one who should be worrying. When the study door closed behind them, Veronika whispered, "My family is old-fashioned. My father is very protective. He forgets that I am a grown woman."

If that is so, he must be blind, thought Colling.

The restaurant that Colling suggested was called *Der Höfischer Garten*. He had noticed it because its tables were behind a hedge, shaded under several large trees. He was relieved when Veronika agreed with his choice. Once they were seated, she told him that her family had often dined there before the war. The place had been closed after the bombing became serious, and had re-opened only at the beginning of the summer.

With Veronika's permission, Colling ordered *Wienerschnitzel* for both of them, but the waiter informed them that unfortunately, veal was not available. After receiving the same news regarding three other choices from the menu, Colling finally asked what *was* available, and pork pies and a potato casserole were suggested. When the food came, they discovered that the pies contained no visible evidence of meat. Veronika laughed when Colling repeated the old story about the name "pork pie" being justified because a pig ran through the kitchen when they were being made; making him wonder whether she was being polite, or that the joke had actually failed to reach Germany.

As they emerged from the restaurant, Veronika asked if they might walk to her house, rather than take the streetcar. Colling had been trying to think of something that they might do to pass the remainder of the day, and was more than pleased at her suggestion. It would give him the opportunity to spend more time with the attractive brunette, and, he thought, to get to know her.

As it turned out, she demonstrated an interest in him first, asking Colling to tell her about America and his home. He described America in general, and Bel Cors in somewhat more detail, after which he went on to tell her about his parents and sisters. When she inquired whether he intended to pursue a military career, he laughed and told her he wanted nothing more than to finish his education and return to Bel Cors to run the family business. She seemed impressed that his father was the owner of a pharmacy, remarking that in Germany, the *Apotheker* was a highly respected professional.

When he explained that the United States government would pay for his attendance at the university under the GI Bill, she expressed her amazement, and wanted to know what the government would ask in return. Colling had not really thought about the post-war education program from that perspective, and after a moment's consideration, he told her that the idea behind the legislation was to reward those who had served in the war.

Colling realized that he had been doing all the talking, and consequently, he asked Veronika to tell him about her family. Rather than speak of her parents, she surprised him by starting with her brothers. She explained that she had three, all older than herself. Wilhelm...Willi...was the oldest, born before the Kaiser's war, as was the next in line, Friedrich. In 1919, during the "hard times" immediately after the first war, Albert Junior came along. She smiled when she said that her parents waited for the currency to stabilize before having her. Colling had gauged her to be a year or two older than himself, but when she mentioned that Germany's massive inflation had ended before she was born, he guessed that she might have been born in 1924 or 1925. He violated convention by asking her birthday directly, and was surprised to learn that Veronika was almost a month younger than he was.

Colling asked where her brothers were, and Veronika replied that the youngest, Albert Junior, had been shot down in 1940, while flying against the English. Albert had always wanted to fly, and had nagged their father until he had relented and permitted him to join a gliding club. Unfortunately, a year later, membership was limited to National Socialists, and Albert again had to pester their father to allow him to join the Hitler Youth. Her parents were not in favor of it, but at last gave in. In early 1940, Albert completed his *Luftwaffe* training, and joined a bomber group. He was given a week's leave the summer after France fell, and that was the last they saw of him. His squadron commander had written a solicitous letter telling them how brave Albert was, but it had been small comfort. While speaking of her brother, Veronika spoke in a level voice, and Colling had the impression that she was being deliberately controlled, almost as if she had practiced what she would say about Albert, Junior, if ever she were asked.

Veronika paused, and they walked in silence for a few moments, until she surprised him by telling him that her family's actual home had been in Frankfurt. This house in Munich was a second residence that they sometimes used when her father had business in Bavaria. He had inherited the place from his maiden aunt and had decided to keep it. Colling asked what the nature of the Schönenberg business was, and Veronika told him that her father had been a furrier. There had been a big house in Frankfurt, as well as an office and warehouses. Everything was gone now, destroyed by the bombing. That was why they had relocated to Munich in the summer of 1944. The decision to retain the house on Kleberstrasse had been fortuitous, otherwise they would have been refugees themselves.

Colling commented that the only people he was aware of who were in the fur trade in Wisconsin were some trappers who seemed to enjoy living an isolated life in the deep woods, but added that more trapping was done in Michigan and north of the border, in Canada. At this, Veronika told him that her father had been an international fur trader, buying pelts in Scandinavia and Russia, and reselling them to customers in Germany, France and the United States, where they were manufactured into coats, stoles and other articles of apparel. Sensing his interest, she told him that her father and older brothers traveled extensively before the war, and that Willi had even made a buying trip to Canada in 1935.

Continuing her narrative, Veronika surprised him by telling him that her family had maintained a residence in Russia for many years prior to the war. Every March for as long as she could remember, her parents and the younger children had migrated to their house outside Moscow. Each fall, they would return to Frankfurt for the winter. Her older brothers remained with their wives and families in Germany to manage the firm, but made numerous short visits to Russia during the summer months. She and her mother had been there when her father sent a message in April of 1941 telling them they should quietly return to Germany. Two months later, Veronika understood the meaning of the warning when the German Army drove into the Soviet Union.

Colling questioned the Soviet government's reaction to their presence, and Veronika explained that the fur trade was important to the Russians, representing one of their principal exports and sources of western currency. Her grandfather had been the first of the Schönenbergs to establish himself in Russia when the country was under the Czars. Even during the hard times and inflation in Germany after the First World War, her father held his funds in his bank in Zurich, and carried out his trades in dollars, sterling or

Swiss francs. As a result, the *Firma* Schönenberg continued to be welcome to do business in the Soviet Union.

Besides, she added, Hitler and Stalin were close friends during the early 1930's, and the German community in Russia frequently entertained the future *Luftwaffe* pilots that were being trained by the Red Air Force. Albert Junior's enthusiasm for flying became stronger after meeting and talking to the "Young Eagles," as he called them, and the young man continued to avidly follow the news accounts of their service with the Condor Legion during the Spanish Civil War.

Colling asked if she had learned to speak Russian, and Veronika responded by saying something that sounded to Colling like the Russian he had heard spoken in Poland. The slightly puzzled expression on his face made her laugh, and she and asked him if he had understood what she said. He admitted that he had not, and she laughed again.

Colling commented that her skill at Russian must have proven useful during the war, causing Veronika's smile to vanish. She said that it was not until late in 1944 that she was asked to come to work for the government. No one ever explained what bureau was employing her, but she reported to work each morning at a *Wehrmacht* office in central Munich. They had assigned her to translating Soviet publications into German, which she added, was all with which she was trusted.

Colling's curiosity was aroused by her last statement, and he asked why she would not be trusted, given that her brothers were German officers. When Veronika responded that they were not officers, he realized that his assumption that Willi and Friedrich had received commissions was in error. Veronika explained that both men had been called up in 1942, awarded the highest non-commissioned rank of *Stabsfeldwebel* and assigned together to an army group quartermaster purchasing unit, buying goods in Russian territory that had been occupied by Germany. Their fluency in Russian was the basis of their appointment, but they could not be made officers because, as Veronika explained it, they were "politically unreliable." Later, the buying of Russian foodstuffs, timber and other goods turned into confiscation, and her brothers' language skills were put to use in the interrogation of prisoners.

Willi had written one letter to her, employing a childhood code of his own that he had explained to her when she was a little girl, so that it had escaped the censors; and he was able to convey his disgust at the behavior of his superior officers and other German soldiers. That had been in December of 1943, and there was only sporadic correspondence from him and Friedrich until the war ended. The last letter, from Friedrich, had been dated in February, 1945, and said little except that he was alive.

Veronika went on to say that Willi's wife and two children were living near Chiemsee, well out in the country, where he had re-located them shortly after the first Allied bombing raids on Frankfurt. Friedrich had arranged for his own family to move to Dresden, and although she was uncertain of their fate, they had not been heard from, and Veronika was of the opinion that they had perished when the city was fire-bombed.

When the three men living over the garage had arrived in May of 1945, they had reported that they had last seen her two brothers in Czechoslovakia, when their convoy of supply wagons had been attacked from the air. The trio had lost track of the Schönenberg men and began their own cross-country trek westward, until they were able to surrender to the Americans.

When Veronika described the coded letter from Willi, Colling had conceived some idea why the Nazis might have believed the Schönenberg brothers "politically unreliable," but as he considered it, concluded that there must be more to it, and consequently, voiced his thoughts to Veronika.

Veronika began by stating that the political matter was because of her father. In 1936, a ranking Frankfurt official in the Brown Shirts, the Nazi *Sturmabteilung*, or SA, had called her father in and informed him that he was to buy out four of the furrier firms in the city that were owned by Jews: Biedermann, Goldman, Wellich and Cohn. The Brown Shirts would apply pressure in the right places to assure that the *Firma* Schönenberg would be able to purchase at rock bottom prices. When her father asked why the Party did not just seize the Jewish firms, he was told that these particular four had international connections and reputations that would make confiscation embarrassing. A purchase by a prominent private concern, such as Schönenberg's company, would be more acceptable, since the sales would appear to be voluntary.

The Nazi storm troop leader assured Veronika's father that there were smaller Jewish concerns that Party officials would be buying later for small change. Realizing that he had some leverage for negotiation with the Nazis, however small, *Herr* Schönenberg said that he would do as requested if the owners of the firms and their families would be given authorization to leave Germany, together with the purchase money. As an excuse, her father said that he did not want the Jews loafing about in the country, spreading defamatory lies about him. The SA leader said that problem could be eliminated by sending them all to Dachau, but her father responded that that would be worse. Everyone would think he had had them imprisoned so that he could steal their businesses. After some additional argument, during which he had to use crude names for Jews and act as if he believed in the stereotypes perpetuated by the Nazis, *Herr* Schönenberg got his way.

Colling estimated that the Schönenberg family's wealth must have increased considerably when the old man bought out the Jewish companies, and that they must be looking back on the years that Hitler was in power with nostalgia. However, he was still confused as to why, after participating in a quasi-confiscation of Jewish property, they would be considered "politically unreliable." His question was answered by Veronika, who said that her father paid 50,000 reichsmarks, which in those days amounted to $20,000, to each of his former colleagues in return for the transfer of their businesses to him. Afterwards, the SA man laughingly told her father that he had "out-kiked the kikes," by paying 200,000 reichsmarks for companies that were worth millions.

For once, the Nazis kept their word and allowed the Jewish furriers and their families to leave Germany. Removing the purchase money from Nazi Germany was another matter. Later her father was to learn that the banknotes in which the government required

Jews to be paid were not permitted to be exchanged for foreign currency, rendering the payment for their businesses meaningless. True to form, all of the Jews' other funds and assets had to remain in Germany and were frozen. It was Veronika's belief that eventually, everything was confiscated by Party officials or one *Reichsministerium* or the other.

But, Veronika explained, it was truly the Nazis who were out-smarted. During discussions leading to the acquisition of the firms, and at other times, *Herr* Schönenberg privately promised each of his former business colleagues that the profits from their compa-nies would be paid into a bank or banks in Sweden, and be made available to them. With his ability to legally transfer funds out of Germany on the pretext that they were for the purchase of furs in the Scandinavian countries, Veronika's father, with some unusual book-keeping, could divert cash to the former owners of the companies that had been added to the *Firma* Schönenberg. The fur business was very good during the years leading up to 1939, and for almost three years afterward. The *Luftwaffe* needed fur-lined flight suits and boots, and SS Panzer officers wanted winter uniforms of leather lined with wolves' fur. The scheme to siphon money to Sweden was continued from 1936 until well into 1943, with hundreds of thousands of reichsmarks flowing through the accounts established in Stockholm.

It was at this point that Veronika asked Colling if he had ever wondered why her father was in a wheelchair, and Colling replied that he had assumed that he had been injured during an air raid. She told him that his assumption was incorrect.

One day in 1943, her father was summoned to Gestapo head-quarters in Frankfurt. Such an invitation was something that no one wanted, but he had seemed calm about it, and sought to allay the fears of her mother and herself, telling them that because he had done nothing, there was no reason to be fearful.

Later that day, he returned, visibly shaken. There was an interest in his transfers of money out of the country. He tried to explain to his interrogators that prices of pelts had risen because of the war, and that if he was to continue to supply the armed forces, that foreign sources would have to continue to be used.

Twice more, her father was brought in for questioning. The last time, someone telephoned from the police station to tell them to come and pick up *Herr* Schönenberg. The family possessed no automobile by this time, but Veronika and her mother were able to locate a taxi driver who was willing to help them. Once the two women saw the condition that her father was in, they knew that he must be transported to a hospital. Among his many injuries, he had been beaten severely on his back, and vertebrae had been fractured.

Colling asked whether they had received any communication from the Jews her father had helped, and Veronika told him that to receive anything from overseas from a Jew at that time would have been a death sentence for them. Veronika believed that in the days before the war, on those occasions when her father or brothers visited their bank in Stockholm, that the manager would have messages for him from New York, but he never shared anything with herself or her mother.

They had arrived at the doorstep of the Schönenberg house, and Colling asked Veronika if she would be interested in a job at the hospital. He sensed that his making an offer to intercede on her behalf was not particularly welcome, but she said she would consider it. In accordance with European custom, she shook his hand and thanked him for the meal and for the pleasant afternoon.

Colling inquired when he might next see her, and with a somewhat puzzled look, she said that she had expected that he would see her tomorrow. Colonel Barrowsmith had telephoned, now that they once again had a telephone, and had announced that he and his wife would be taking up residence on Sunday. Colling explained that he was aware that he would be accompanying the Barrowsmiths as interpreter, but that he had been asking when the two of them might be able to go out by themselves. Veronika smiled and said that perhaps if he asked the question the following day, she could tell him.

CHAPTER 6

JULY, 1947

Sergeant Gayle had left a note tacked to Colling's wall locker, informing him that the Barrowsmiths' train was not expected at the Munich *Hauptbahnhof* until 1430 hours. As a result, on Sunday morning, Colling ate a leisurely breakfast and afterwards spent over an hour composing letters to his parents and his oldest sister. He had heard nothing from Elizabeth since April, and true to the promise he had made to himself, he did not bother to write to her. After completing his correspondence, he methodically arranged his uniforms and equipment so that he would have little to do in preparation when his quarters would next be inspected. At noon, he went to the mess hall, looking for the colonel's driver, whose last name he now knew was Everson, and joined him at his table. As they ate, Everson speculated as to what Mrs. Barrowsmith would look like, and Colling responded that she was probably a nice middle-aged lady, and for the PFC not to get his hopes up.

They were at the main railway station at 1400. Colling told Everson to stay with the staff car while he went to meet the Barrowsmiths. On his way, Colling checked the large blackboard where arrivals and departures were posted and saw that the train from Frankfurt was supposed to arrive on time.

He found two porters to follow him to the designated platform and wait with him. The train from Wilhelmshaven arrived, and after the line of passenger cars hissed to a halt, Colling spent several minutes scanning the crowd before Colling spotted Colonel Barrowsmith. Exactly as Colling had predicted, he had a very pleasant-looking middle-aged woman on his arm. The colonel greeted Colling warmly, introducing his wife before Colling took the bags they were carrying. Colling asked for the claim checks for the rest of their luggage, but Colonel Barrowsmith shook his head, telling Colling that he would have to send another vehicle to handle it all.

Everson gave Colling a "you were right" look as the driver held open the sedan's door for the colonel's wife.

Colling heard Mrs. Barrowsmith use his name, and turning in his seat said, "Sorry, ma'am, I couldn't hear you."

She responded, "I said, Sergeant, do you think I'll be able to get over the language barrier with the Schönenbergs?"

"I imagine so, ma'am. The Colonel said you were taking a Berlitz in German."

"Yes, I have. *Wie geht's* and *Auf wiedersehn* are about the limit for me so far, though."

The colonel interjected, "Now, Martha, don't sell yourself short. You did very well in Spanish when we were in the Philippines, and you even picked up a little Tagalog to boot."

Colling's interest was aroused by the colonel's comment, and he asked, "You were in the Philippines, sir?"

"Yep. We came home in July of '41, thank God. Spent two years there."

His wife added, "It was such a lovely place. Heaven knows what it's like now. From the newsreels, everything in Manila has just been totally destroyed."

Colonel Barrowsmith looked at Colling and said, "You know Major Elliott served in the Philippines?"

"No, sir. She's never mentioned it."

"She was. That's where Mrs. Barrowsmith and I first met her. She was a first lieutenant then. Fine girl, and an excellent nurse."

All Colling could say was, "Yessir," before the colonel continued, "She was still there when the Japs came. I understand she was with one of the field hospitals on Bataan, but then got pulled back to Corregidor, luckily. She was one of those nurses that got evacuated by sub a couple of weeks before the surrender."

Mrs. Barrowsmith added, "I never could figure out why, when she got back to Australia, she just didn't ask to come back to the States. She could have done so without anyone thinking the worse of her."

The colonel said, "But, she stayed in Australia, and ended up attached to a field hospital. She was in New Guinea, then later, back to the Philippines with MacArthur. Probably would have been in on the invasion of Japan if it wasn't for the A-bomb."

Colonel Barrowsmith frowned slightly as his wife interjected, "But you know the Army, they didn't make her a major until she got here to Germany, after the war was over."

Colling was developing a greater respect for Major Elliott as he listened. He had given no thought to the nurse's service during the war, and had assumed that she had been assigned to one of the large facilities in the States, or a station hospital in England. Because she had never mentioned being with a field medical unit, there had been nothing to make him believe otherwise.

Mrs. Barrowsmith had begun commenting on the appearance of the neighborhoods through which they were passing, and Colling provided a running commentary, describing the buildings and landmarks with which he was familiar. When they reached the Nymphenburg district, her reaction betrayed her favorable impression. Colling noticed her take hold of Colonel Barrowsmith's arm as they caught sight of the Schönenberg mansion, confirming his expectation that the colonel's wife would be pleased.

Veronika met them on the front steps with the cook and maid, both wearing crisp uniforms that Colling speculated had also been taken out of storage. Veronika introduced Hilde, the older woman who would be preparing their meals, and her daughter, Annelise, who curtsied when Veronika announced that she would serve as housemaid. Colling translated the exchange, assisted by Mrs. Barrowsmith, who tried out her rudimentary German. Colling smiled as Veronika responded politely to the American woman's laboriously-pronounced phrases. There was another tour of the house for the benefit of Mrs. Barrowsmith, and Colling once again acted as interpreter. Afterwards, Veronika ushered them all into the study to meet with her parents.

While Mrs. Barrowsmith had exhibited no particular reaction when she saw that *Herr* Schönenberg was in a wheelchair, when they were back in the foyer, she said to her husband, "Whatever happened to that poor man?"

Colonel Barrowsmith responded, "I would imagine it was the bombing," but then asked Colling if he knew.

"From what I understand, sir, he was beat up pretty bad by the Gestapo."

"Oh my heavens!" said Mrs. Barrowsmith, "What did the poor man do?"

"He did some things that the Nazis didn't like, ma'am," continued Colling, unwilling to relate all that Veronika had told him. "I wouldn't imagine he'd want to talk about it. Maybe some day, he'll let you know."

"Martha," said the colonel, "It's like men who've been in combat. They'd rather not dredge it all up again. When they want you to know more, they'll tell you."

Everson was standing in the foyer next to the Barrowsmith's luggage, waiting for instructions. Colling noticed him and asked Veronika which bedroom the colonel and his wife would be occupying. Indicating that Colling and Everson should follow her, she led them up the stairs, where they deposited the baggage in the largest of the second floor rooms.

As he and Everson were leaving, Colling had a few moments at the door to speak to Veronika, where she told him that she would be pleased to see him again on Saturday. As Everson drove them back to the hospital, the PFC commented that Veronika was a "real looker," and told Colling he was a lucky man. Colling agreed with Everson's assessment, and although he knew that further comment was expected, he said nothing.

Among the mail that Colling picked up on Monday was a letter to himself, bearing a return APO address from a Corporal Joseph Appleby. Colling did not know anyone named Appleby, which caused him to look again to make sure the envelope was correctly addressed. Satisfied that he was supposed to be the recipient, Colling tore it open; and inside discovered a folded sheet of note paper with a handwritten message.

Jim –

We need to talk. I'll be in the woods near where you and Liz used to picnic. Come by Schwinn if you can, suggest local garb.
Saturday the 12th, between 10 and noon.

Quarles

Colling was surprised that the missive was from Lieutenant Colonel Andrew Quarles, the Army intelligence officer with whom Colling had become acquainted the previous year. Colling was never completely free of suspicion when it came to Quarles' motives and intentions, and his first inclination was to throw the note away, but his curiosity was aroused.

The place where Quarles would be waiting was between Grabensheim and Camp 146, nearly a hundred kilometers from Munich. Colling would have to take a morning train to Grabensheim, if there was one running on Saturday morning, and then find a way to travel from there to the rendezvous. Quarles was obviously suggesting that he travel by bicycle and not wear his uniform. The civilian clothes he had brought back from Poland had been cleaned, washed and pressed and returned to his suitcase. They would do, but he couldn't get through the hospital gates dressed in them.

While he was considering how hard it might be to borrow a bicycle, he remembered his date with Veronika on Saturday. If he went to meet Quarles, he would not be able to keep it. For a moment, he was on the verge of electing not to meet with the intelligence officer, but then he decided instead to ask Veronika if they might postpone things until Sunday afternoon.

Colling had been expecting either Annelise, the maid, or Mrs. Barrowsmith to answer the telephone at the Schönenberg house, and was pleasantly surprised when he heard Veronika's voice instead. He explained that he had some "Army duties" he must perform on Saturday afternoon, and inquired whether he might come to see her on Sunday afternoon instead. Veronika replied that she understood that his military responsibilities must come first, and agreed that their afternoon could be postponed one day.

Finding a bicycle was not as difficult as he had expected. Fritz Meltzer knew someone who would loan him one for the day for a carton of cigarettes. Colling told Meltzer to bring the bike to the main railway station early Saturday morning. He had confirmed that there was a 0730 train to Grabensheim, and then asked Major Elliott if he could have a weekend pass. When she agreed, Colling told Sergeant Gayle that he would not be available for the weekly inspection, and said he would ask Hardesty if he could take over for him.

Colling met Meltzer on the steps of the *Hauptbahnhof* at 0600. He changed from his uniform into the civilian clothes he had brought with him in his knapsack, gave Meltzer a carton of Luckies, and shouldering the bicycle, bought a second class ticket to Grabensheim. A man with a bicycle was less conspicuous among the wooden benches of the cheaper accommodations than he would have been in a first class compartment.

The train station in Grabensheim had not changed since his last visit. Two MPs were still stationed on the pavement outside, and paid scant attention to the German bicyclist in the rumpled tweed suit who walked past them, then rode away.

The lack of vigorous exercise in his assignment as a hospital medic became painfully evident to Colling within a few minutes, as he pedaled the cobblestone streets of Grabensheim. His calves soon began to ache, and he started cursing Quarles under his breath for the intelligence officer's brilliant idea.

When Colling reached the road leading from town, the terrain was flatter, and he found it easier going, but by the time he approached the little country inn where he and Elizabeth had often picked up a lunch basket to eat in the surrounding forest, he was breathing heavily, and his shirt under the wool jacket was wet with perspiration.

Colling found the track leading off the main road into the woods, and dismounted, pushing the bicycle. After a few dozen meters, he emerged onto a grassy hillside that provided a view of the nearby hills of which Elizabeth had been particularly fond. Colling glanced around, and seeing no one, thought that he had been the first to arrive. He dropped the bicycle on its side, and as he did so, a sound behind him caused him to turn. Lieutenant Colonel Andrew Quarles, dressed in brightly embroidered *Lederhosen*, and wearing a Bavarian hiking hat with a ridiculously long pheasant's feather in its band, stepped from among the trees, and motioned to Colling to join him in their shadows.

"I see you remembered where to come," said Quarles.

"How could I forget, sir?" responded Colling.

"I guess not," said Quarles with a grin that contained just enough of a hint of salacious implication about his relationship with Elizabeth to annoy Colling.

"Still on the intelligence side of things, sir?" asked Colling.

"Yeah. We've got a radio-intercept operation in place."

"You had plenty of experience with that, I guess. That was your job in Italy, wasn't it? Eavesdropping on the Germans?"

"Yeah, only now it's the Reds," said Quarles.

Colling had to force himself to conceal his irritation before he asked, "Begging your pardon, sir, but what does that have to do with me?"

"That part doesn't, but I'm also involved in getting Red defectors over to our side. A colleague of mine started the operation in Austria. We call it the " 'Rat Line '."

"Named after the line that rats use when they leave a sinking ship, sir?" asked Colling.

"You get the picture," said Quarles.

"Before you say any more, sir, count me out. If you want me to go behind the curtain again and bring someone across, forget it. I don't want to have anything to do with any more Russians, not since last time, no matter what."

"This is a little different," said Quarles, reaching into a pocket for a pipe, which he tapped on the palm of his hand before lighting. "It's a job you might be interested in. No Russian defectors involved," and when Colling did not immediately respond, he added, "No Nazis, either."

The lingering annoyance that Colling had been feeling came to the fore, "Sir, You forget that I've never actually done a job for you. The first time, I didn't even know who you were. Elizabeth was the one who got me involved. And the second time, when I went to Poland to find Elizabeth, it was for me, not for you."

"For someone who wasn't working for me, you sure didn't hesitate to accept the pay," replied Quarles.

Colling did not respond immediately, aware that Quarles had given him $5,000 when he had put him on the plane from Hamburg in March. "Most of what you call 'pay' was to replace my own funds," said Colling.

"Granted, but you always got back more than you put in, didn't you?"

"Not quite true, sir. I had to forfeit six months' pay and allowances the last time."

"That was partly your own fault. You were the one that decided to free-lance, and then get yourself killed so I couldn't set up a cover story for your absence. There was really no choice but to let it go down as an AWOL. You did take the summary court, didn't you?"

"Yeah...sir...," said Colling, "But Vincent was the exec, and he hit me with the maximum."

"And I now understand you have your stripes back, and six months' pay was peanuts. Besides, you got your money from me in greenbacks."

"All right, all right, sir," replied Colling, "I'm tired of arguing. Give me a good reason why I should even listen to you."

Quarles paused before smiling and saying, "Because, the fact is, I think you like the challenge. You've gone behind the Iron Curtain twice and brought people out...important people, I might add. I think if I explain what has to be done this time, you'll be interested. And, this time I *will* pay you more than your expenses. How does another $5,000 sound?"

Colling's curiosity was aroused, "What's it all about," he asked.

"Let me give you a little background first. Right now there are over a million Soviet troops in Eastern Europe, staring down our throats. The political climate on our side is such that nobody wants to send more of our guys to guard Western Europe, so over here, we are operating on the proverbial shoe string. The only thing that keeps Stalin at bay is the A-bomb, which we have and he doesn't. He's figured out that four A-bombs would cause the USSR the same amount of casualties and damage as they suffered in the war, and he's willing to let that many more Russians die. Only problem Stalin has is, he doesn't know how many bombs we have. If we got more than four, he's screwed."

"So what does that have to do with me?" asked Colling.

"I'm coming to that. In order to keep the Russkies off balance, our flyboys, mostly Navy guys, but some Air Force types, make 'test runs' at them. They fly planes in real close to Soviet territory, finding out what kind of radar and other warning systems the Russians have got, and to see how they'll react. How many fighters they'll put up, and so on. They call them 'ferret' operations. The idea is, we want to look like we're always getting ready to drop the big one on them.., or lots of big ones, if you will."

"I still don't get it."

"One of our planes went down in Poland last month. A B-29 with nine men aboard. I'd like you to take a shot at getting them out."

"I have no desire to go to Siberia," said Colling.

"Don't need to," replied Quarles, "They're in Germany."

"I thought the Reds shipped all our fliers to Siberia."

"Not this time. They decided to use the services of a former *Luftwaffe* interrogator and a real nasty fellow from the security branch of the SS to work on our guys."

The reputation of the Nazi internal security agency, the *Sicherheitsdienst*, or "SD," was well known to Colling. Torture was their specialty, and it was said that anyone who fell into their hands seldom survived the experience. "So the Reds have got the Nazis working for them," he commented.

"Birds of a feather," said Quarles.

"Yeah," said Colling, "So why should I stick my neck out?"

"So you maybe can save some of our guys from taking a bullet in the back of the neck, or worse, really going to Siberia, or both.

And plus, you'll enjoy the challenge," replied the intelligence officer, with too much of a smile to suit Colling.

"Who knows I'm going in?" asked Colling.

"Nobody but me," said Quarles.

"$5,000?" asked Colling.

"Yep."

"If I don't make it, paid to my folks?"

"If you want. But you'll make it. After all, it's the challenge," said Quarles, smiling again.

"This time, I want a cover story so I can be absent from my outfit," said Colling.

"Done. You've been accepted to a course in tropical diseases in a French Army hospital in Oran. That's in Morocco. You applied for the slot months ago. At least that's what the paperwork will show. If you give me a 'yes' today, the orders will be in your CO's office on Wednesday."

"And if somebody happens to make inquiries in Morocco?" asked Colling.

"You'll be in the desert, studying the Tsetse fly or some such. I have a friend in the French secret service who's running an operation in North Africa. He owes me a favor from Italy, and he'll make sure there's paperwork to show you arrived and are where you say you are," replied Quarles.

"Okay, sir, I'm listening," said Colling.

Quarles pulled a map from his jacket pocket and unfolded it, pointing to a pencil mark in the Soviet Zone, near a town named Hohenwald. "The place is a former SD camp the Nazis called '*Stalag S-1.*' They built it in '38, and first used it for Czech officers that they wanted to give special attention to, if you know what I mean. Later, they brought Poles, French and British prisoners there for questioning, and then Russians and Americans. As far as we can tell, only a handful of the inmates ever got out alive, and nobody escaped. The Russians took over the place and have been running it themselves."

Colling scanned the map, and then asked, "What makes you think the B-29 crew is still alive?"

"I don't, but I do know that the Russians will want to keep them alive."

"Because they know something they want to know real bad," said Colling.

"Right," replied Quarles.

"And could you tell me what it is?"

"Without going into any detail, the plane was carrying a piece of equipment that's used with the A-bomb. Don't ask me how. I haven't been told, and I doubt if I would fully understand it, anyway."

"So why didn't the Reds just take this thing, whatever it is?"

Quarles answered, "I'm told it's rigged with a booby-trap. If you don't know how to take it out, it goes boom."

"And the Reds are questioning the crew to find out how to do it?"

"Right. They captured a B-29 with one of these things aboard that went down in Siberia, a year or so ago, and apparently a couple of their technicians and some high-ranking Soviet officers were killed when the explosives went off. They don't want to make the same mistake again."

While listening to the intelligence officer's responses to his questions, Colling began to assess all the things that might spell disaster in an attempt to extricate the airmen, and he asked "How sure are you that they're at this particular camp?"

"I have a contact. He goes by 'Vogelsang,' but that may or may not be his real name. A ex-*Waffen* SS type. He has a few people in the area who have been resisting the Soviet occupation. Kind of like what we were experiencing the last couple of years on our side, only he's kept at it. I've been sending a few Mausers to him, and he provides me with some help."

"So the Reds employ Nazis, and we do the same," commented Colling.

"Whatever works, my friend. This guy might be your ticket out of East Germany, so don't let yourself get too morally strict about it."

"Can you trust him?"

"I don't know. But as long as I supply him with arms, I figure he'll stay on our side."

Colling thought for a moment before he asked, "How do you figure to go about getting them out?"

"I thought you might hook up with Vogelsang, watch the camp, and wait for an opportunity to bust in and get them. I already set up a little diversion...I got the State Department to demand the flyers' return, and insist that they were known to be in a specific camp in Poland. The Russians are denying everything, of course, and hopefully they'll think we don't know where our flyboys really are."

A plan had begun to form in Colling's mind, fueled, by the "challenges" the mission presented, to use Quarles' terminology; as well as a faint sense of confidence that it might actually succeed. He was also attracted by the possibility of saving the lives of the Air Force men who were surely doomed if he did nothing. Colling thought back to the disappearance of Elizabeth's husband, who had been part of a B-29 crew that went down in Russian territory during the war, and who was never heard from again. Maybe someone needed to do more than just use "official channels" to demand the return of American servicemen in Soviet hands.

Colling had not spoken while turning these thoughts over in his mind, and he noticed that the intelligence officer was quietly waiting for him to say something, so he said, "I'll do it."

"Good man!" said Quarles.

"But I do it my way. I decide when to contact Vogelsang, and you don't give him any advance notice I'm coming. I'll need some expense cash, and the next time you hear from me, I hope, is when I'm back in the U.S. Zone. And don't have anyone following me around before I go."

"Done," said Quarles, taking another piece of paper out of his pocket and handing it to Colling. "This is a list of the names of the men in the B-29 crew. You might want to memorize it. And the map is yours to keep. If you ask the proprietor of the tavern in Hohenwald for Vogelsang, he's supposed to be able to contact him."

"I'll leave as soon as the orders for Morocco arrive," responded Colling. "What about the expense money?"

Quarles reached into his jacket and handed Colling an envelope, saying, "There's five hundred there. I can't get any more to you before you leave, so if it's not enough, use your own cash, and I'll reimburse you. And by the way, if you need to reach me, use the APO address for Joe Appleby, and I'll get it. Watch the content of anything you write; it might not be totally secure."

The intelligence officer reached out to shake Colling's hand, "Good luck, Jim. If things begin to go sour, forget the mission and get the hell out of there."

"You can count on that, sir."

It was clear that their business was concluded, and Colling had picked up his bicycle and was swinging his leg over the seat, when Quarles said, "I hope you can convince everyone when you get back that you've become an expert in tropical diseases, you know, like malaria and beri-beri."

"Beri-beri's a nutritional disease," said Colling.

"Yeah, but it sounds tropical," said Quarles

CHAPTER 7

JULY, 1947

Concentrating on what had to be done to prepare for the task ahead of him meant that Colling was not conscious of the aching in his legs while pedaling back to Grabensheim. When he reached the town's outskirts, he decided that rather than immediately returning to Munich, he would look up an old friend, Klaus Zinsmann.

Zinsmann was a building contractor whom Colling had first met soon after Colling had arrived in Germany in the fall of 1945. Because of Colling's ability to speak German, he had been asked to find local labor to repair the kaserne in which Colling's infantry battalion had been quartered. The German builder had been chosen to do the work, and afterwards, had been hired by the Army for other projects. As far as Colling was concerned, however, he had proven more valuable in other ways. Zinsmann, whom Colling had reason to suspect had served in the *Waffen* SS, had taught Colling how to use a Luger pistol, and had provided him with advice in obtaining forged documents before Colling had gone to Poland to rescue Elizabeth.

When Colling knocked on the door of Zinsmann's apartment at Number 8, Trebensallee, he was surprised when a man he did not recognize answered. Colling asked for Zinsmann, and was told that he no longer lived there, but the man added that he worked for the contractor, and that Zinsmann had moved into a house on the south side of the town. The man gave Colling directions, and fifteen minutes later, Colling was pedaling up the lane leading from the road to a neat two-story house that appeared to be newly constructed. Two children were playing in the yard, and when they sighted Colling, they ran into the house, shouting that someone was coming.

Before he could dismount from the bicycle, Zinsmann was out the front door and greeting him effusively, "My friend! How goes it? I heard rumors that you were dead at the hands of the damned

Russians, and then that you arose from the grave," said the German, as he clapped Colling on the back.

Forcing himself to ignore how Zinsmann would have heard that he had been killed in Poland, Colling grinned and said, "Dead I am not, my friend."

"That I can see," laughed Zinsmann. "What brings you to Grabensheim?"

"I came to see you. As usual, I have a favor to ask."

"Anything, Colling. What is it you require?" said Zinsmann, as he led Colling into the house.

"First you must tell me how you have come to acquire such a fine residence," said Colling, while Zinsmann urged him to take a seat and brought out a bottle of Bourbon whiskey and two tumblers.

"Business is good," said the German as he poured the liquor and handed Colling one of the glasses. "I have almost thirty men working for me now, twenty of them regularly, and eight trucks. Next month, your Army promises me they will let me buy a surplus earth-mover, how do you say in English, 'A bulldozer.' Your Army permits me a gasoline ration for the work I do for them. There has been even more construction to be done for my countrymen. That damned thief Hessler has made so much money with his tavern that he had it expanded. He has influence with your Army so that your soldiers are not prohibited from patronizing his place."

Colling could not recall who Hessler was, but he nodded and took a sip of the whiskey. He almost coughed at the burning sensation in his throat, but fought against the urge. Colling's alcohol consumption was usually limited to beer, and the occasional glass of wine with meals, leaving him un-used to stronger drink. When he had recovered his breath, he said, "It pleases me that you have done well."

"Myself as well, Colling," replied Zinsmann. "Tell me what it is that I might do for you."

"I need some things. Some German uniforms that are no longer of use, perhaps, and some documents. I have American dollars to pay."

"The uniforms are not a problem. There is a man in the town

who deals in used clothing, and I know my workers purchase such items from him from time-to-time. Documents are another matter," said the German.

"False documents are not what I seek," said Colling. "I wish, instead, to obtain perhaps some old *Wehrmacht* or *Luftwaffe* pay books and identity papers. I know that many of these were discarded shortly after the war's end, but such things are also sometimes saved."

"True enough," said Zinsmann. "My friend in the town also possesses *Soldbuchen* left behind by soldiers wishing others not to know that they had served in the military."

Zinsmann insisted that they use his Opel truck to drive to the used clothing shop. The contractor boasted as they drove that the little vehicle had only 40,000 kilometers on its odometer. He had stumbled on it in a barn, where it had been hidden by its owner in 1943 to avoid confiscation by the old government, and then later, the Americans, after they came on the scene. The farmer had little practical use for the truck, having no influence or money to obtain gasoline; and Zinsmann had been able to take it in exchange for some renovations to the man's house and outbuildings.

The shop to which Zinsmann drove was situated in the last building on Grabensheim's main thoroughfare, just before the street turned into the country road leading west to Kummersfeld. The store's facade had not been painted for a long period of time, and the single plate-glass window was so grimy that it was almost impossible to see into the interior of the place.

Colling had just said that the shop looked as if it were closed, when Zinsmann jumped out of the truck and began banging on the front door, shouting for 'Otto.' Eventually, a window on the second floor was thrown open and a man's head appeared. It became apparent to Colling that the man must be Otto when Zinsmann told him to open up, that one of his men needed some work clothes.

Otto admitted the two of them, then locked the door behind them, grumbling about needing his Saturday afternoon off. Still complaining, he led them into the rear of the shop, where every available surface seemed to be piled with articles of clothing. Colling asked to see military items, and Otto showed him a large table stacked high with used *Wehrmacht* and *Luftwaffe* uniforms. Colling and Zinsmann sorted through the pile, Colling holding up trousers, shirts and jackets, seeking those in his size. When Colling asked about shoes, Otto pointed to a cluttered row of footware along the base of the back wall.

After a half-hour's search, Colling had selected two pairs of German Air Force trousers, a tunic to match, a couple of well-worn shirts, underwear, socks and heavy shoes that Zinsmann assured him were *Luftwaffe* issue. The German contractor also pulled an overcoat from a rack and tossed it on top of the other items. Colling asked Otto if he had a rucksack in stock, and the shopkeeper rummaged in a wardrobe before bringing out a gray-blue canvas bag intended to be slung over one shoulder. Otto explained that he had no backpacks in stock, and Colling would have to take what was offered. When Colling hesitated, Zinsmann remarked that such bags were commonly used by German Air Force personnel.

Otto was folding and stacking the clothing that Colling had selected when Colling said that he understood that the man might have some discarded *Soldbuchen* for sale. Zinsmann nodded his approval, and Otto left the room, returning a few minutes later carrying a cardboard box. Colling pulled back its flaps, and saw that it was nearly full of German pay books, labor force identity books, and other reminders of the Nazi bureaucracy's obsession with everyone always having the proper "papers."

Colling flipped through the pay books, looking for the dark gray covers of those issued to German Air Force troops. After examining the identity photographs in several of them, he settled on one that had belonged to a young man with a reasonably close resemblance to himself. While Colling was engaged in his search, Zinsmann was also rifling through the contents of the box, and as Colling settled on his choice of *Soldbuch*, the contractor handed him an old military railway pass, some ticket stubs, and several snapshots of groups of young soldiers in *Luftwaffe* uniform, telling him that they might prove useful.

Because it should have been clearly apparent to Otto by now that he and Zinsmann were interested in more than work clothing,

Colling was becoming concerned about the probability that the storekeeper would spread tales about his two Saturday afternoon customers. When Otto left them alone for a few moments, Colling whispered his thoughts to Zinsmann, who told him not to worry.

When Otto returned, Zinsmann asked him how much the various items would cost. The man responded that 500 marks would do, and Zinsmann turned to Colling, who took out $100 in U.S. currency. Colling placed half of the money in Otto's hand, and as he gave him the remaining fifty dollars, he told the man that for the extra payment, he expected total silence about his purchases, and that all memory of his visit would be erased. Zinsmann had a particularly threatening expression on his face as he added that any slip-up on Otto's part would have serious consequences. When the storekeeper's face went pale at Zinsmann's remarks, Colling was reasonably confident that he would not talk.

They returned to Zinsmann's house to retrieve Colling's bicycle. Colling was invited inside, where the German left him waiting in the living room, reappearing after several minutes with his hands full. He gave Colling a small battered compass and gray-painted tin box that looked as if it had once been some sort of first aid kit. When Colling opened it, he found it contained a safety razor, an open package of blades, a small piece of soap and a shaving brush, all wrapped in a scrap of towel. The German also handed over a worn copy of a paperback book titled *Panzer Vorwärts!* Its cover pictured a German soldier waving a tank forward. Zinsmann said, "It would be best if you read a little of it, in case you are asked about it."

The German next gave him two five-franc banknotes overprinted for Tunisia and another of 100 francs from France with a 1942 date. As he did so, the German advised, "Keep this money, but be sure to have a few Allied military marks on you, and buy a bread roll or two for your pockets, and a bottle of beer to put in your pack. If you can find a little cheese, that too would be good."

After offering this advice, Zinsmann produced a piece of paper on which were written the names of individuals, dates, and what appeared to be the numbers of German military units. "I think I know what you intend to do, Colling, and you have made a good choice. If you are to be a *Luftwaffe* veteran, it is best to be of a flak unit. They were often attached to larger commands, and came and went frequently, so that it would be hard to trace the history of any one of them. Besides, it will mean you will be expected to know nothing about airplanes."

Running his finger under two of the names that were listed, Zinsmann continued, "These two men, I know to have been *Volks-deutchen*, raised in America and returned to Germany when Hitler called. I knew these men when I served in Africa and then later in the Fatherland. I do not know whether they live or not, but they were Germans who spoke English well. The other names are those of officers I knew, and the rest are the numbers of flak detachments that were with the panzer grenadier battalions in which I served. Of the last, there were two also, the 35th and the 267th. These names will, perhaps, give you an edge when you are questioned.

"The man Pretzmann, I know to have been placed in an Allied prisoner of war camp in Tunisia to deceive the prisoners that he was an American. I recommend that you not be arrested by the Americans while you pretend to be Pretzmann, as he was responsible for the deaths of American war prisoners, and for certain is likely to be classed as a war criminal."

The German concluded by saying, "I trust that you may find this information of use. I wish you much luck, my friend. You must this time try not to get yourself killed."

Zinsmann drove Colling to within a block of the railway station, pulling the Opel to the curb at a place where it could not be seen by the MPs who were still standing outside its entrance. Colling thanked the German for his assistance, and with the canvas bag full of his purchases over his shoulder, pedaled his bicycle over the cobblestones to catch the afternoon train to Munich.

In Munich, Colling removed the documents from the carryall, changed back into his uniform, checked the bag containing the civilian clothes at the *Hauptbahnhof* baggage counter, and went to see if Meltzer was there to pick up the bicycle as promised. The German was waiting for him at the place where he said he would be. Colling handed over the bicycle and boarded the streetcar for the hospital.

Hardesty was enjoying Saturday night on the town, so Colling had their room to himself. He began by going over the map that Quarles had provided, doing his best to memorize the location of *Stalag S-1* and the features of the countryside around Hohenwald. He looked over the list of names of the B-29 crewmen, and after some juggling, discovered that their last names could be arranged to spell out CHARTWELL. By a quirk, Caldwell, the pilot, and Hammerslee, the co-pilot, headed the list. Confident that he would be able to recall the name of Churchill's estate, and consequently those of the airmen, he turned to his own identity.

Colling took out the paper that Zinsmann had provided. The German contractor's help was a stroke of luck. Colling had been concerned about how he would create a plausible background for himself, and had considered asking Quarles for some last-minute assistance on that score. But using the APO address that Quarles had given him would be too slow, and with the possibility of the Heidelberg telephone lines being tapped by the Soviets, the prospect of making a call did not particularly appeal to him.

Colling read and re-read the information about the *Luftwaffe* and panzer units, and the names he must be able to recall with ease. When he was able to visualize the paper in his mind and could say each item softly without reading it, he felt he had mastered its contents.

Colling next scrutinized the *Soldbuch* he had purchased from Otto, and memorized the information about Heinrich Denschler, its former owner, that had been filled in on its pages. When he was certain he could repeat back everything about Denschler, he added the pay book to the other documents and hid everything in an inside pocket of his U.S. military overcoat that was hanging in his wall locker.

These preparations completed, Colling composed a letter to his parents, explaining that he had been selected for special training in Morocco, and would not be able to write for several weeks. He post-dated the letter to Wednesday. He made a mental note to be sure to drop it in the mail before he departed.

Veronika answered the door when Colling arrived at the Schönenberg house about an hour after noon on Sunday. He had intended to ask her where she might wish to eat lunch, but before he could pose the question, Veronika invited him into the kitchen, where she said a meal had been prepared. He took a place at the long table that filled the center of the room. Veronika sat next to him, and Annelise shyly helped her mother bring their plates. Once everyone had a dish in front of them, the cook and maid joined Colling and Veronika and after crossing themselves, began to eat.

Colling was amazed at the relish with which the three women attacked the slices of Spam that comprised the principal part of their lunch. Veronika remarked that the American tinned meat was wonderful, adding that they were very fortunate that Mrs. Barrowsmith had generously brought them several cans from the commissary. For his own part, Colling thought the diced fried potatoes more remarkable, and the boiled cabbage had been seasoned to perfection. About half-way through the meal, Colling thought to diplomatically ask whether Veronika's mother and father had been able to enjoy such delicious food, and she informed him that they had been served first.

After lunch, Colling and Veronika once again strolled along the shaded sidewalks in the Nymphenburg district. They exchanged small talk, regarding how warm the summer had become this year in Munich, and about how kind the Barrowsmiths were to Veronika's parents. Eventually, there was a lull in the conversation, and after they had walked in silence for a few moments, Colling slipped his hand into Veronika's, and was pleased when her fingers closed warmly on his own.

Veronika began to speak of her childhood in Germany and Russia, and as she did, Colling found that he could not keep his eyes off her. While he was consciously registering what she was saying, his mind was filled with the impression of her dark hair shining in the sunlight filtering through the leaves above them, and how her violet eyes seemed to sparkle when she smiled. She suddenly let go of his hand to point to a bird that had landed in a tree ahead of them, and Colling seized the moment to put his arm around her waist. He was disappointed when she pulled away and brought her hand back into his.

Veronika stopped and turning to face him, said, "Jim, I must tell you something. I was once betrothed. To a young man who was so wonderful. But he came back from the Eastern Front with only one leg. I went to Tölz to visit him in the convalescent hospital, but it was not good, and he has told me never will he see me again. He is so angry, and now I have heard that he has married another."

"This is of no consequence to me," replied Colling, "Unless you remain in love with him."

"I am not," said Veronika, "But it is important you know this. It was wartime, and we thought that we had little time. What my father has said to you about me...you see...."

The young woman was clearly searching for a way to say that she was not a virgin, but was having difficulty in saying so, prompting Colling to come to her assistance by saying, "But a father does not always know everything, is that not true?"

With a look of relief, Veronika responded, "Yes, that is so. That is a good way to put it."

Colling did not share the preoccupation with female virginity of most of his male colleagues, and consequently, had no difficulty in telling Veronika, "This also is of no consequence to me. We shall not speak of it again."

Veronika's hand was still in his, and as Colling gazed down into her eyes, he felt something inside himself that he had never experienced with any other woman. Her eyes were fixed on his, and he had to stop himself from saying that he was in love with her. Fully expecting Veronika to express some similar emotion of her own that would complicate matters, and wishing to forestall it, Colling said, "We are friends, yes?"

"Yes, for sure, yes," replied Veronika.

At this point, Colling decided that the moment had arrived to inform Veronika that he would be going away for a time. He told her that he had been accepted at an Army school in Morocco, and did not know how long he would be in Africa. The school was in the desert, and he could not promise that he would be able to write to her, but added that he would do so if he could.

Colling's news resulted in their being decidedly subdued as they concluded their walk and returned to the Schönenberg house. Rather than saying farewell on the front steps, Veronika led Colling to the mansion's rear and down the set of steps leading to the basement kitchen. They stopped outside the door, and Colling promised her that the school would not last long, and she told him that she would look forward to his return. Veronika reached out to shake hands, and on an impulse, he drew her to him and kissed her. She returned his embrace, her lips on his, but then pulled away sooner than he would have preferred. With one last soft, "*Auf wiedersehn,*" Veronika turned quickly and left him, shutting the door behind her.

Sick call on Monday morning was busy, consisting of a high proportion of the usual intestinal maladies resulting from the intemperate consumption of alcohol over the weekend. There were also several soldiers concerned about having contracted venereal disease, all of whom wanted an injection of penicillin. Because only one of them was exhibiting the symptoms of gonorrhea, he was the one whose request was granted by Major Elliott. Colling distributed swabs and specimen envelopes to the others with which they could take smears to be sent to the laboratory for culturing, and they were then instructed concerning the signs of infection for which they should watch. Colling assured each of them that they would be informed about the results of the tests, and if positive, they would be directed to return for treatment.

When he returned from lunch, Major Elliott told him that he was to report to Sergeant Gayle. As expected, the master sergeant notified him that he had been chosen to attend a school in tropical diseases in Morocco. Gayle expressed his disbelief that Colling been accepted for the training, and asked suspiciously when Colling had applied. Colling responded that he recalled requesting to go to the classes when he heard about it a year or more previously, and admitted that he had forgotten about it. Gayle said that he could always decline the assignment, but Colling said he was still interested, and added that it would give him a chance to say he had been to Africa. Gayle grumbled that Colling would be leaving on Wednesday as he handed him his orders.

That night, Colling wrote a letter to Quarles, using the name and APO that the lieutenant colonel had given to him, and the "Corporal Joe Appleby" return address. Being as brief and anonymous as possible, he asked Quarles to have the U.S. Constabulary put out an alert regarding Robert Pretzmann, an American citizen who had served in the German army, and who was responsible for the deaths of American POWs in North Africa.

CHAPTER 8

AUGUST, 1947

Meltzer agreed to accompany Colling to the Munich railway station on Wednesday. In the men's room, Colling changed out of his uniform into the civilian clothes that had been hidden in the bottom of his wall locker. Dressed in his Cousin Jerry's old suit and carrying his suitcase, Colling went to the baggage counter and checked his Army duffel bag, now containing the uniform he had worn to the terminal, and retrieved the canvas carryall he had left there on Saturday afternoon. He passed Meltzer on his way out and handed him the new claim check and the suitcase. He had arranged for the German to pick up the other bag and keep them at his home in his absence.

The closest town to the border with the Soviet Zone that possessed a train station was Zilsdorf. Colling bought a ticket to the place, and waited patiently until his train arrived. He had decided not to use the false passport he had carried when he was pretending to be his Cousin Jerry, and consequently the only documents on his person were those related to Heinrich Denschler, and they were tucked away in the canvas shoulder bag. Colling was gambling that there would be no one examining the identity papers of travelers within the U.S. Zone, and he took it as a favorable omen when it turned out that he was correct.

At Zilsdorf, Colling left the train, stopping to buy a beer and two of the *Brötchen* that were being offered by a old lady plying her wares from a cart on the station platform. With the carryall over his shoulder, Colling hiked out of Zilsdorf until he found a side road leading to the east. Eventually, he encountered a track that intersected the road, and followed it into the trees. Once in the woods, he changed into the German air force uniform. Afterwards, he searched for a place where he could easily dig a hole by hand, and buried his civilian clothing. The *Soldbuch* and other documents needed to complete his disguise were in the pockets of his *Luftwaffe* tunic when he touched a match to the map and lists given him by Quarles and Zinsmann and scattered their ashes.

Colling traveled through the forest, remaining parallel to the road, until it ended in a farmyard. A man was tilling a garden next to the house, and Colling watched him work until a woman called to him from its doorway. The farmer dropped his hoe, and wiping his hands on a rag, went inside the house, presumably to eat his midday meal. Colling circled the perimeter of farm, remaining concealed as much as possible, until he reached a more densely forested area.

With the sun directly overhead, Colling was no longer certain of the direction in which he was traveling. Admitting that he would never have thought of the necessity for a compass, Colling blessed Zinsmann as he used the one that the German had given him to get his bearings. Following the compass' needle, he used a large hill that he could see in the distance as a landmark that would lead him to the Soviet Zone.

Demarcation between the two occupation zones proved easy to find. A 200-meter wide swath of open ground had been cleared, presumably by the Russians, and Colling could see a crew working on the construction of a guard tower about a kilometer from where he had stopped at the edge of the trees on his side of the line. There was no fence in evidence, and Colling considered whether there might be landmines planted in the cleared area that he would have to cross.

Colling was watching the men nailing cross-ties on the legs of the tower when out of the corner of his eye, he noticed movement, causing him to draw back into the underbrush in which he was hiding. Two Soviet soldiers on horseback were riding on the far side of the cleared gound, PPSh submachine guns slung on their backs. They gave no indication that they had seen him and continued past his position. The presence of the patrol in the open field was probably an indication that there was no risk of mines. Colling decided he would wait until nightfall to cross into the forest opposite.

By Colling's estimate, the horse patrols passed by at one hour intervals during the remainder of the day. Because he had no watch, he decided that after it was fully dark, he would move as soon as possible after the first pair of Russians rode by. He rested on his back, waiting for the forest to recede into darkness. When night came, there was no moon, and all was in shadow. Colling rolled over watching and waiting for the patrol to make its rounds. After what seemed a long time, Colling made out the dark forms of the riders traversing the field in front of him. When he could no longer see their shadows, he continued to listen carefully for the sound of the horses. When he was certain they had moved off into the distance, he ran crouching across the field, dashing breathlessly into the cover of the trees on its opposite side.

Quarles' map had shown a road close to the Soviet side of the border, which Colling had expected to find quickly, even at night. However, when he had been walking through the darkened forest for what seemed a long period of time, and he had still not found the roadway, he decided to settle down and wait for the sun to come up. Once he lay down, he instantly fell asleep.

The dim light of dawn was just showing through the trees when Colling was awakened by the sound of an engine. He looked through the branches of the bushes behind which he had been sheltering and watched as a military truck drove by on a dirt road not more than fifty meters from his resting place. Once the vehicle had passed out of sight and sound, Colling drank some of his beer and ate one of the *Brötchen*. When he had finished, he picked up his canvas bag and resumed his journey.

Colling headed north, keeping to the trees, but in sight of the road. Aside from the truck, there was no motor traffic, although he did pass a wagon heaped with hay moving slowly in the same direction as himself. When he spotted another cart carrying no cargo headed the opposite way, Colling emerged from the forest and with his hands held high, approached the driver with a friendly greeting, making sure to keep a smile on his face as he did so.

"*Kamerad!* I mean you no harm," said Colling, "I wish only to know the way to Hohenwald."

The white-haired old man driving the cart leaned forward in his seat, and Colling could see that there was a hatchet close to his right hand as he said, "Stand back. That is close enough."

Colling stopped in his tracks, and again said, "I seek only the way to Hohenwald, sir."

The driver was now scanning the trees behind Colling, clearly trying to discern whether Colling had friends hiding there. Colling said, "I am alone, sir. I only wish to find my way." Pulling the bottle of beer from his bag, Colling popped open the ceramic cap and offered the man a drink. At this, the old fellow reached down and took the bottle and raised it to his lips. After a long swallow, he handed the beer back to Colling. Gesturing over his shoulder, the driver said, "Hohenwald is that way. Not far. Be careful of the Russians. They pick up wanderers and put them to labor."

Colling thanked him and returned to the trees. Once he was in among them, he watched as the cart moved slowly off along the road.

The forest ended on the outskirts of Hohenwald, and Colling was forced to walk into the town, ready to flee or attempt to conceal himself should he encounter any Russians. The map had indicated that he must go to the south of Hohenwald before finding a side road that would lead to *Stalag S-1*. He passed a few people, several of whom looked at him with curiosity as he tried to display an air of purposefulness while he strolled through the town. None of them spoke to him, and he simply nodded a greeting as he walked by. He hoped that the sight of former German soldiers was not so unusual as to cause any of them to mention it to someone in a position of authority.

The turnoff that Colling guessed would take him to the camp was a rutted dirt track that disappeared into a dense stand of pines. He decided that it was no time to be timid, and he whistled a German hiking song as he walked along. After about a kilometer, he walked out into an open field. The prison camp was set in its center, fifteen or twenty wooden barracks surrounded by a double barbed wire fence, guard towers at each corner and in the center of each side. The dirt track had changed into a gravel roadway as it emerged from the forest, and Colling's shoes crunched underfoot as he walked briskly towards the two upright poles that marked the camp's entrance. When he saw faces in the towers turning in his direction, Colling knew that he had arrived at the right place.

When Colling was about a hundred meters from the gate, a man wearing a German army uniform stepped out of one of the sentry boxes flanking it. As Colling drew closer, he was able to see that the guard's uniform had been stripped of its former insignia. The soldier had a German submachine gun held across his chest, its sling over his right shoulder. Colling took some comfort in the fact that the guard did not aim the weapon at him as he asked, "What is it you want here?"

"I have heard you need English-speakers," said Colling, coming to a halt.

"Where have you heard this?" asked the guard as he walked forward and stopped in front of Colling.

"Different places," replied Colling, watching for any sign that the muzzle of the gun was about to be pointed in his direction.

The man was close now, his eyes alert as he stared at Colling. "What different places?"

"Is it of more importance to you to know where I have heard this? Or that I can speak English well?" asked Colling.

Colling was surprised when the man laughed and told him to follow him. They stopped at the gate, and the guard called to another man dressed as he was who had been watching from inside the camp. "Go to the *Obersturmbannführer* and tell him we have a flyboy here who says he can speak English."

As they waited for the message to be delivered, the guard turned to Colling and asked, "What unit?"

"Flak detachment," answered Colling.

"No flying then?"

"Never," said Colling.

"I am *Waffen SS*," said the guard, "You were on the Eastern Front?"

"No, the Fatherland only."

"You were fortunate. You could surrender to the Americans."

"Perhaps," said Colling, trying to sound non-commital.

The other man had returned to the gate, and swung it aside, gesturing for Colling to follow him. Colling glanced about as they walked towards a building that he assumed was where the camp commander was located. There were no prisoners visible in the camp's yard, and if it were not for the guards, the place would have been deserted.

The frame building was somewhat larger than the barracks that comprised the majority of the camp's structures. A covered wooden veranda ran the length of its front. The structure bore none of the usual signs indicating that it might serve as a headquarters. Colling followed the guard up the steps and through a double set of battered doors, into what he discerned was the orderly room.

Three men wearing German uniforms without insignia were waiting for them. One of the men dismissed the guard who had accompanied Colling, and barked, "Put your bag on that table. Your pockets are to be emptied as well. Then go with Schultz."

The man's bearing and tone were those of a sergeant, no matter what army, and Colling decided it would be prudent to address him accordingly. Colling snapped to attention and responded, "Yes, *Feldwebel.*" and immediately dropped the canvas carryall onto the table at which the man had pointed. Colling hurriedly turned out his pockets into a small pile beside the bag. The last item he removed was the remaining hard roll, and as he placed it on the table, a second soldier had already dumped out his carryall onto the table and was sorting through its contents. The man held up the bottle of beer to the light to measure its contents, and seeing that it was almost empty, set it down on the table.

The third soldier took Colling by the arm and conducted him into what turned out to be a latrine and shower room. He ordered, "Remove your clothing," and stood watching with his arms folded. When Colling had stripped bare, the other man told him to turn around in a circle, then said, "At least you are not a Jew," and ordered him to get dressed.

The NCO was looking at Denschler's pay book when Colling was brought back into the outer room. He began firing questions about Denschler at Colling, glancing up to look at Colling as he gave his answers. Seeming to be finished with the *Soldbuch*, the NCO asked, "With what units have you served?"

"Several, *Feldwebel*. Most recently, the 453rd Antiaircraft Detachment. I was there when the order to cease fighting came."

"To what unit was your flak *Abteilung* attached?"

"The 267th Panzer Battalion, *Feldwebel*," replied Colling.

"And where did you serve?" asked the NCO.

"That was in the Fatherland, *Feldwebel*. In the west, near Coblenz, I believe, *Feldwebel*."

"Where have you been after the cease-fire?"

"An Ami POW cage, *Feldwebel*. Then, after a few weeks, the Ami's told all of us who were of low rank to go home."

"You had no home?"

"Not that I knew with certainty, *Feldwebel*. Right away the Ami's ordered that I must work clearing rubble, but it gave me something to eat and to earn a little money to be able to find my family. At last I was able to walk to Augsburg. That is from where I had last received a letter from my father and mother."

The NCO asked, "If you are here, you must not have found them."

"Truly, *Feldwebel*. From Augsburg, I have found work from time to time, and from place to place."

"Why have you not settled somewhere?"

"I was raised in the United States, Sergeant. It is best that I avoid the Ami's."

"Ahh," said the NCO, "That says much."

Colling was told that he could refill his pockets, and that his canvas bag would be kept safe for him. When Colling was finished replacing his belongings, the NCO said, "You will wait here and then you must speak to the *Obersturmbannführer* who is the commandant of this place."

The NCO went to one of the doors behind him, knocked, and when a muffled assent to enter was heard, did so. A few minutes later, he emerged and held the door open for Colling.

When Colling walked into what he gathered was the commandant's office, there were two men seated at a large ornate desk, waiting for him. The German seated directly behind the desk, whom Colling took to be senior, was a large man wearing field gray. The second man, who had taken a chair to one side, was thinner, possessed dark piercing eyes, and was wearing *Luftwaffe* blue. Neither wore any rank, decorations or other insignia, although the air force man did have the wreathed-eagle badge of a pilot on the left breast-pocket of his jacket. Colling came stiffly to attention in front of the man wearing *Feldgrau*, saluted, and said, "*Herr Obersturmbannführer!* *Gefreiter* Heinrich Denschler reporting!"

"Your pay book, Denschler," said the officer.

Colling fumbled his *Soldbuch* from inside his tunic and handed it over. The German slowly thumbed through the book, asking Colling the same questions that the NCO had previously posed about his date of birth, place of birth, residence and other information from its pages. Colling continued to stand at attention, responding briskly to each.

Glancing up from the pay book to Colling's face, and then back to the book, the officer said, "Your photo is a poor likeness."

"True, *Herr Obersturmbannführer*. I was younger when that portrait was made," replied Colling.

"No one appears today as they did when their *Soldbuch* photo was taken," interjected the air force officer.

After seeming satisfied with his interrogation regarding the pay book, the German said, "I am called Colonel Kottbach. This is *Oberleutnant* Grau, late of the *Luftwaffe*. I am of the SS, the SD, to be precise. This camp is my responsibility, and Lieutenant Grau is my second in command. How do you come to be here?"

"I have heard that one who speaks English might find employment here."

"Where did you gain such information?" asked the colonel.

"I was in Munich, and a man in a tavern spoke of it."

"Of this camp, specifically?"

"No, *Herr Obersturmbannführer*," replied Colling nervously, "It was said only that in the Eastern Zone, that persons who speak English might be useful. I heard of this place in Hohenwald when I asked where such employment might be possible."

"And the name of this person who told you this?" asked Kottbach.

"I know it not, sir. I stopped beside the road to eat my breakfast, and this man who was traveling, as was I, came and sat beside me to eat, and we talked. He was a former flak soldier, as was I, and when we parted, he told me of this place."

Colling was momentarily taken off balance when Lieutenant Grau asked him in English, "Who was the first President of the United States?"

"George Washington, of course, sir," said Colling. "Would you like me to name as many other Presidents as I can?"

"That will not be necessary. Tell me how you learned to speak English."

Colling spoke in English as he explained that he had been born in Stuttgart, and taken to the U.S. as an infant. He had grown up there until at age 15, when his father decided to return to Germany. He described living in Milwaukee, and spun a tale of his father's working as a taxi driver. At Grau's probing, he provided addresses, dates and names to bolster his imaginary biography. When he was asked where his family was, Colling told the two officers that as far as he knew, they had been in Augsburg. He related that he had gone there, but had been able to find no trace of them. Kottbach asked about his own service, and he told him that he had been an ammunition loader in a light antiaircraft battery. Throughout his narrative, Colling was conscious that Grau was listening to his accent and evaluating his mastery of colloquial English.

Finally, Grau stopped him and said, "You speak English like an American, and German like a Northerner. Yet your pay book says you were born in Stuttgart."

Aware that Kottbach was watching him closely, Colling shrugged his shoulders and said in German, "*Herr Oberleutnant*, you have a greater knowledge of local accents than I do. I have no explanation for this, other than that I speak German as my parents did." Switching to English, Colling continued, "And I speak English like the other kids in my schools in Milwaukee."

Grau smiled and nodded in Kottbach's direction. "He will do," said the air force lieutenant.

"You will join our unit, Denschler," announced Kottbach, "Lieutenant Grau will give you your instructions."

Colling saluted again, thanked the SD man, and turned on his heel and marched out of the room. Grau followed, and once in the outer reception area, the *Luftwaffe* lieutenant asked Colling to come with him to his own office. He instructed Colling to be seated, and inquired whether Colling believed he could write a report in German. Colling assured him that he had attended a German school in Milwaukee where the children of German parents were taught to read and write the language of the Fatherland. Seeming to be satisfied, Grau informed Colling that his assignment would be to examine the personal effects of American soldiers and prepare a report concerning what the documents and artifacts might disclose about each of them.

At the conclusion of his instructions to Colling, Grau shouted, "*Feldwebel* Wolfjäger!"

The man whom Colling had earlier guessed was a sergeant appeared in the doorway, "Yes, *Herr Oberleutnant?*"

Grau said to the NCO, "Take this man, Denschler, and find him a billet. Instruct him about the camp rules. He will be paid fifty marks a month. He speaks and reads English, and is to be assigned to Section D."

To Colling, Grau said, "This is Sergeant Wolfjäger. He is your sergeant. Obey him as such."

"Yes, *Herr Oberleutnant*," replied Colling.

Colling followed Wolfjäger to a barracks adjacent to the headquarters. Inside, the sergeant pointed to the top tier of a double bunk and told him it was his. Three nearby large pegs set in a horizontal piece of the structure's framework would serve to hold his gear. Wolfjäger took Colling to a room at the end of the building and unlocked it. Arrayed along its walls were *Wehrmacht* uniforms on hangers suspended from a line of pegs similar to those in the barracks. After a short search, the German NCO found two jackets, two pairs of trousers, and three shirts which he handed to Colling. Sets of underwear and socks were drawn from a bin at one end of the room. A pair of well-used but re-soled German army shoes was placed on top of the pile which filled Colling's arms, and Wolfjäger pronounced him fully outfitted. The sergeant left Colling to sort out the issue of clothing, instructing him that as soon as he had finished, he was to get into his new uniform and report back to the headquarters for further instruction.

Wolfjäger's instructions consisted of reciting the camp rules, which were similar to military regulations that Colling had encountered previously, with the exception of a restriction on the guards' leaving the camp. None of the camp personnel, except those assigned to drive the supply trucks, were permitted out of the camp unless the commandant personally approved the absence. Wolfjäger added that approval was a rare occurrence.

The German sergeant went on to explain that "entertainment" was provided once every two weeks by women brought in for that purpose. A canteen in the guards' mess hall was open after duty hours each day, where beer could be purchased. Schnapps would be made available on special occasions. Wolfjäger did not specify what those special occasions might be, and when the sergeant ended by asking Colling if he had any questions, Colling did not ask for clarification of that, or any other particular issue.

Colling's introduction into the camp concluded, Wolfjäger reminded him that Lieutenant Grau had ordered him assigned to Section D. The German sergeant explained that Section D involved the examination of captured documents and personal effects of enemy soldiers. Even though Grau had already described the type of work that he would be expected to perform, Colling listened politely, and when asked, assured Wolfjäger that he could do the job. He did not mention that the sergeant was repeating what the air force officer had told him.

Section D was housed in a room to the rear of the headquarters. The room to which Wolfjäger brought Colling had a single window that had not been cleaned in some time. Through it, Colling could see a barbed wire fence separating the administrative buildings and guards' quarters from a row of a dozen or so wooden barracks that he assumed housed prisoners.

The room was furnished with a table and a single chair. Plank shelves filled with stacks of papers, file folders and ledger books lined one wall. While Colling was taking in his surroundings, Wolfjäger left him, returning a few minutes later with a large cardboard carton. Placing it on the table, the German sergeant informed Colling that he was to prepare a report on the contents of each envelope in the box, pointing out the pads of paper and cupful of pencils on a nearby shelf.

After Wolfjäger departed, Colling opened the carton to find it filled to the top with manila envelopes. As he removed the first half-dozen of them from the box, Colling surmised by their weight and shape that they probably contained wallets, jewelry and other personal items. He ceased taking out any more, instead turning to the one that had been on top of the pile, and was the first that he had placed on the table.

The light brown envelopes had an odd type of wire clasp that differed from the American style Colling was used to. It took him an extra moment to figure out how to undo it. When he did, he dumped the contents of the envelope onto the table. The first item Colling picked up was a folded wallet. The Army Air Force identity card inside it declared that its owner was a lieutenant named Charles Finley, whose name was not on Quarles' list. Colling recollected that American airmen were not supposed to carry documents containing personal information when flying over enemy territory, and he was surprised that Lieutenant Finley would be so careless as to disobey those orders.

Among the other items in the wallet was a photo of a young woman and two small children with the names Bernice and Susan and Tommy written on the reverse, dated May, 1944. There were also membership cards for various base officers' clubs and a number of other organizations. An Indiana driver's license for Finley was behind a celluloid panel, and a folded letter from someone named Thelma, dated July, 1945, was tucked away in one of the wallet's compartments. There was no U.S. currency, but there were three pieces of Allied Military Currency denominated in yen, of a design that Colling had not seen previously, and some colorful bills from the Central Bank of China. A second, smaller envelope held a gold wedding ring, a class ring from a James Madison High School, class of 1938, a set of silver first lieutenant's bars, and silver Air Force wings with the bomb device indicating Finley must have been a bombardier.

Colling spread out the articles, and began writing in English. At the top of the page, he placed Finley's name and rank of first lieutenant and noted that he was a bombardier. After that, Colling went on, combining the factual aspects of each item with the logical conclusions that might be drawn from them. Based on the snapshot, he stated that Finley appeared to have a wife and two children. The driver's license, which had expired in May, 1942, suggested that Finley was a resident of Elkhart, Indiana, before joining the Air Force. A membership card in the Indiana Underwriter's Association dated 1941-42 likely meant that he might have sold insurance or worked for an insurance company in civilian life. Colling commented that the two country club membership cards indicated that Finley must have made a decent income prior to the war. A golf scorecard showing a hole-in-one on the third hole on September 2, 1941, probably meant he used his memberships to play the game.

The officers' club membership cards showed that Finley was stationed at MacDill Field in Florida, Kellerman Field in Texas, and an un-named airfield on Saipan. It was likely that the lieutenant flew from an air base located in some part of the former Japanese Empire, perhaps Okinawa, since he was carrying currency issued by the Americans that looked as if it were for use in the Japanese homeland. The Chinese money could mean that he had made some flights to the mainland as well. Colling speculated that Finley was having an affair with "Thelma" from the tone of her letter to him. After completing the report, Colling read it through, and began translating it into German.

Writing German proved more difficult than Colling had anticipated. While he was wholly comfortable speaking the language, it had been two years since he had been called upon to express himself on paper. He had to concentrate on correct spelling, capitalization and punctuation. As a result, it took him well over an hour to complete the report, then additional time as he transcribed everything into a flawless final draft.

Colling placed both the English and German versions aside, and lifted a second envelope from the box. He had begun sorting through its contents when Wolfjäger opened the door and informed him that the workday was over, and he could go eat his supper.

The mess hall was in the separate compound allocated to the camp guards and support personnel. Colling entered the line of soldiers working its way past a serving counter, picking up a tray made of something that looked like Bakelite, on which he placed a fork, knife and soupspoon. A metal bowl of cabbage soup, and a tin plate holding boiled potatoes, a slab of black bread, and half a thick sausage were placed on his tray as he moved along. When his tray was filled, Colling looked around until he saw a vacant place at a table with several other men. The guard who had conducted him from the gate to the headquarters dropped down opposite him a second later.

"I am called Rudolf Kessel," said the guard.

"I am called Heinrich Denschler," replied Colling.

"It is said you are from America," said Kessel, "Is this so?"

"This is true," said Colling.

Some of the other soldiers at their table were overhearing the conversation, and along with Kessel, began asking questions about the United States. Colling repeated the same answers he had given at his previous interrogations, but embellished his account by assuming the superiority he had noticed was sometimes displayed by some Germans who had visited America. Speaking with an air of authority, he combined braggadocio with matter-of-factness, and expounded on the wealth and size of the United States. At the same time, he tempered his description by expressing his disgust with the greed and materialism of Americans in general.

A man who gave his name as Schiller asked Colling where he had served, and Colling related a brief history of having been an ammunition handler in a light flak battery, and that he had remained in Germany throughout his term of conscription. Fortunately, no one posed any questions related to the technical side of the 37 millimeter antiaircraft gun.

They had finished eating before Colling had the opportunity to ask a general question regarding the military experience of the other soldiers, and heard most of them say that they had been German Army, and had been assigned as guards at prisoner of war camps.

Kessel was silent, listening to the responses of the others, and when they had finished, he said, "Myself, I am not shy to say I am SS. The rest of you will not say it, but you also were SS. You, Bötscher, were at Gross Rosen when I was, yet you tell this youngster you were a POW guard."

The other men seemed to Colling to become uncomfortable at Kessel's remonstrance, and they began getting up from the table in twos and threes, ultimately leaving Colling and Kessel by themselves. Colling did not want to appear curious about the camp's inmates, and had carefully avoided raising any question along those lines. He had anticipated that eventually someone would provide information without any prompting, but when Kessel leaned across the table, a conspiratorial expression on his face, and said, "You know the Russkies really run the camp?" he was surprised that it had happened so soon.

Colling nibbled at a piece of bread, saying nothing, waiting for Kessel to continue, and the SS man said, "Yes, it is true. The Russkies have only brought Kottbach and Grau here to make questions to the Americans."

"Americans?" said Colling casually.

"Yes, for sure. Grau was *Luftwaffe*. It is said he was very good in the interrogation of Ami flyers. They brought him here for this purpose."

"I have seen no Russians about," said Colling, trying to seem uninterested in the Americans.

"Ach, they are quartered in the brick building on the other side of the camp. They do not make themselves obvious. There is a Red Army colonel and two other officers, and a dozen or so men from the ranks."

Colling took another small bite from the remnants of his bread, and commented, "So we do the work, and the Russkies loaf, eh?"

Kessel scowled and said, "That is so. Every day or so, women are brought in for their pleasure. We poor sods must wait for two weeks to see a woman."

"Unfair, it seems to me," said Colling, "But what can one do? Nothing, of course."

"Very true, my friend," said Kessel, "We are as much prisoners here as are those that are called prisoners."

"But it is not so bad here," commented Colling, "I have been even in an Ami POW camp, and it was worse than this."

"Yes, for sure, things could be worse. The Russkies never hesitated to shoot German prisoners, and those that were not are even now in Siberia."

The mess hall was empty, and Kessel suggested that they go to the canteen for a beer. Colling explained that he had no money, and the German said if he would tell him more about Milwaukee, he would advance the cost of two or three drinks.

Kessel and others who joined them in the canteen provided Colling with more information and gossip with each additional glass of beer that was consumed. He learned that Wolfjäger had been an SS sergeant major, or *Hauptscharführer*, who had served with Kottbach. The rumor was that Wolfjäger had been the senior NCO of a squad in Poland and Czechoslovakia that had the task of executing German deserters and traitors. The guards feared him as much as they did the Russians. Kessel speculated that the reason that the Russkies had let Wolfjäger live was because the SS sergeant major had killed more Germans than he had Russians.

Towards the end of the evening, talk turned to the camp's inmates. The discussion went on around him without Colling having to ask a single question, and he was made aware that there were only about a dozen individuals being held in *Stalag S-1*, despite its having room for two to three hundred. The most important prisoners, for the moment, at least, were some American flyers.

They were held in their own barracks, but even at that, there was a dispute among those at Colling's table as to how many of them that there were. The German guards had been forbidden to know their identities, but some of the Ami's had nevertheless tried to give their names to their warders. When one of the guards, somewhat drunker than his companions, mentioned the name "Lindsey," there were fingers brought to lips all around, accompanied by whispered warnings to keep quiet.

Lindsey was on Quarles' list, and Colling felt a sense of relief in the knowledge that he had probably come to the right place. Now all that remained was to find a way to contact the flyers and then to escape from the camp. Colling was not sure how that was going to happen...yet.

Chapter 9

September, 1947

For the next several days, Colling sifted through one manila envelope after another, diligently composing reports about what their contents suggested regarding their owners. As he regained his familiarity with written German, Colling ceased preparing an English version of his opinions. The last time he had had to write a German composition was when he had taken German literature as an elective during his second year of college, two years previously. Now, he found that with practice, old skills returned, and he was able to express himself directly into German without using English as a foundation to organize his thoughts.

The routine was interrupted after a little more than a week, when he arrived early one morning, and Wolfjäger informed him that Lieutenant Grau wanted to see him. The smug expression on the sergeant major's face when he delivered the message made Colling uneasy, and he entered Grau's office expecting that he was to undergo what he suspected would be another interrogation.

The *Luftwaffe* officer let him remain standing in front of his desk, saying nothing as he blew a stream of tobacco smoke upwards. Colling maintained his composure, focusing his thoughts on the possible causes of the officer's chain-smoking, attested to by the ashtray full of discarded cigarette butts that was on the desk.

"You are not Heinrich Denschler," declared Grau.

Colling did not respond. He had been expecting his deception regarding Denschler to be discovered, and waited to see if Grau would say how he had come to know the truth.

Grau seemed slightly disconcerted when Colling said nothing, and his voice rose as he continued, "We have made certain inquiries, and have learned that *Gefreiter* Heinrich Denschler was reported dead in April, 1945. Would you have me believe that you have risen from the grave?"

"No, sir," said Colling, "I must admit that I took Corporal Denschler's pay book from his body. We had been strafed from the air by the Americans. He was hit, I was not. I thought it best, because I was, in truth, born in America, to take his identity. He was born in Stuttgart, as you know, but he was never in America."

"That, too, we have discovered. He grew up and attended schools in Stuttgart. The matter remains, who are you?"

"I am by name, Robert Kuhlmetzen. I was born in Chicago. My family moved to Milwaukee when I was quite young. All the information I am providing you and Colonel Kottbach about my childhood in the U.S.A. is true, I swear it," said Colling

"I remain unconvinced,...Kuhlmetzen, is it? You will give me your service number."

"Yes, *Herr Oberleutnant*. It is Hamburg XXI/24/16/3246E." said Colling, providing the fictional military serial number that he had previously fabricated and memorized.

Grau had written the number as Colling had spoken, and the lieutenant looked up as he finished, and said, "You know we will make inquiries about this?"

"Yes, sir. Of this I am aware."

"Tell me once more why you decided to take Denschler's identity?" said Grau.

"Sir, I have been born in America. I wished to conceal that from the Ami's. If I am born in Germany, and just lived in the United States, the Ami's leave me be. If I am born there, I am a citizen, and a traitor. I have heard that the Ami's hang traitors. I do not wish to be discovered to be an American. This is the reason, sir."

"A plausible explanation, soldier. It is no wonder that Colonel Kottbach noticed that your pay book photo was not a good likeness. And if you were enlisted in Hamburg, that explains your northern accent. What was your rank in the *Luftwaffe*?"

"Private, sir," replied Colling, "I was in truth an ammunition loader in a light flak battery...along with Denschler. He was my mess-mate."

"Very well, Kuhlmetzen. As you were a private, your pay is re-duced to forty marks each month. I will inform Wolfjäger to enter you in the rolls as 'Robert Kuhlmetzen.' You are dismissed."

Wolfjäger went past him into Grau's office as Colling exited. Colling was at his table, examining the personal effects of American airmen when the sergeant major came into the room.

"So it is 'Kuhlmetzen' now?" said the SS man.

"For truth, *Hauptscharführer*, that is my name," replied Colling.

"You had best pray that you are not found to be telling another lie," threatened Wolfjäger.

"All I wish is to stay here and earn my keep," said Colling.

The SS sergeant gave a derisive snort and left Colling to his work.

Colling was trying to decide how he would tell his fellow camp personnel that his real name was Kuhlmetzen, but Kessel beat him to it at the noon meal, by loudly announcing to the men at their table that "Heinrich" was not "Heinrich," but "Robert." Colling just smiled and shrugged his shoulders. Kessel laughed, leaned across the table and said in a stage whisper that just about everyone who worked in the camp had used one or more false names. One of the other guards added that not everyone was as proud to have been SS as Kessel, which elicited a great deal of laughter from the group of soldiers.

Colling had, soon after joining the U.S. Army, formed an opinion that the food provided in American mess halls was not particularly appetizing, but compared with the fare served in *Stalag S-1*, it was Cordon Bleu. Breakfast in the camp mess hall always consisted of grainy black bread, and coffee that had an odd taste that Colling suspected was due to its being made in part, at least, from nutshells. Both lunch and supper consisted of some variant of potatoes and cabbage, with an occasional piece of sausage thrown in. The bread was served three times a day, and the two or three times that it came with a chunk of margarine did little to improve it.

Aside from the promised biweekly visit of the prostitutes, which Colling had not yet had to deal with, off-duty activity was limited. In the evenings, he went with Kessel to the canteen, sipped at the one glass of beer that he allowed himself, and listened to the guards' discussions about the state of things in Germany now that the war was over.

After becoming Robert Kuhlmetzen, Colling was left to his assigned task of analyzing personal effects. Three days after meeting with Grau, he had used most of the morning to complete reports regarding the contents of two envelopes. He had yet to run across any of the names that he had been given by Quarles. It was not quite time for lunch, and Colling decided to take one more envelope from the box. When he dumped everything inside onto the table, there was a wallet, a small leather portfolio, dog tags, first lieutenant's bars, Air Force wings, a gold necklace with a crucifix, and the usual class ring.

Colling picked up the portfolio first, and when he flipped it open, saw that it held a photograph. He almost dropped it when he realized that he was looking at a color portrait of Elizabeth Hamilton. Colling's hands were trembling slightly, and his mind raced, unable to mentally absorb this unexpected turn of events.

Across the bottom of the photograph, Elizabeth had written, "All my love, Liz." Tiny gold letters in the lower left corner spelled out "Spencer's, Philadelphia, Pa."

Colling left the photo frame open and upright on the table. He picked up the wallet and found an Air Force identity card inside in the name of Captain Brian Moorehouse. Colling had expected to see "Hamilton," but then recalled that Elizabeth had always been referred to as "Miss" Hamilton. The time or two that she had mentioned her husband, it had been "Brian." In fact, as he thought back to their months together, he realized that she had never told him her married name, which led Colling to speculate that perhaps she had never actually taken Moorehouse's name as her own.

Colling removed everything that was in the wallet. Any currency that it had contained was gone. There were some business cards, one from a garage in Texas, another from a restaurant in Los Angeles, and one from the Royal Hawaiian Hotel in Honolulu. Moorehouse possessed two driver's licenses, from Pennsylvania and Texas. He had been carrying several officers' club membership cards. Two of them had oriental characters printed on them in addition to English, and Colling made a guess that the clubs might have been located on Air Force bases in China.

A number of snapshots made up the remainder of the wallet's contents, including two of Elizabeth. In one, she was wearing shorts, standing in front of a simple frame cottage, and Colling remembered her having told him about living with her husband in Texas. The second snapshot was of Elizabeth on the steps of a brick building that Colling would have guessed was located on a college campus. The rest of the pictures were of groups of people whom Colling did not recognize, some in civilian clothes, and others in Air Force uniform.

Colling had picked up the portrait of Elizabeth again when he realized that Wolfjäger was looking over his shoulder. For some reason sensing that the sergeant was watching him to see what his reaction to the picture would be, Colling held it up for the German to see and said, "Have you seen this?" And when Wolfjäger smiled and nodded his head, Colling added, with a salacious grin, "Would it not be wonderful to hump this Ami bitch until her eyes popped out?"

Wolfjäger took the picture out of Colling's hands and said, "More likely, from the look of her, it would be she who would make your eyes pop out."

Colling smiled as he said, "So true, *Hauptscharführer*. But it has been so long since I have had a woman, I fear that it would be the blink of an eye, not the popping of the eye."

Wolfjäger found Colling's clumsy play on words hilarious, and he laughed and slapped Colling on the back, saying, "Ach, Kuhlmetzen! You speak the truth for all of us. You will have to pay for a whore on Saturday, and improve your vision."

It was Colling's turn to laugh with the sergeant, who was unduly amused by his own attempt at humor. As Wolfjäger left him, the SS man was still chuckling to himself and repeating, "A blink of the eye! So true!"

Colling wrote his report on his evaluation of Moorehouse's effects, passing over Elizabeth as possibly the man's wife or fiancé.

When he was finished, he returned Moorehouse's things to the envelope and placed it back in the box. Still unsure whether or not Elizabeth's portrait was intended to be some sort of test, Colling decided that it was important that he not show any further interest in Moorehouse's effects, particularly the portfolio with Elizabeth's picture inside.

Wolfjäger's prediction about women being available on Saturday was accurate. One of the camp's trucks delivered them to the compound in the afternoon. There were seven of them, and the soldiers who were not on duty at the gates and towers crowded around as they were assisted from the back of the vehicle. Colling remained inconspicuously in the rear.

The women were dressed in what Colling assumed must pass in postwar East Germany for provocative attire. Instead of the somber baggy dresses, gray aprons, stockings and headscarves that most of the local female population seemed to favor, they had on light-colored dresses, and wore their hair loose. Make-up consisted of a single shade of bright-red lipstick, and pink rouge, liberally applied. The prostitutes looked better-fed than the women Colling had seen in Hohenwald, but he would not have characterized any of them as pretty or attractive.

It was obvious that the men of the camp were familiar with their female guests, shouting out their names and lewdly propositioning them, which the women gave back in kind. Two of the younger girls were singled out and led off by Wolfjäger to the headquarters building, where Kottbach and Grau were billeted, while the others were escorted by two of the sergeant major's immediate subordinates to the barracks that housed the guards' canteen.

Colling followed, and ordered a beer before seating himself at a table. An adjoining room had apparently been fitted out so that the women could provide their services. Colling observed that priority was according to rank, and as the most recent addition to the camp's complement, and a private as well, that his turn would come after the other thirty or so men in the canteen. It was also possible that the other half-dozen men standing sentry duty outside would have their chance at the prostitutes before he did. Colling had never had any particular desire to utilize the services of a prostitute, and the current crop did nothing to change his mind. On the other hand, turning down this opportunity might incur suspicions that he did not want raised.

Kessel, smiling and buttoning his jacket, came out of the adjacent room, stopped to pick up a glass of beer, and joined Colling at his table.

"Ach, that Trudi, she is the one!" said the SS man.

"You were first in line, my friend?" asked Colling.

"*Nein*, I was after Sergeant Schuster. But she washed up in between. Ask for her when it is your turn, Kuhlmetzen. You will not be disappointed."

"I fear I shall not be able to take your advice," said Colling.

Kessel's face showed disbelief, "What is this? You do not need a woman?"

"I do, my friend," said Colling, and then lowering his voice, he added, "But I have caught the gonorrhea from a whore three years ago, and I do not wish to repeat that experience."

"You have it still?" asked Kessel.

"Ach, no. The sawbones gave me something, but it took weeks before the burning when I pissed stopped. And the medicine made me nauseous for the whole time."

"I myself could not have such strength," said Kessel, "Too long without a woman is not good for a man's health."

"Before I arrived here, I worked for a farmer for a couple of days, and I had a go at his daughter, so for me, it has not been all that long. If I could sneak out of here some time, I will visit her again."

Kessel chuckled, "Do not try it, my friend. They hang deserters...it saves ammunition."

"Well said," replied Colling, raising his glass to his lips and turning it up.

It was two days later that Colling was again ordered by Wolfjäger to come with him to Lieutenant Grau's office. The SS sergeant major remained blocking the door behind Colling as he stood before the

Luftwaffe officer's desk. Grau was not smoking, a departure from his normal behavior that made Colling's palms begin to sweat.

Grau picked up a sheet of paper from his desk and held it out so that Colling could see it.

"Once more, you attempt to deceive, soldier," growled the air force officer.

Colling could see that Grau was holding a flyer with his picture on it, announcing that Robert Pretzmann was wanted by the American authorities as a war criminal. Colling swallowed and blinked his eyes, deliberately supplementing the actual anxiety which he was feeling, in order to appear completely un-nerved.

"*Herr Oberleutnant,* I wish to explain."

"Are you Pretzmann?" asked Grau.

"Yes. But I wish to explain...,"

Grau cut him off, "This is the third identity you have given us, soldier. I can have Sergeant Wolfjäger take you out and put a rope around your neck."

"Please, sir," pleaded Colling, "The Ami's are searching for me. I wish only to avoid them. I wish only to stay here and earn my keep."

"What is it you have done that the Americans want you?"

"It was long ago, *Herr Oberleutnant.* Some American POWs were shot because of information I provided."

"You will tell me everything about this, soldier," said Grau.

"Yes, sir. It was in Tunisia. Many Americans had been captured, and I was called out of my flak detachment because I was able to speak English in the American manner. I thought I was to be assigned to interrogate prisoners, but instead, my superior officer said that I was to wear American uniform and go in among the POWs. I was to gather information, and to give warning of any plans of the Ami's to escape."

"Who was your superior officer?" asked Grau.

"Colonel Strumpfer, sir. I do not know his unit."

"His Christian name?" asked Grau

"I regret that I do not know, sir."

"What was your unit in Africa?

"The 87ᵗʰ Flak *Abteilung*, sir. Attached to the 35ᵗʰ Panzer Grenadier Battalion," answered Colling.

"And this POW camp, soldier. Where was it?"

"I cannot say precisely, sir. Near Tunis, I believe."

"Were you taken by the Americans when Tunisia fell?" asked Grau.

"No, sir. I contracted malaria, and Colonel Strumpfer saw to it that I was evacuated to Italy by airplane. I was most fortunate, sir."

"This Strumpfer must have thought much of you. Why did he not see that you received a promotion?"

"I was *Luftwaffe*, sir, and he was *Wehrmacht*. It is my belief that he made such a recommendation, but once I was released from hospital, nothing came of it. I was assigned to another flak unit in the Fatherland. I thought it best not to pursue it," explained Colling.

"Was Colonel Strumpfer captured by the Americans?" asked Grau.

"I know not, sir."

Grau stared intently at Colling for what seemed like a long period of time. "Tell me once more, how is it that the Americans have said that you are a war criminal?"

"Some of the Ami POWs had plans for escape. I informed Colonel Strumpfer of this, and several of them were shot and killed when they attempted to carry out their plans. There was also a prisoner who was thought only to be rank and file infantry. I discovered that he was a signals officer with knowledge of codes. He was taken away for questioning, and I heard later that he was dead. I think that this is the reason for the Ami's saying that I am guilty of war crimes."

"How is it that the Americans know that you did these things?" asked Grau.

It was Colling's turn to be silent for a moment. "I do not know for certain, sir. But it may be that other American prisoners suspected that I was a German soldier, and when repatriated, gave this information to the Ami authorities."

"If Colonel Strumpfer was himself captured, he might have provided this information," mused Grau.

"I know that not, sir," said Colling, certain that his implicating a former superior officer in a betrayal would not be a wise course of action.

"It is against my better judgment, but I will permit you to remain here, Pretzmann. That is your name, is it not?"

"Yes, *Herr Oberleutnant*. For truth, that is as I am called."

"And the service number you provided for Kuhlmetzen?" asked Grau.

"For truth, Lieutenant, sir, it is mine, except for the last three numbers. The true number is Hamburg XXI/24/16/3624E."

Grau was writing down the serial number and, without looking up, he said, "You are dismissed, Pretzmann. Return to your work. And by the way, you shall lose two months' pay for lying to me."

Wolfjäger smiled mirthlessly at Colling as the two of them exited Grau's office, and once the door had closed behind them, said, "Once again you escape the noose."

CHAPTER 10

SEPTEMBER - OCTOBER, 1947

Kessel and his fellow guards made Colling's predicament the main topic of discussion in the canteen that night. They commiserated with him over his loss of pay, but found his frequent change of identity to be extremely entertaining. Late in the evening, one of the former SS men, after he had consumed several beers, confided drunkenly to Colling that he also had used many false names in evading the Russians and the Poles, but then he bared his upper arm and showed Colling the tattooed SS runes. Amid gales of laughter from the other Germans, the SS man declared that he had never been able to figure out why his deception was never successful.

One favorable aspect that Colling noticed about his displaying a good-natured attitude about the teasing was an apparent greater acceptance by the camp personnel. Even Wolfjäger told him with a wry smile that he was too clever for his own good. He returned to his assignment evaluating personal effects, from which he was learning nothing useful to his objective. However, a day or two after his meeting with Grau, Colling was surprised when the SS sergeant major brought him a new cardboard box of manila envelopes. Wolfjäger informed him that Lieutenant Grau wanted him to stop what he had been doing and to work on the new batch of material.

Curious at the change, Colling approached his assignment in the same manner as he had previously. The first envelope he selected contained a wallet whose owner was a staff sergeant named Allen Lindsey. Colling recognized the name as one of those he had been given by Quarles. Aside from the wallet, which contained his Air Force identity card and some personal snapshots, there were few other clues to its owner.

Restraining the inclination to rummage through the other envelopes to see if they might pertain to others on the list of crew members of the B-29, Colling followed his customary form in writing his report regarding Staff Sergeant Lindsey. He pointed out that there was little to go on that would provide more than a minimum of personal information about the man.

After he had finished and had re-read it to make sure he was satisfied with the result, he drew a second envelope from the carton. The only form of identity in the envelope was a set of dog tags belonging to Milton Evans, together with a major's rank insignia and Air Force observer's wings. Evans was the "E" in Colling's CHARTWELL acronym. *Two out of two,* thought Colling. A fountain pen and a wedding ring made up the remainder of the envelope's contents, leaving Colling with the impression that Major Evans took the flight crew security rules even more seriously than had Lindsey. Colling's report of his findings on Evans was even shorter than the one on the staff sergeant. As he completed his review of what he had written, Colling experienced a grim suspicion that Evans' dog tags were in the envelope, while Lindsey's were not, because the major was dead.

By the end of the day, Colling had finished going through all of the envelopes that Wolfjäger had given him. They contained the personal belongings of everyone on the list: Caldwell, Hammerslee, Abrams, Roberts, Tunsholder, Wilmont, Evans, Lindsey and Lomax. In addition, three other men, all Navy personnel, were represented, but Colling did not recognize their names.

Colling reported to Wolfjäger that he was done, and the sergeant told him to deliver his reports to Lieutenant Grau before leaving for the evening meal. It was the first time that Colling had met with the *Luftwaffe* officer without the SS sergeant major or another NCO being present, and Colling was surprised when Grau told him to be seated while he quickly read through the sheaf of papers that Colling had handed him. One of the ever-present cigarettes was in his hand.

After a few minutes, the lieutenant looked up, exhaled a stream of smoke, and said, "Pretzmann, have you not wondered why it is that you have been assigned the drafting of these reports?"

"No, *Herr Oberleutnant,* I have not," replied Colling.

Grau smiled and said, "The expected response from a German soldier. You follow orders and have learned to have a minimum of curiosity."

"Yes, sir," answered Colling.

"I would have thought that your American upbringing would have left you with some little of the Yankee independence of thought."

Switching to English, Colling replied, "I was raised in the Midwest, sir, among good German stock. Yankees are from the Northeastern part of the country, and do tend to be more troublesome."

Grau responded in German, "An interesting observation, Pretzmann, but perhaps a useful generalization on your part. Even though you decline to admit that you have not even one tiny bit of curiosity, I have decided, for reasons you will learn, that it is nevertheless necessary to tell you what our reasons are for being in this camp."

All that Colling could think of to say was, "Yes, Lieutenant, if that is your wish."

"You have discerned by this time, I would expect, that this camp operates at the direction of the Russians?"

"That is what is said in the barracks, sir," said Colling.

"And you no doubt have heard that we have Americans here, as well?"

Colling did not respond for a moment, trying to give the impression that he was concerned about implicating his fellow soldiers.

Grau prompted him, saying, "Do not be concerned, Pretzmann, I am aware of the gossiping that goes on."

"I am told that this is a secret, *Herr Oberleutnant.*"

"A secret well-known within the camp, it is true."

"Yes, sir," replied Colling.

"Very well. Accept that the Americans are here. Of particular interest is a group who are the crew of an American bomber, a B-29. You are familiar with this aircraft type?"

"We received training about it, sir. But, in truth, I have never seen one. It is supposed to be the largest made by the Americans."

"I myself never encountered one, either. But that is neither here nor there," said Grau. "Colonel Kottbach and I were brought to this camp by the Russians to interrogate these men. The Reds have their own methods, but they frequently result in the demise of the subject. In this case, they are being more cautious. These men were captured by the Reds when their bomber was forced down in Soviet territory."

"Is it allowed that I know why you and Colonel Kottbach were selected, Lieutenant, sir?" asked Colling.

"It is. Suffice to say that I have some experience in extracting information from Americans. I was grounded after being wounded, and because I had some English, I was assigned to a POW camp for nearly two years afterwards. I found that Americans wish to be liked, and are easily duped into saying more than they should by a friendly English-speaker. For me, it was never necessary to resort to physical means."

"Do you wish me to interrogate these men?" was Colling's response.

"That has not been decided, but already you have had a chance to become familiar with them."

Colling raised his eyebrows in feigned surprise, and said, "How is this so, sir? I swear that I have never spoken to any prisoner."

Grau smiled and said, "Have no fear, Pretzmann. The reports, man, the reports!" said Grau, holding up the sheaf of papers that Colling had given to him.

"Ach, I see, sir," said Colling, sighing as if relieved.

"You know their names, and a bit about each of them."

"There were few personal items, compared to those of others who I have examined," replied Colling.

"Just so. But you have been the best at evaluating what you have been given. I wish you to now listen to their conversations, and tell me what you think."

"How is that to be done, sir?"

Grau blew another cloud of smoke towards the ceiling before replying, "A hidden microphone, of course. We listen and record all that they say."

"Pardon, sir, but have you not, by such means, been able to find out all that you...or the Russians...wish to know?"

"So far, no. Perhaps you will notice something that I have

not."

Grau rose from his desk, took his cap from a rack near the door, and told Colling to follow him. They crossed the compound to a smaller building. Inside, there were two Germans sitting side-by-side at a table, earphones on their heads. In front of the men was equipment that Colling initially thought was a radio, but then realized was some sort of amplifier. An apparatus with two slowly spinning wheels was at one man's elbow. Tape recorders had been used in movies Colling had seen, but this was the first time he had ever seen one in real life.

The *Luftwaffe* officer introduced Colling to the soldiers, both of whom Colling recognized from the canteen, and told them that Colling would be working with them for awhile. Grau gave orders that Colling would be using one set of the earphones, while the other two tended to the equipment. After Grau departed, the man whom Colling knew as Gruber gave up his seat, and showed him how to put on the headset. The other soldier, whose name was Fischer, pointed out the volume control on the amplifier, and Colling settled in to eavesdrop.

At about 1700, Gruber and Fischer were relieved by two other men named Kant and Schmidt. Colling was told that there were three eight-hour shifts involved in manning the listening post. As Grau had not indicated how long he should stay on duty, Colling remained until 1900, when the *Oberleutnant* dropped by and told him he was relieved, and to get something to eat.

At breakfast, Kessel asked why he had not been in the canteen the evening before, and Colling, assuming an air of secrecy, responded that he could not discuss it.

Continuously listening in on a hidden microphone turned out to be one of the most boring activities that Colling had ever experienced. For long stretches, there was nothing to hear except silence,broken occasionally by the sounds of shuffling feet, snores, grunts, and other noises, the origin of which Colling could only speculate. His fellow eavesdroppers found it amusing that the quiet was punctuated more frequently than might be expected by the sound of someone breaking wind.

Colling quickly learned that Gruber and Fischer used small slips of paper to mark the tape when they were overhearing something. Because only one recording machine was available, replacing a completed tape with a new one was done in haste, if possible at a time when it appeared that there would be nothing important to record.

By the end of his first day, Colling was convinced that the occupants of the prison barracks were aware that a microphone had been installed. His staying late on his first day of duty taught him that in the evenings, the prisoners talked more than they did during the morning and afternoon, but not about anything of a military or personal nature. There was lots of joke-telling, and they seemed to take turns recounting stories, most of which were the plots of American motion pictures. One wag even attempted to imitate the voices of some of the stars. Once or twice, someone would teach a class on some academic subject. At Grau's request, Colling reviewed one recording of a lecture on the Civil War battle of Vicksburg, about which the speaker seemed to have extraordinary knowledge.

What personal conversations there were seemed to be concerned with the next meal or speculation about the league standing of the New York Yankees. There was one heated debate about whether Jimmy Cagney was tougher than George Raft. Colling had to admit to himself that the argument that Raft was reputed to have actually been a gangster was compelling.

Colling was listening to the sounds made by the prisoners at their morning meal when Grau arrived and asked for the tapes from the previous day. Fischer handed them over and the lieutenant left. Gruber explained that the *Luftwaffe* officer had a machine in his office, and reviewed all the recordings. The paper tabs at the places where voices had been heard helped to accelerate the process.

Colling had not noticed any of his fellow eavesdroppers speaking English, and when he asked, he learned that they possessed only a rudimentary knowledge of the language. They simply marked where someone was speaking.

When Grau brought back the tapes shortly before noon, Colling had just turned over his earphones to Gruber, and he asked if he might speak to the lieutenant. They stepped to one side, and Colling said, "Lieutenant, sir, I am hearing nothing of value. I am thinking that these Americans know that they are being listened to."

"You are most probably correct, Pretzmann. We even have a man on the inside, and it was my opinion that if he could not learn anything, that the use of a microphone was of no value."

"A man on the inside?" asked Colling.

"Yes. The Russians had their own man on the aircraft. That is how it was possible to cause it to land and be taken intact," said Grau, "He is not in a position to ask any questions concerning what we wish to find out, else he be exposed as a spy. Unfortunately, he does not possess any skill at initiating a conversation that might draw out information. I suspect that he is a traitor, an American communist, rather than a Russian who has been taught English and had training in espionage."

"Lieutenant, sir, it seems as if this is an impossible task," commented Colling.

"Unlucky for all of us if that is so," said Grau, "If we do not succeed, we will without doubt be sent back to labor camps in Russia. Most of the men here are of the SS, and it will go badly for them."

"But what of us who are not SS?" asked Colling, allowing a hint of anxiety to surface in his tone of voice.

"Not as bad, perhaps. You have never been in a Soviet camp. I have, and it is not a pleasant experience. It is likely to be a life sentence, if you understand my meaning."

The lieutenant's ominous prediction reminded Colling of Quarles' final advice to get the hell out if things got tough. That night, he lay awake in his bunk, taking stock of his situation. He had located the men he was supposed to rescue, even though he did not know exactly where in the camp that they were being held. He believed he had gained the confidence of their jailers. But he did not have any idea how he could extricate the men from *Stalag S-1*, much less convey them through hostile territory to the American Zone. Furthermore, it was clear from Grau's comments that time was growing short. Before he fell asleep, he had decided he would have to find a way to contact Vogelsang and arrange for some sort of assistance.

Unfortunately for Colling's planned course of action, and fortunately for his own safety, his contact with Vogelsang came sooner than he had imagined it would, and in an unexpected way.

Grau had informed him that he was required to spend only eight hours in the listening post each day, and consequently, Colling had resumed spending his evenings in the canteen. Colling had ordered his customary single glass of beer, when he noticed a man in civilian clothes sitting with Kessel and some others. Kessel waved Colling over, and as he slid into onto the bench beside the SS man, Kessel said, "Pretzmann, you must meet our friend, *Herr* Vogelsang."

Colling took the man's hand, and said, "My pleasure, sir."

Kessel continued, "Vogelsang here lives in the village. Today he brings us a bottle of brandy." The SS man emphasized the declaration by holding up the bottle of liquor, and waving it, after which, he poured himself a drink and tossed it back.

"Can he make it possible for me to pay a visit on a local farm girl?" asked Colling with a sly grin.

Kessel laughed, and said to Vogelsang, "Pretzmann avoids the whores. He has had the gonorrhea, and wishes not to repeat the experience. But a little clean *Fräulein* remains to his liking."

Vogelsang said, "Alas, not within my power, my friends. You have to get Kottbach and the Russkies to give you a pass from the post."

"Not likely to occur," said one of the other men at the table.

Kessel poured some of the brandy into a clean glass and pushed it over to Colling, inviting him to drink. Colling swallowed the liquid in one gulp, and coughed as the fiery alcohol singed his throat. This caused his table companions to laugh, and when Colling protested that he had not had schnapps for several months, this seemed to cause even more amusement.

In a voice hoarse from the brandy, Colling asked Vogelsang, "What brings you here to our happy home, sir?"

This elicited more laughter, and Kessel said, "Pretzmann has not been in our midst long enough, comrades." The SS man turned to Colling and explained, "Vogelsang here is the partisan leader in these parts."

Colling put a shocked expression on his face that brought another round of laughs, and Kessel continued, "It should be said that Vogelsang is *supposed* to be the partisan leader, but in truth, he works for the Reds. The dumb-head Ami's send him money and guns, believing he is on their side."

All the while, Vogelsang had been watching Colling with interest, and when there was a pause in the conversation, he leaned forward and said, "It was I who brought the notice to Kottbach that you are a wanted man, Pretzmann."

Vogelsang's statement caused the table to become silent, leaving Colling to smile and say, "My reputation will be ruined by you, *Herr* Vogelsang, telling everyone that the Ami's want me to swing at the end of a rope."

This caused a stir among the guards, and Colling was amazed that the camp's usually-efficient gossip mill had not spread the news about his alter-ego, Pretzmann, being a war criminal. Vogelsang laughed, and Kessel asked, "Pretzmann, what is it you have done to deserve the attention of the Ami's?"

"I followed orders," was Colling's sullen response, which elicited a murmur of empathy from the crowd of soldiers.

"You and many others, comrade," commented a man standing behind Kessel, prompting a chorus of "*Ja*'s and "That is right!" from the crowd.

Vogelsang seemed disconcerted by Colling's response, and his apparent acceptance by the camp's personnel. He shouted for another round of beer for himself and Colling, and reached across and slapped Colling on the shoulder.

Colling stayed for an hour or so longer than his usual custom, and then excused himself on the grounds that Grau would have his head if he were not alert in the morning. That there was a certain truth in his excuse for leaving the canteen became evident when he felt his head spinning on his way to his barracks. The three beers and one shot of brandy had challenged his tolerance for alcohol, so much so, that when he fell into his cot, he was asleep in moments.

With any help from Vogelsang out of the question, Colling began reviewing various schemes that might lead to his freeing his fellow Americans. There were few options, and he grew more discouraged as each day went by. As time passed, he also began to doubt that there was any possibility of his engineering his own escape from the camp.

When Wolfjäger informed him that he had been summoned by Kottbach and the "Russky Colonel" to a meeting in the SD officer's office, Colling surmised that something had been discovered in German military or civil records that had unmasked Robert Pretzmann as a fabrication. By the time he found himself with Kottbach, Grau and two other men in Red Army uniforms, he had resigned himself to having no chance of survival, hoping that he would not disgrace himself under torture.

Grau spoke first, "Pretzmann, I wish you to meet Colonel Penakov, and Captain Visinsky."

Colling decided it was best to salute, after which he said, "I await your orders, sirs."

The Russians stared at him through lowered eyes, and the one Grau had pointed out as Penakov said something to his fellow Soviet officer that Colling could not understand. Visinksy answered and the two continued to speak quietly with one another for a minute or so. Colling noticed that Grau and Kottbach were standing rigidly at attention, and guessed that the two Germans were no more able to comprehended Russian than himself.

Penakov finally told them in heavily-accented German to stand at ease. The Russian Colonel pointed at Colling and asked Kottbach, "You think this one knows English enough that he will pass as an American?"

Grau interjected, "Colonel, sir, his accent is perfect. He did, after all, grow up in America."

Colling found himself confused by where things seemed to be going. What he had expected to happen to him before he entered Kottbach's office was momentarily forgotten as he tried to comprehend what was actually occurring. Why would his command of English be important unless the Russians planning to use him as some sort of spy?

Speaking their native language, Visinsky seemed to be giving advice to Penakov that the Red Army officer was considering, and with which he seemed not to fully agree. He turned to Grau and said, "Perhaps we will have a Russian speak with this man, to see if what you say about his English is true."

Kottbach interjected, "Colonel, sir. That would be most appropriate."

Penakov sneered as he responded, "I do not need your permission, Nazi. I do as I wish."

The SD Colonel stammered nervously, "Yes, of course, Colonel, sir."

Visinsky stepped forward until he was face-to-face with Colling, then he said in English, "You have been American man, is it so?"

Colling answered, "Yes, Captain. I grew up in Milwaukee, U.S.A. Until I was fifteen, when my father took us back to Germany."

"Say to me, mister, what you do in U.S. of A." asked Visinsky.

"I went to school. Elementary school, junior high school, then high school. James Madison High School, in Milwaukee...for one semester. I had a paper route. I played baseball with my friends. That's about it."

Visinsky said something to Penakov, who said to Grau, "My captain says your man speaks good English. You may put him with other Americans. If our man believes they become not to trust him, then he comes out. You understand?"

"Yes, Colonel, sir. It will be done as you command," replied Grau.

Kottbach and Grau saluted the two Russians, and Colling followed suit. The Red Army officers did not return the courtesy before leaving the office.

The *Luftwaffe* lieutenant sat down heavily in a chair, at the same time, Kottbach dropped into his own. The two Germans looked at each other and let out a sigh. Colling was still standing, and moments passed before Grau took notice of him.

"Sir, if I may ask," said Colling to Grau, "What is this about?"

The air force officer pulled a pack of cigarettes from his pocket and lit one. After he had inhaled deeply and blown a cloud of smoke upwards, he said, "Pretzmann, you are to be an American soldier once again. You will go among these prisoners. You will repeat your previous performance."

"No, sir," protested Colling. "I cannot do this again."

"But you will," said Kottbach angrily. "You obey your orders, as a German soldier."

"Please, *Herr Obersturmbannführer*, if I do this thing the Ami's will be even more diligent in their search for me. I will never be at rest," pleaded Colling.

"We have no choice," said Grau. "It is this, or we all go to the east. And you must be successful, Pretzmann."

Colling shook his head resignedly and said, "What is it I am to find out, Lieutenant, sir?"

"For now, how many of the B-29 bombers are in England, where they are based, and how many atom bombs the Americans have," replied Grau.

Colling had expected some reference to the equipment that Quarles had told him was aboard the downed plane, and wondered why it was no longer a matter of interest. He paused before responding to Grau, "In truth, Lieutenant, sir, it is strange that the man the Reds have on the inside does not know this already, if he was of the American air force."

"For some reason, it appears that he does not. You have your orders, Pretzmann. Wolfjäger will see that you have an American uniform," said Grau.

"Sir, is it not also possible that I might have the chance to read some American newspapers? The Americans will, without doubt, ask me about things, such as their sports. If I appear ignorant of them, they will immediately suspect that I am not one of them. Colonel

Stumpfer required me to prepare myself thus in Tunisia."

Grau turned to Kottbach and said, "See, Colonel, sir, I told you this one would know what to do."

"He has not yet been successful," replied Kottbach sullenly.

Colling was taken to Grau's office, where he waited for over an hour until Wolfjäger brought him an American khaki uniform with PFC's stripes on it. The German also handed him a set of olive-drab underwear, socks and brown shoes. Colling asked the SS man where the clothing had come from, and was told not to ask questions. After he had put on the uniform, Grau came to see the result. The air force officer brought brass enlisted-men's insignia with him, which he pinned on the collar of the shirt. Colling was relieved to see that Grau had positioned them accurately. If he had not done so, Colling was in no position to correct him without revealing more knowledge than he was supposed to possess. The uniform was rumpled and the brass and shoes needed polishing, but Grau advised Colling to leave things as they were, in order to bolster Colling's tale that he had been in Russian custody for some time.

The story of his capture in Berlin was suggested by Grau, who briefed him regarding the names of American barracks and some street names in the city. Colling said that he would use "his own" background about living in Milwaukee. The *Luftwaffe* officer told Colling to say that when he had been taken into custody by the Russians that they had taken his dog tags, leaving Colling to adopt any name he wished. Colling said he would have to think about it, but might use the name of one of his boyhood schoolmates.

As an apparent final touch that Colling had not anticipated, Grau summoned Wolfjäger and told him to slap and punch Colling in the face. The SS man obliged by knocking Colling down with his first blow, and then kicking him in the ribs. When Colling struggled to regain his feet, Wolfjäger hit him twice more before Grau ordered him to stop. As Colling got up from the floor and stood swaying, Grau examined the damage to his face while the SS sergeant major watched, an expression of pleasure on his face. After wiping the blood from Colling's upper lip, and seeming satisfied, the *Luftwaffe* officer told Wolfjäger he was dismissed.

When they were alone, Grau told Colling to be seated. The German lieutenant rummaged in a filing cabinet, and then pulled out several old issues of *Stars and Stripes* which he handed to Colling. Grau sat behind his desk and smoked while Colling read the newspapers. The most up-to-date issue was dated in November, 1946, and Colling had already seen most of them, but he dutifully leafed slowly through all of them. When he was finished, he said, "*Herr Oberleutnant*, these are old. I do not know what I shall do if more recent events come up."

Grau responded, "These Americans have been locked up since June. They will ask you for news that they cannot verify. Tell them what you wish."

"I fear that they will ask about American sports, sir, especially baseball, and I cannot be ignorant of what has happened this summer. That is the season for baseball. Is it possible to obtain news from the radio?"

"A good thought, Pretzmann," said Grau. "I will ask the Russians for one. You will remain here. I do not want your fellow guards to see you in American uniform, and with bruises and a bloody nose."

Colling waited, and as he continued to page through the old *Stars and Stripes*, a twinge in his stomach reminded him that he had not eaten since breakfast. Over an hour had passed before Grau and Captain Visinsky returned, followed by a Russian enlisted man carrying an old table-model radio. The Russian soldier made an elaborate show of placing it on Grau's desk and plugging it in, while Grau and Visinsky watched. The radio's dial lit up as he switched it on, and then he began to tune it, searching for a broadcast in English. Colling heard the American announcer first, and waved his hand and told the Russian to stay on that frequency, but the soldier did not understand German, and continued twisting the dial. Finally, Grau spoke to Visinksy, who shouldered the man aside and tuned the radio until swing music was heard. When the song had finished, a voice announced that they were listening to Armed Forces Radio.

Colling sat listening to the familiar broadcasts for most of the evening. The Russians remained in the room, clearly reluctant to let the radio out of their sight. Visinsky paced, while Grau sat at his desk, each of them smoking one cigarette after another, almost as if they were engaged in a contest. The Russian enlisted man sat upright in a chair, staring straight ahead, his hands on his knees. At one point, Wolfjäger brought a tray of food for Colling. The fourth news program, which included a sports update like the first three, concluded at midnight, and was followed by the Star Spangled Banner, as Armed Forces Radio signed off for the day.

Grau asked if Colling believed that he had learned enough to fulfill his role as an American soldier, and when he replied in the affirmative, the former *Luftwaffe* officer called in Wolfjäger and told him to escort Colling to the Americans' quarters in the prison barracks.

CHAPTER 11

OCTOBER, 1947

Wolfjäger switched on the lights and shouted at Colling as he shoved him roughly into the room where the American airmen were being held, deliberately, in Colling's opinion, disrupting everyone's sleep, and reducing his chances of being a welcome addition.

The Americans were confined in a barracks fitted out with about two dozen cots and what Colling took to be a mess table and benches. All but five of the available beds were unoccupied. Two of the bunks near the door were in use, as were four others at the opposite end of the room. Both men who had been sleeping closest to the door were sitting up, staring at Colling. Those farthest from the entrance had pulled their blankets over their heads, and someone asked that the lights be doused.

In response, the man nearest to Colling said, "Captain, we got a new guy."

Colling said nothing, and watched as a head emerged from under the covers of one of the cots at the other end of the barracks. Colling assumed that it must be that of the individual who had been addressed as "Captain." The man remained in bed while he took his time looking Colling over, then asked him who he was.

"Jim Roper, sir," said Colling.

The officer climbed out of his bed and while pulling on his trousers, he said, "You're wearing a uniform, soldier, so how about acting it."

Colling came to attention and said, "Yessir. PFC James J. Roper, sir."

"How'd you get here, Roper?"

"Don't rightly know, sir. A bunch of Red soldiers jumped me, and threw me in their stockade. Next thing I know, I'm in the back of a truck and here I am."

"You have any idea where you are now?" asked the officer, who was standing in front of Colling, hands on hips.

"No, sir. All I can guess is some kind of a prison camp."

"Well, Roper, it looks like you know as much as we do. Welcome to your first concentration camp. My name is Bill Caldwell, Captain Bill Caldwell. United States Army Air Force. Those two guys over there by the door are Tech-four Jimmy Tunsholder, and Staff Sergeant Bert Lindsey. And in the officers' quarters at the other end of the hall are Lieutenants Hammerslee, Roberts and Wilmont. For some reason, the Krauts, or the Russians, who I must guess really run this place, have decided not to segregate enlisted from commissioned. I'm senior, and will expect you to conduct yourself properly at all times. Is that clear?"

"Yessir," replied Colling.

"You can stand at ease. And saluting is deferred for the duration. Take that cot over there," said Caldwell, pointing, "We'll talk in the morning."

"Yessir, right, sir," said Colling, before unrolling the thin mattress that had been provided for the bed that the captain had selected for him. There were no sheets, blankets or a pillow, but Colling kicked off his shoes and stretched out. He had pulled himself into a fetal position in order to attempt to stay as warm as possible, when something soft hit his back. When he turned over, he found that it was a gray German army blanket. Lindsey said something about it being an extra before he wrapped himself in his own bedclothes and rolled over.

Colling was awakened by Captain Caldwell's shouting for everyone to get up. Colling had not undressed, and he was putting on his shoes when he realized that Caldwell had the other air force men in two ranks, officers in front, and was about to begin leading calisthenics. Colling hurriedly completed tying his shoelaces, then took a place beside Tunsholder.

The Air Force captain led them through the usual exercises, and the session came to an end precisely upon the arrival of three guards bringing their breakfast. Two of the Germans stood by, rifles in hand, while the third doled out chunks of black bread and coffee. When each of the Americans had received his ration, the soldier brought out a small chunk of cheese and two apples and placed them on the table. When Caldwell asked how they were supposed to divide the apples, the German smiled, took out his bayonet, and sliced each of the apples into six pieces, and pushed two of the resulting twelve sections towards each of the prisoners. He then repeated the process with the cheese, cutting off six fairly equal slices.

Colling was contemplating how ironic it was that breakfast for the camp's jailers normally consisted of only bread and coffee when Caldwell spoke to him, "Roper, where were you when the Reds picked you up?"

Colling hesitated for a moment, chewing a mouthful of bread, before replying, "Well, sir, it was like this. I was in bed with a little frow-line, when all of a sudden, a bunch of Red soldiers bust in and drag me onto the floor and begin kicking the hell out of me...excuse me, sir, I didn't mean to cuss, but they gave me a good punching. Then they drug me down the stairs and threw me in a truck and took me to some stockade someplace. You know, a jail."

"I know what a stockade is, Roper. What I want to know, is where was this that you were in bed with this...a...a...German woman?" asked Caldwell.

"Oh, yessir. In Berlin. An apartment house on Seltzer or Saltzer street. Something like that. Mostly a bombed-out place."

"Were you Berlin occupation?"

"Yessir. Twenty-first Infantry."

"How long have you been in Berlin?" asked Caldwell.

"Going on six months, sir," said Colling.

"And in the Army?"

"About nine months, sir. I went in right after New Year's."

Tunsholder interjected, "Where'd you do basic?"

Colling hesitated momentarily before answering, "Fort Dix."

"What about advanced?" was Tunsholder's next question.

"Same. All at Fort Dix," said Colling.

"Where you from?" asked Lindsey, before he tore off a small piece of bread and popped it into his mouth.

"Milwaukee," replied Colling, "We lived out on Walnut, right off Fon Du Lac."

Captain Caldwell had been listening intently to Colling's responses, and Colling knew that the officer was gauging both the substance of his answers and his command of English. The officer seemed about to say something when Lieutenant Wilmont spoke up, "I used to go to Milwaukee to visit my grandparents. You know where Mitchell Park is?"

"Yessir," said Colling, "Right off South Layton Boulevard. The Horticultural Observatory is out there, isn't it?"

Wilmont looked at Caldwell, and raised his eyebrows in an apparent demonstration of his satisfaction with the answer.

Colling asked, "Sir, that's a nice neighborhood. Do your grandparents still live there?"

"Yeah," said the lieutenant.

For the next half-hour, the Air Force men asked Colling questions about Milwaukee, his parents, his schools, and his father's occupation; clearly seeking to reach a conclusion as to whether he was what he claimed to be. He believed he had convinced them when they reacted with either glee or dismay to the news that the Yankees had won the first game of the World Series. Caldwell, who was clearly a Dodgers fan, vowed that Brooklyn would prevail.

Eventually, as they seemed to become comfortable with his persona as Roper, Colling cautiously advanced some questions of his own. Lindsey revealed that they were the crew of a B-29 that had been forced down, and that they had been based in England. The home towns of the five men were offered without any inquiry from Colling, and he listened as they talked about their parents, where they had attended school, and other similar matters.

At one point, Colling informed the airmen that a few days earlier, they had all become members of a new separate United States Air Force. This information resulted in a minor celebration that Congress and Truman had finally done something that should have been accomplished years earlier.

By the end of the morning, Colling was confident that he was being accepted. He was hesitant to inquire regarding anything that Grau had told him the Russians wanted to know, preferring to wait until some turn in the conversations he was having with the prisoners would present an opening for a question about heavy bomber dispositions in the British Isles, whether there were A-Bombs at the bases, and how many of them there might be.

The mid-day meal consisted of more black bread, tepid cabbage soup, and tea. A small portion of margarine had been put on each chunk of bread. There was a chorus of complaints about the food, and Colling asked if this was what they were usually given to eat. His question was greeted by laughter, and Lindsey commented that he was looking forward to Christmas, when he was convinced that they might find a piece of turkey in their soup.

They had finished eating when the guards reappeared and ordered Caldwell to come for interrogation. Lieutenant Roberts voiced his observation that the daily inquisition had been delayed, and attributed their being left alone for the morning to Roper having joined them.

After about an hour, Caldwell was returned to the barracks, and Wilmont was summoned. This procedure was repeated throughout the afternoon, as each of them in turn was taken for questioning. The evening meal did not materialize, apparently delayed until everyone had been interrogated. Colling was the last to be called, and his departure was accompanied by pleas from the airmen to do what he could to keep his session short so that they could get something to eat.

Grau was waiting for him, and Colling began to speak German before the lieutenant remonstrated, telling him to speak English.

"Yessir. English it is. I'm not finding out anything."

"They seem to accept you," said Grau, lighting a fresh cigarette from the remains of the one he had been smoking.

"Maybe, sir. I had to think quick when they asked me about my training. I had heard the Ami's talk about Fort Dix when I was in Tunisia, and I must've said the right thing. I need more information about their military bases. If they ask me where I sailed from the U.S., I have to have an answer."

"New York is always a suitable response, Pretzmann. You can say you arrived in Wilhelmshaven. The Americans have the use of that port from the British. I do not think that you will be asked such questions now, however."

"Which one of the Ami's is the Russians' man?" asked Colling.

"It is best you do not know," replied Grau, "It could lead to your making a mistake and exposing you both."

Colling responded, "If he's been among them for longer than I have, and he hasn't found out anything yet, I doubt that I'll be able to."

"You are new to them, and it is reasonable that you should be curious. An opportunity will arise, do not fear."

"Does this guy know that I'm not Roper?" asked Colling.

"Yes, he has been informed of this," said Grau.

Colling said nothing in response, hoping his silence would suggest dissatisfaction at the unequal treatment he was receiving. When he sensed it was time to say something, he asked, "Lieutenant, sir, can you give me any advice about how to get them to talk?"

"They have already told you that they were based in England, so you might ask what that country is like. That may lead to other revelations. In a day or two, I will arrange that you and the other two enlisted men are separated from the officers, and you can express complaints about officers, and see what they may say."

"I'll try, sir, but I think they may still not trust me."

"Remember, Pretzmann, that it is natural for an ignorant man to ask questions. So far, you have said nothing to make them think that you are clever. I suggest you do nothing to change their minds," said Grau with a smile.

"I understand, sir," replied Colling, trying to give the impression that he had not noticed the sarcasm implicit in the German's advice.

Grau asked Colling to provide his thoughts regarding each of the imprisoned Americans, taking notes as Colling expressed his opinions about the abilities, motivations and character of each of the men. When Colling had finished, Grau reached into his desk and brought out a deck of cards, a pad of paper and a pencil, and a box containing a chess set. He gave them to Colling, instructing him to tell Captain Caldwell that his request for recreational materials had been granted. Grau added that the paper was not to be used to write letters or otherwise try to communicate with anyone.

Caldwell expressed his amazement that Grau had agreed to provide the items for which he had asked weeks previously. The captain wondered out loud why the *Luftwaffe* officer had given them to Colling. The captain's question raised a concern with Colling that Grau might have made a mistake that would destroy whatever confidence he had earned with his fellow prisoners, and make them suspicious that Colling was collaborating with their jailers.

It did not take long for Colling to became used to the prisoners' daily routine: Caldwell's morning exercise session, breakfast, a thirty-minute walk around the perimeter of the wire enclosure next to their barracks, followed by individual interrogations. Lunch and supper were brought in at the times when all six of them had been returned to the barracks during the questioning sessions. After supper, they were left to themselves for an hour or so before lights out. Grau's having provided them with cards and the chess set meant that there was an alternative to the activities that Caldwell had organized: Spinning yarns, telling jokes or taking turns teaching some subject that the lecturer was familiar with.

Colling refused any invitation to play chess on the grounds that the game was too difficult for him. He did participate in the nightly poker game, where they wagered slips of paper marked with their initials and "5," "10," or "25" cents, to be derived from the back-pay that was supposed to be due to each of them. With a dollar-limit rule, Colling's customary cautious and low-key style of play meant that he began to accumulate markers for a fair sum of money. More than once, he reluctantly conceded to himself that his winnings were likely to be meaningless, given that he had not yet thought of a way in which to get any of them out of the camp and to the American Zone.

That changed two days later, when an idea came to him. He

had to admit that the likelihood of success was slim, and his scheme would require a level of sophistication that had not been a part of any of his previous endeavors. Its complexity would mean it would be replete with risk, but he was already deeply in danger of being transported to a Siberian prison camp for German POW's. He also knew that time was running short, and the Russians were likely to decide at any time that Kottbach's and Grau's methods of extracting information were useless, and the inevitable journey to the east would occur.

He brought up the subject of the Russians' impatience with their progress with Grau at their next meeting, causing the lieutenant to exhibit even more nervousness than usual in fiddling with his cigarette. The *Luftwaffe* officer admitted that the Russians were growing restless, but voiced a confidence that Colling found hollow.

When Grau was finished, Colling spoke German, not bothering to conceal his dejection, to ask, "*Herr Oberleutnant*, what are we to do?"

"We must follow orders, Pretzmann. Like good German soldiers," came the reply.

"But, lieutenant, sir, these Ami's are cautious. They are well trained, and say nothing of any value. The only people that they would trust would be a company of American paratroopers coming from the sky to rescue them."

Grau stood and leaned over his desk, "You have not done what I told you to do. You fail to ask the right questions."   "But, sir, I have asked about England, as you said, yet all they will say is that it rains much and that English girls are friendly."

"Tonight you will set a new course. You will ask if they know any of those men who dropped the atom bomb on Japan. You will voice your opinion about their bravery, and ask if they have any worry about having to do the same to Russia," instructed Grau.

Colling pushed his chair back and stood at attention, "Yes, *Herr Oberleutnant*! I will do as you say."

"Good. Return to your barracks."

Tunsholder was stretched out on his bunk when Colling was shoved into their quarters, and the airman asked, "Hey, Roper, how'd the interrogation go?"

"Not bad," said Colling. "Lots of yelling and accusing me of being some kind of spy. The dumb Krauts can't figure out I'm just a dog-face soldier who don't know nothing."

"Wait 'til they decide to start using the clubs and rubber hoses. I ain't figured out yet why they been holding off with the rough stuff," said Tunsholder.

"Well," replied Colling, "I ain't looking forward to it. Them Russians who picked me up gave me a couple of good goings-over, and they wasn't even asking any questions. I ain't going to think about it. Only thing I'm going to think about is taking you guys' money at poker."

"Keep dreaming," said Lieutenant Wilmont, who had walked up behind Colling. "You're too far ahead, Roper, and you have to start drawing some bad cards sooner or later."

"Yessir," said Colling, "With all due respect, sir, this is the first time I ever played cards with officers, and it sure is nice to be owed money by someone who gets paid enough to make good on their IOU's."

Wilmont snorted and turned away, saying, "I'll get mine back, Roper. I feel lucky."

The American lieutenant's prediction was inaccurate, as Colling won the first three pots that evening. Remembering Grau's instructions, Colling asked whether any of them were acquainted with anyone who was part of the crews of the B-29's that had dropped the A-bomb on Hiroshima and Nagasaki. Caldwell said he had known Colonel Tibbets when he was a major in the same bomb group in England, earlier in the war. This developed into a general discussion between poker hands about what it would take for an air crew to drop an atomic weapon. But when Colling, trying to make himself sound ignorant and guileless, wondered out loud how many of the bombs the U.S. had, the conversation ended abruptly. When the hand finished, Caldwell leaned across and hissed in Colling's face, "That's classified information, soldier. Don't bring it up again."

When he was led out to his interrogation session the next day, Colling was prepared to be castigated by Grau for having lacked finesse in his attempt to follow the *Luftwaffe* officer's instructions. Instead, he found Colonel Kottbach with Grau in the lieutenant's office.

"Sit down, Pretzmann," said the Colonel.

The two German officers eyed him for a moment, saying nothing, then Grau broke the silence, "The *Obersturmbannführer* has come up with a plan which may result in the Americans providing the information that is sought."

"Yes," said Kottbach, "I believe that the Ami's will have trust in you if they believe you have been sent to rescue them."

Colling feigned an expression of surprise as he asked, "Colonel, sir, how is this to be accomplished?"

"I have been contemplating this," replied Kottbach, "And it is clear that the Ami's will not believe a rescue is taking place unless they actually think themselves to be free."

Colling shook his head, "Sir, with respect, that would require that they leave this camp, and the Soviets will never allow such a thing to happen."

Kottbach smiled and replied, "Ach...that has been anticipated, Pretzmann. I have gained the approval of Colonel Penakov. The so-called escape will be closely watched by Penakov's troops so that it does not turn into the real thing."

"But, Colonel, sir, if that is so, how am I to be certain that I am not shot by the Russians by mistake, or to cover their tracks once they have the information they seek?"

"That is a hazard you will have to accept, Pretzmann," said Grau. "If you succeed, all of us are better off. If you do not, the result will be the same at any rate."

Colling shrugged his shoulders and said, "So it shall be, Lieutenant."

Kottbach unfolded a map on the desk, and Colling saw that it showed the area surrounding *Stalag S-1*. The SD colonel, speaking in a conspiratorial tone, outlined his plan for the false break-out from the prison. He described how Colling would tell the Americans that he has been sent by U.S. intelligence to free them. He would confide that he has accomplices in the camp, and they have arranged for Colling and the prisoners would be smuggled out of the camp in one of the trucks assigned to the *Stalag*.

At Kottbach's request, a cottage in the forest between the prison and the border had been set aside as a "hideout" for the escapees while they were to await their chance to leave the Soviet zone. The cottage would be fully equipped with listening devices, and Soviet soldiers would be waiting nearby. Once it appeared to the prisoners that they were safely ensconced, Colling was to tell the Americans that he was under orders that the airmen verify that they are in fact, the crew of the *Sassy Lassie* by confirming where they were based, how many planes there were in their unit, and how many A-bombs they knew to be stored in England. After the information was obtained, the Russians would move in and take everyone back into custody.

Colling listened without comment to the SD man's plan, and when Kottbach was finished, he said that Caldwell and the rest were too intelligent to be taken in so easily. Colling expressed his concern that if all that was done was to move the Americans out of the camp, and then demand the same information that their interrogators had been trying to extract from them for weeks, that they would say nothing. While Kottbach was mulling over Colling's comments, Grau interjected his opinion that Colling was correct. It would be necessary to be more subtle in their approach.

Colling suggested that it would be more convincing to the Americans if, at the house where they were to take refuge, there are civilian clothes, money and papers for nine men, the original number in the crew. Colling went on to explain that this would have been the number of men that American intelligence would have expected to have to provide for in an escape. Colling added that it would also be a nice touch if there were a radio, and if Colling could appear to have the ability to communicate with his superiors on the other side of the border. The radio could be wired to the same listening post as that for the cottage's microphones, permitting an apparent two-way transmission to take place.

Grau agreed enthusiastically with Colling, assuring Kottbach that he had someone who was sufficiently fluent in English to play the role of the radio contact in the U.S. Zone. As the *Luftwaffe* lieutenant was speaking, Kottbach began to pace, clearly taking it all in, nodding his head in agreement, and saying, "*Ja, gut, gut,*" as the deception became more elaborate and hence, seemed to have a chance to be believable and successful.

Once he had confidence that the two Germans were willing to listen to his recommendations, Colling timidly suggested that the final element needed to convince the Americans might be a pistol or two at the house. The two Germans raised their eyebrows at this, and Kottbach held up his hand in a gesture of disapproval; but Colling went on, explaining that anyone from U.S. intelligence would be expected to be carrying a weapon on a mission of this sort. The Americans, who were renowned for their love for, and trust in their firearms, would absolutely believe Roper to be an American agent when they saw that he possessed a loaded gun.

Kottbach objected to the idea on the grounds that the Russians would not permit such a thing, but Grau suggested that they might approve, if the pistol were loaded with blanks, or altered so as not to fire. Colling shook his head at this, and responded that the Americans would without doubt wish to examine any firearms, and if they found them to have been disabled, they would immediately know that they were victims of a ruse.

Colling continued to press his point, arguing that perhaps the Russians' concerns about the prisoners resisting their ultimate arrest would be alleviated if they knew that only he or their "man inside" would be the only one to have a gun in his hand when that time came. Kottbach nodded his head in agreement, and said he would make an attempt to explain it all to Penakov, but also voiced his doubt that he would approve.

Grau, who had been exhaling cigarette smoke towards the ceiling during the exchange between Kottbach and Colling, commented that if they obtained the information they were looking for, that it might be appealing to the Reds if the Americans could all be fatally shot while resisting recapture. Colling responded that provision would have to be made for himself to be spared from any such unhappy conclusion, or he would refuse to participate. Grau assured Colling that he was merely thinking out loud, and that he had nothing to worry about.

With Kottbach and Grau concurring with Colling's embellishments to the original plan, it was proposed by Grau that at Colling's next interrogation session, he would be informed as to the exact time that the "escape" from the camp would take place, and whether Colonel Penakov had agreed to a pistol being in the cottage. As they were about to dismiss him, Colling asked Grau who would be at the wheel of the truck that they would use. The German lieutenant replied that Colling would do so, and Colling confessed apologetically that he did not know how to drive. Kottbach told Grau to see that Colling had some instruction in operating a motor vehicle.

The man assigned to teach Colling the ins and outs of the Lend-lease 2½-ton Dodge truck, that the Russians had provided as part of *Stalag S-1's* transportation requirements, was named Niemyer. With Colling sitting in the driver's seat, the German explained the various switches and dials on the vehicle's dashboard, and the purpose and locations of the floor pedals. Colling acted as if he were seeing everything for the first time, and asked questions so that Niemyer had to repeat his explanations more than once.

After he had finished with the preliminaries, Niemyer led Colling through the process of starting the engine, and then instructed him in the use of the clutch, gearshift and brakes. Seemingly unafraid of what the result might be, the German told Colling to put the truck in gear, release the clutch and press the accelerator. There was a lurch forward, and the engine died. Niemyer patiently told Colling to re-start the vehicle, and on the second try, Colling drove smoothly forward, but made sure to twist the steering wheel erratically, as if in panic, causing the Dodge's forward progress to be a series of twists and turns. Niemyer responded with his own genuine panic, leaning over to grab the wheel and fight Colling for control, in order to keep the vehicle on a straight path.

After several more stops and starts, Colling pretended to gain familiarity with driving, and when he successfully circled the compound adjacent to the camp gate two or three times, Niemyer pronounced him competent to operate the truck.

At his interview with Grau the following day, the German informed him that all was in readiness, and that the fake escape would take place in two days. The Russians' insider had been let in on the plan, and Colling was to use written notes to let the other Americans know that there were microphones planted in the prison barracks. After that, he was to reveal that he was an American agent sent to rescue them. Grau suggested that Colling use the name of the new U.S. intelligence organization, the Central Intelligence Agency, or "CIA."

Colling was to say that he had accomplices in the camp, and that they had arranged for their escape. They would overpower the guards bringing them their meals, after which, Colling would lead them to the truck. Colling would have taken the uniform of one of the guards, and would drive out the main gate with the Americans hidden in the back of the vehicle. Once outside, he would head directly for the cottage, conceal the Dodge in the woods at the edge of the road near the cottage, and proceed on foot from there to the house.

At the conclusion of Grau's instructions, Colling said he wanted to visit the cottage to make sure he was familiar with the place. After all, in order to have stocked it with clothing and the other items needed for the escape, and to be sure of its location, he would have to have been there at some time prior to going to Berlin to get himself picked up by the Russians and sent to *Stalag S-1*. At this, Grau reminded him that he would have to have an explanation as to how he was able to be imprisoned at this particular camp, and Colling suggested he would say that the CIA had someone among the Russians in Berlin who was able to arrange such things.

Grau informed Colling that he would see him the next morning, and if a reconnaissance of the cottage was permitted by Colonel Penakov, then the German lieutenant would take Colling there. Before returning Colling to his quarters, Grau smiled and commented that he thought that the scheme just might work.

CHAPTER 12

OCTOBER, 1947

As it turned out, Grau was not smiling when Colling was ushered into his office early the following day. The German was behind his desk as usual, a cigarette in his hand, but the confidence he had seemed to have had in Colling when he had last seen him was absent.

"What sort of a game are you playing, Pretzmann?" asked Grau in German.

Colling felt his heart leap in his chest. Its beating was so pronounced that he imagined Grau must be able to hear it. His mind raced, trying to figure out what Grau meant, and searching for a proper response, he replied, "*Herr Oberleutnant*, what do you mean?"

Grau's hand came from under his desk holding a small pistol, which he pointed directly at Colling's chest. "I suspect you truly *are* what you have convinced Kottbach and Penakov you are pretending to be. Might it be true that you are not a German born in America... not *Volksdeutsche*, but a true American?"

Colling was mentally measuring whether he should rush Grau, despite the desk between them, or turn and try to make it out the door. He had opted to attack, and was tensing in anticipation of the distance he would have to cover to reach the German, when Grau lowered his weapon. Colling decided to hold his stance, while remaining alert to the possibility that an opportunity of disarming the officer might still present itself.

Continuing to hold the pistol in his hand, Grau said, "I will not bother to ask your true name. Three identities are more than sufficient. Are you not curious to know how it was that I came to realize that you are, in fact, an American agent?"

Colling made no reply, staring at the *Luftwaffe* officer and keeping track of the direction in which the muzzle of his pistol was pointing.

"I must admit that you had me completely fooled. I took you for a lad with no morals and something to hide, who wanted to appear more of a dolt than he was. I was of the opinion that you were guilty of more than some POW camp activities in Tunisia, but you were useful, and I put that aside. You were very clever in engineering this escape thing. I did not realize that you deliberately planted the seeds for it until you slipped up and I knew you for what you are."

Seemingly amused with Colling's silence, Grau continued, "You planted two seeds, in fact. First, that story about having had experience with POW's in Africa. I know not how you selected the location, or this 'Colonel Stumpfer,' but whether you knew it would be so or not, I was unable to find anything that might refute your tale. Or confirm it, for that matter.

"The second seed was your comment about American paratroopers coming to rescue the prisoners. You were so good, that I actually thought that I myself had conceived the idea of using a counterfeit rescuer to gain their confidence. I was displeased when Kottbach took credit with the Russians for what I believed was my idea."

Colling commented, "Is not allowing a superior officer to take credit for the ideas of the subordinate the path to promotion for the subordinate?"

Grau laughed, "You sound like Moltke or Clausewitz, philosophizing about the traits that a true soldier must possess."

"I am neither, *Herr Oberleutnant*. Only a lowly private, trying to survive," said Colling.

"You continue to amaze me, Pretzmann. I have you cornered, and still you play the innocent. Perhaps if you understand how I am sure that you are no German anti-aircraftsman, you will cease your charade." When Colling did not respond, Grau said, "You made a mistake when you asked that clothing for nine men be placed in the cottage. It came to me later...you were never told how many were in the crew of the B-29, not by anyone in this camp, that is."

Seizing on the slim opportunity that he still might be able to talk his way out, Colling protested, "But Lieutenant, sir, one of the

Americans did mention this to me."

"Nonsense!" said Grau, returning his pistol to its original position targeting Colling's chest, "I checked the recordings from the microphones in the barracks. None of the Americans said anything of the kind. You had to have known this information from somewhere else. Do you want to tell me, or am I to turn you over to Colonel Penakov? He will, no doubt, be able to loosen your tongue."

Colling slumped forward, his hands on Grau's desk, his posture reflecting his acceptance of defeat. For the first time since he had been interned by the British in Lübeck, when he had believed that he might be returned to the mercies of the NKVD, he considered the virtue of avoiding such a fate by seeking a quick end to his own life. He was about to lunge at Grau simply so that the German would put a bullet through his heart, when Grau said, "I wish to go with you."

"What did you say?" asked Colling.

"I wish to go with you. What choice do I have? If I give you to the Russians, it will be an admission that I was duped. The experiment to extract information using my methods will be proven a failure, and I will be returned to a Soviet camp. I will suffer no better a fate than shall you. And in truth, you must have thought this through with great care, so that there is a better than even chance you will pull it off. Consider also, that I am able perhaps, to provide additional help to make success more likely."

Colling found himself in a state somewhat akin to shock. A moment before, he had been in utter despair, preferring death to what he knew from experience awaited him at the hands of the Soviets, and now he felt almost euphoric with the realization that the odds seemed to have turned in his favor. He decided to drop all pretense, and said, "What of Kottbach? Is he to come with us?"

"Nay," said Grau, "If I were to tell him of this, he would betray us in the forlorn belief that the Russians would reward him for it. Besides, many Czechs and Poles, not to mention Germans, have died because of the SD. I can find no pity for him."

"What of the others?" asked Colling.

"The same. None of them can be trusted, and all are of the SS.

Their time has come."

"Is it possible that we are being overheard at this very moment?" said Colling, glancing around the office.

"The microphones are there, but I have disabled them temporarily," replied Grau, "It helps to know where the wires run. I will reconnect them before we go to the cottage. On our way, we will talk some more."

Grau rose from his desk, slipping his pistol into his pocket as he did so. He then reached behind a bookcase, and did something that Colling guessed involved re-establishing the listening devices. The lieutenant took his cap from a coat stand near the door, and adjusted it to a jaunty angle. Grau also tossed Colling a guard's uniform jacket from the same rack, telling him to put it on over his American khaki's, in order to be less conspicuous, and to ward off the chill outside. When Colling had the coat on, Grau motioned for him to follow.

A small Opel utility truck had been made available for their drive to the hideout in the forest. While Grau drove, Colling made a mental note of the route and distance, estimating that about twenty minutes were required to make the trip.

While they traveled, Grau talked about being shot down while flying a Messerschmitt, intercepting Allied bombers over France. His legs had been broken, and he was given little hope of flying again. When he was able to walk, his command of English resulted in his being assigned to an interrogation unit in the German air intelligence service, and assigned to work questioning British and American flyers. He discovered he was quite good at it, and as the war went on, he fully expected to remain in Germany, interrogating POW's, until the end. Things did not work out as he had anticipated, however. In late 1944, the shortage of qualified pilots resulted in his recall to a fighter squadron based in Poland. At the end of the fighting, Grau was in Czechoslovakia, captured when his air base was overrun by the Red Army. He had managed to survive in a Russian labor camp for nearly two years afterward, until someone in the hierarchy of Soviet intelligence decided to bring him back to Germany and *Stalag S-1*. Colling suspected that the German's revelations might have been intended to elicit a reciprocal disclosure about his own background, but Colling said nothing.

The cottage was at the end of a dirt track off the main road. They had not passed through Hohenwald, and Colling surmised that they were south of the village. They pulled up in front of a small, unpainted wooden structure that looked more like an over-sized tool-shed than a place of human habitation. There was glass in the windows, however, and its stout door was secured by a padlock that bore the "Yale" trademark. Grau commented as he loosened the lock, that it had come from Captain Visinsky, who had laughed when he told Grau it was "American Lend-lease."

Colling's opinion that the cottage was only marginally fit to live in was confirmed once they were inside. There was one large room, half of which had been devoted to serving as a make-shift kitchen. There was a small coal stove between a plank counter and a square sheet-metal sink that was outfitted with a hand pump. Colling was pleasantly surprised that there was at least an indoor supply of water. When he opened the doors on the two cabinets over the counter and the sink, Colling saw that there was a supply of canned American Army rations that Collins supposed had also been Lend-lease to the USSR.

A piece of lath had been nailed horizontally to the wall at the rear of the wooden counter, designed to serve as crude rack for an assortment of cooking cutlery. The largest of the knives appeared to have been locally forged, and was at least ten inches in length. Colling slid it from behind the lath and tested its edge with his thumb. Its slightly-curved blade was as sharp as a razor, ending in a point that was equally acute. Instead of replacing the knife where he had found it, Colling set it on the counter, pushing it back until it rested against the wall.

A rough table and several chairs were in the center of the half of the room allocated as its kitchen, while a pair of bunks constructed from boards occupied the remaining half. Colling noted that when the seven, of them were there, five, would be relegated to sleeping on the floor. The beds both held piles of well-worn clothing. Through the window located over the wooden counter, Grau pointed out a privy about twenty meters into the woods behind the cottage.

An old wooden cheese crate was resting on a small table under the window that overlooked the dooryard. Grau lifted the box, revealing the radio that Colling was to use to appear to contact his CIA superiors. Colling stepped closer to examine the apparatus, and the *Luftwaffe* officer identified it as a German field radio, demonstrated how to turn it on, and invited Colling to try the earphones. All that Colling could hear was a whining sound, which prompted him to twist the dial in the radio's center until it sounded like an appropriate frequency had been found. Colling picked up the microphone that rested in front of the set, looking at Grau, but hesitating to speak into it.

"No one is yet on the other end," said Grau, "Tomorrow you will be speaking with my man in English. It will be best if you make contact soon after your arrival. Ask for instructions, and you will be told to move westwards after nightfall. There will be some code words that you will pretend to understand. You will use the name 'Runner' to identify yourself." Colling voiced his understanding, and the German replaced the crate covering the transmitter.

Grau gestured for Colling to step outside with him, where he produced a different map than the one Kottbach had shown Colling when they had discussed the spurious escape a few days previously. The *Luftwaffe* lieutenant's version was hand-drawn, and had been marked to show where the Russians had pitched a tent to house their eavesdropping equipment. There was also a small circle closer to the cottage and behind it, which Grau explained represented an observation post where two Russians would be watching through binoculars.

Pointing to the map as he related his information, Grau said, "They will have a company of border troops waiting on this road near the tent, ready to surround the house once they hear the Americans tell you about the aircraft and atomic bombs. They are only about a hundred and fifty meters away, so they will be upon you in less than ten minutes. The soldiers assigned to keep the house under visual observation have a field telephone, and will sound an immediate alert if they see anyone appearing to flee."

Colling's spirits fell with the realization that every avenue of escape seemed to have been closed. His face must have betrayed his dismay, because Grau continued, "Do not be down-hearted, Pretzmann. You will have some help. You will leave the truck in which you escape the camp in the underbrush near the main road. The Russians will have concealed a radio transmitter in the vehicle, to remove any difficulty in tracking it, should there be any attempt made to drive to the border. I have arranged for someone to drive the truck away. This will serve as a distraction. Before the truck is started, the two men in the observation post will be eliminated after the wire to their field telephone is cut. There will be some shooting, which shall be the signal to you to flee from this place. If the Russians overtake the truck, it will be destroyed by explosives.

"To the east, through those trees, lies a stream. When you flee, it is in that direction that you must go, and you must cross the stream in order to confuse their dogs. If the distraction that has been planned works, the Russians will be trying to head off and pursue the truck. You perhaps will hear an explosion that will indicate that they have managed to stop the truck. For awhile, the Russians may believe that all of you have perished in the blast, allowing you and the Americans to put some distance behind you."

Grau concluded by saying, "Once you are across the stream, keep moving through the forest until you reach this road here."

Colling asked, "To whom will we owe our thanks for this assistance?"

"Wolfjäger will take the truck and drive it as far as he is able," replied Grau, "A man named Vogelsang and some of his men will provide the explosives and liquidate the observation post."

"Was it not you who has said that the SS men at the camp are not to be trusted?" said Colling, "And I have been told that Vogelsang works for the Russkies."

"Wolfjäger has this one chance to himself escape," was Grau's response, "And he is the only one who is tough enough to do what must be done. As for Vogelsang, he bears no love for the Russians, and will do this thing for his own reasons."

"And how far to the east is it that you expect us to run?" said

Colling.

"To this road here," said Grau, his finger tracing the map, "It will be over three kilometers. Wait here, at this point, hiding in the forest, and I will join you."

No firearms had been evident in the cottage, leading Colling to inquire, "What about the guns?"

"Ah, yes," said Grau, "Come, let us return to the house, and I will show you where they are concealed. Be cautious in what you say, the listening devices are in place already."

The German lieutenant reached on top of the cabinet over the sink and brought down a Luger. He handed it to Colling, who pulled back the slide to test the weapon's action. He found that the magazine was full, and he peeled off the top round to feel its weight and check the primer. Grau whispered that the ammunition was good, and when Colling handed back the pistol, the German returned it to its hiding place. Without speaking, his fingers to his lips, Grau reached under the wooden counter and produced another Luger. Colling examined the second pistol as he had the first, and found it satisfactory. Grau replaced the gun where it had been concealed, and suggested that it was time to return to the camp. After replacing the padlock, the *Luftwaffe* lieutenant made sure that Colling was aware that he had hidden the key on the ledge above the door.

As they walked to the truck, Grau folded the map and handed it to Colling, saying, "The second Luger is known only to you and myself. Penakov and his men prepared the house, and their man on the inside knows the location of the first. Be cautious that he does not take possession of it before you do."

"It would be wonderful if you would tell me who he is," said Colling.

"Alas, I am not able to do so," replied Grau, "Only the Reds know him, and I know not even how they communicate with him. I suspect that they use the opportunity of the weekly shower allowed to the prisoners to somehow do so."

"It will be a great problem to have an informer in our midst," commented Colling.

"Your problem will, for truth, begin when he discovers that

your intent to escape is real," was Grau's response, as he started the Opel's engine.

Colling had pulled himself halfway into the cab of the truck when he stopped and informed Grau that he had to return to the cottage. Colling heard the *Luftwaffe* officer speaking as he crossed the yard, telling him not to take too long. He used the key to quietly re-enter the house and go quickly to the cabinet where the first Luger was concealed. Colling removed it and hid the pistol under the thin mattress of the nearest bunk.

The orchestrated escape was scheduled to take place when the guards brought their breakfast the following morning. Before the food arrived, Colling wrote a note which he showed to Caldwell, stating that he, Roper, was a CIA agent who was there to free them from the camp. At the same time that he handed the captain the piece of paper, Colling put his finger to his lips and pointed upwards, sending a warning about eavesdropping. The Air Force officer nodded his understanding, after which Colling wrote another message informing him that the guards at breakfast had been bribed, and that they could be easily over-powered.

Caldwell quickly gathered the other prisoners and let them see what Colling had written, simultaneously repeating the wordless gestures that Colling had used with him regarding the presence of microphones. When everyone had indicated that they understood, Colling pushed each of the men into positions flanking the door, and they waited.

Grau had apparently done a good job of coaching the three Germans who brought their breakfast, because they put up virtually no resistance when the Americans seized them and pushed them to the floor. Colling continued to silently caution against making any noise. The guards cooperated by foregoing any attempt to cry out or make a commotion while they were being tied up with strips torn from bedding.

Wilmont and Roberts had picked up the Mauser rifles that two of the Germans had been carrying. While Colling was stripping off the jacket and trousers of one of the soldiers, he hissed at the two lieutenants that the guns were loaded with only a few rounds of ammunition, and useless; and that they should be left behind. The two lieutenants propped the weapons against the wall, and after Colling had pulled on the uniform and clapped the owner's cap on his head, he put his head out of the door and glanced around, then waved for the others to follow him.

The area outside their barracks was empty, and Colling led his companions in a crouching run through the spaces between the rows of other buildings until they emerged into the lot where a line of vehicles was parked. Colling pointed to the closest, the Dodge deuce-and-a-half, and urged Caldwell to get his men into the back and cover themselves with the tarpaulin that they would find there.

Colling climbed into the cab and switched on the electrical circuit and then the ignition. The engine came to life, and he pushed the accelerator pedal a time or two, listening to the satisfying roar that resulted. He put the truck into gear, and drove to the camp's front gate. Colling wondered whether anyone would notice that his handling of the vehicle was considerably improved since Niemyer's driving lesson.

The sentry at the entrance to *Stalag S-1* nodded at him and asked in a bored voice where he was going. Colling replied that he had orders to pick up some foodstuffs in Hohenwald, and he was casually waved through. He followed the route that Grau had taken, but instead of driving up the dirt track leading to the cottage, he did as Grau had directed, and parked the truck behind some underbrush where the track to the cottage intersected the road.

The others were already clambering over the truck's tailgate when Colling joined them. He ordered everyone to follow him, and began walking rapidly towards the hideout, glancing over his shoulder occasionally to make sure everyone was close behind him.

The key to the padlock was on the narrow ledge where he had left it, and Colling quickly opened the door and ushered everyone inside. He invited the airmen to change into the civilian clothing that was piled on the bunks, as he began to remove the guard's uniform.

Colling was the first to finish dressing, probably due to his not being particularly selective with regard to the size or condition of what the Soviets had provided. He had grown used to wearing dirty, ill-fitting, threadbare clothing when he was in Poland, and experience had taught him that when acting the part of a refugee, the shabbier one appeared, the better.

Hoping his actions were convincing whichever of the Americans was a traitor that the charade was going as planned, Colling lifted the crate off the concealed radio and turned it on, while slipping the earphones, over his ears and twisting the tuning dial. He said, "Runner here, Runner here," in his best Hollywood imitation of an OSS agent, and he was momentarily startled when he received a reply, "X-Ray here, Runner, do you read?" Colling responded that he did indeed hear whoever X-Ray was, and then said, "Do you have instructions, X-Ray?"

"Proceed after nightfall, Runner. West to border. Truck will be waiting. That is all, out," and the voice ended. As he switched off the radio, Colling became aware that Caldwell and Hammerslee were on either side of him, their ears close to his. Caldwell said, "Well, it looks like we wait here awhile, until it gets dark, right?"

Colling responded, "Yessir, that's the drill. As soon as it gets dark, we head for home."

This caused the Americans to set up a quiet cheer, smiling and softly clapping their hands. Colling added, "It ain't over yet, sir. We need to get through about twenty kilometers of woods before we reach the U.S. Zone."

Breakfast had been deferred because of their escape, so Colling recommended that they eat. When he picked out three cans of C-ration pork and beans from the supply in the cabinet and showed them to the airmen, he was surprised that they murmured their approval. In less than five minutes, Colling had a fire going in the stove and their food was heating in a cast-iron pot. He found U.S. Army issue ground coffee and ladled a few spoonfuls into a battered tea kettle full of water, which he set on the stove beside the pot of beans.

Caldwell was going from window to window, glancing outside, while the others discussed their good fortune at having escaped. Colling made no comment, waiting for the food to heat, and the coffee to boil. When he was satisfied that their breakfast was ready, he asked everyone to have a seat at the table, and doled out the C-rations on the tin plates that he had discovered in the other cabinet. The airmen praised the fact that they at last had American food to eat, no matter that it consisted of field rations. Roberts caused them all to laugh when he complained that there was no sugar or cream for the coffee.

When the last mouthful was eaten, Colling motioned for everyone to remain around the table, and he pulled out the pad of paper that Grau had provided along with the cards and chess set. He wrote a note warning that there were microphones in the room, and that they must be cautious about what they said. As he pushed it across so that the others could read it, Colling watched each of them for their reaction. The Soviets' inside man, on realizing what Colling had done, was the first to move, dashing across the room and reaching atop the cabinet for the Luger that was no longer there.

Colling slammed into Lindsey just as he turned from trying to retrieve the pistol, and they went down on the floor in a tangle. Colling had picked up the kitchen knife as he crossed the room,, and as he had been taught in basic training, thrust it upwards below Lindsey's ribs while clamping his hand over the airman's mouth to stifle the scream that followed the penetration of the blade.

The other Americans were frozen, stunned at the spectacle of the two men rolling on the floor. Colling viciously twisted the knife until Lindsey slumped back, blood streaming from his mouth, making a gurgling, choking sound that ended in a long bubbling sigh as he died.

Colling sat up, breathing hard, fully expecting the Air Force men to attack him because of what he had done to one of their own. They were hesitating, wide-eyed, and Colling realized that he was holding the knife, smeared red, and pointing it in their direction. He put a finger to his lips, then forced himself to laugh and loudly say, "Jeez, Lieutenant, did that chair get the best of you? You really fell on your ass that time!"

Colling gestured with both hands, trying to get the other Americans to follow his lead. Caldwell was the first to react, saying, "Wilmont! How the hell many times have I had to tell you not to lean back so far. I told you that the damn chair would tip over sooner or later."

In response to Caldwell, Wilmont said, "Would one of you please help me up, or are you just going to sit there looking at me?"

Colling had regained his feet, and moved quickly around the room, locating the microphones and pointing to them, while signaling for the men to keep on talking. When he was satisfied that he knew where each of the devices was hidden, he returned to the table and began writing another message.

The notes explained that Lindsey was a Russian agent, and that he had tried to reach a pistol that had been concealed on top of the cabinet. Colling demonstrated that he had moved the weapon by producing the Luger from beneath the mattress. After tucking the gun into his waistband, Colling retrieved the other one from beneath the counter and gave it to Caldwell. Hammerslee took a blanket from one of the bunks and tossed it over Lindsey's body. Tunsholder and Roberts had dropped back into their chairs, seemingly unable to fully fathom what had transpired in the last few minutes.

Colling motioned for Caldwell to join him outside, and once Colling had closed the door behind them, he said, "Captain, stay close to the wall here, the Russians have an observation post behind the privy. We need to get the hell out of here as quickly as possible, as soon as we hear shots."

"Okay," replied Caldwell, "What direction will we be heading?"

Colling nodded towards the tree-line to the east of the cottage, "That way, sir."

"I'm not fully oriented, Roper, but I think that's east, away from the border," said Caldwell.

"Right, sir. There'll be a diversion to make the Russians think we're going to take the truck and make a beeline to our zone. We need to go in the opposite direction for awhile to throw them off the scent."

They re-entered the house and Colling used the pad to pencil an explanation for the others. Caldwell nodded his head in confirmation of Colling's instructions. Colling emptied the cabinets, handing everyone some of the C-rations, and then urged the men to quickly roll the blankets from the beds and tie them so that they could be slung over their backs. They had just finished carrying out his instructions when they heard the sound of the Dodge's engine starting, followed immediately by a flurry of gunshots. Colling herded everyone out the door, and as an afterthought, picked up the bloody butcher knife from where he had left it on the counter and shoved it into his waistband.

Colling led them in a run to the woods, urging them onward in a low voice. There was no path, but he pointed out an open space in the underbrush and told them to keep moving. When they reached the stream, he instructed them to cross, and once everyone had passed him, splashed through behind them.

Caldwell had stopped and gathered the others around him as he reached the forest on the other side. Colling caught up to them and after referring to Grau's map, signaled for them to follow him, after which they crashed off uphill through the pines. More firing was going on behind them, and then there was a loud series of bangs, followed by a corresponding series of palpable concussion waves. Colling glanced back to see a ball of fire and black smoke rising above the trees, and wondered if Wolfjäger had managed to get out of the truck before the explosion. Smoke continued to billow upwards from where the blast had occurred, and there was no immediate indication that the Russians were searching in their direction.

They had been laboring through the woods for what Colling estimated to be a little over an hour when they emerged onto the dirt road shown on Grau's map. Colling made a choice to turn to the left, and the others were behind him as he trotted close to the tree line, ready to dive into the forest at the first sign of pursuit. The spot where the *Luftwaffe* officer had said that he would meet them was supposed to be marked by several large boulders beside the track, and Colling was praying that his choice of direction had been the correct one.

He was relieved to see the massive rocks he was looking for jutting up from the earth at the edge of the other side of road ahead of them. They crossed on the run and when they were in among the trees, Colling ordered a halt. As an afterthought, he picked up a fallen pine branch that still had some of its clusters of needles attached, and ran back across the road and used it to sweep out their tracks. He dropped beside Caldwell, and breathing heavily, said, "Sir, we need to get everyone back further into the trees. The Russians will be looking for us."

The Air Force captain instructed his men to conceal themselves more deeply in the forest. Colling remained lying on his stomach on a slight rise above the rock formation, wondering whether he would have to lead his little band to safety on his own, in the event that Grau did not appear as promised.

Colling was contemplating what his next move would be if the German failed to make their rendezvous, when Caldwell dropped down beside him. The captain said, "You speak pretty good German. You also speak English like a Midwesterner. Which one was it you learned in school?"

"Neither, sir. I learned both at my Mama's knee," said Colling, watching the road.

"'Roper' your real name?" asked Caldwell.

"As far as I know, sir," was Colling's response.

"Where you from, Roper?"

"Sir, I don't think I should tell you, and I don't think you should know," replied Colling.

"Fair enough," said the Air Force officer, "I notice you call me 'sir.' I figure that must mean I outrank you."

"Not necessarily, sir," said Colling, turning his head to look directly at Caldwell.

"Right," said Caldwell, "I'll shut up. Think I'll get back to the men."

Colling nodded his head in agreement, and the captain crawled away.

From his vantage point, Colling could see a column of black smoke still rising over the tops of the trees, and he thought he recognized the popping of small-arms fire, which was immediately verified by the staccato sound of automatic weapons. He wondered how long the Reds would be fooled by Wolfjäger's diversionary run, and reflexively reached up to touch his face where the SS sergeant had hit him.

He was considering the irony of their depending on help from a Nazi when he heard a twig snap to his left. He rolled over, taking the Luger from his belt and placing it within reach, then drawing the butcher knife and preparing to use it to deliver an upward blow. Everything was silent, and Colling returned to a prone position, pulling his knees underneath his body and waiting to lunge when the opportunity presented itself.

If Grau had been a Russian soldier, Colling decided later, the Red would have killed him before he could have used his knife. The German officer came out of the underbrush so quietly and quickly that Colling was literally not aware of Grau's presence until he was lying beside him.

"*Guten Tag*," said the *Luftwaffe* lieutenant in Colling's ear, "How goes it?"

"God in heaven!" hissed Colling, "You have scared me out of my wits!"

"Better to die of fright than a blade across the throat," chuckled Grau.

"I did not know *Luftwaffe* pilots were trained as Red Indians," said Colling.

"True enough," replied Grau, "But my boyhood companions and I played at Leatherstockings in the woods above our village. From Karl May we learned of Winnetou, and like him, to move through the forest like shadows."

"A valuable skill, but disconcerting," said Colling, recalling having read portions of Karl May's novels about the American frontier in German class in high school. "What now?" Colling asked.

"We wait until nightfall," said Grau, "Where are the others?"

"Behind us, in the forest," and seeing that the *Luftwaffe* officer was wearing his German uniform, added, "It is best that I go to them before yourself, to spare them alarm."

"So be it," said the *Luftwaffe* officer, "I will remain here to watch the road."

Colling found the five airmen scattered in a circle, concealed separately behind undergrowth and rocks, and in depressions in the ground. He guessed that Caldwell had given orders to disperse, rather than remain in a group, and was thankful that the captain was using his head. When the Air Force officer lifted his head from his hiding place and called Colling's name in a low voice, Colling joined him and said, "Sir, we have to lay low until dark. So far, it doesn't look like the Russians are on our trail. And sir, we have some help, he's up where I was, watching the road. As soon as it starts to get dark, I'll bring him down. For now, keep everyone under cover, no fires and no smoking."

Caldwell replied, "Not a problem, Roper. All of us lost the habit a long time ago. Only time anyone ever got a smoke was when they were questioning us."

When Colling returned to where he had left Grau, the first thing that the German said was that he wished he could light a cigarette. Colling sympathized with him while expressing his gratitude that the German was keeping his craving for tobacco under control. Colling smiled inwardly at the coincidence that his last conversation with Caldwell and his first with Grau had concerned the same subject, and wondered whether it had been Grau who had offered cigarettes to the airmen during their interrogation sessions.

Colling and Grau remained in their position for the rest of the day, periodically shifting their bodies to relieve cramps and improve the blood flow to their extremities. Grau had brought a rucksack, and they took turns using it as a pillow to rest while the other stood watch. The smoke on the horizon continued to drift skyward, a reminder of the black clouds that had been there earlier. There was no sign of movement on the road or in the woods on its other side. Late in the afternoon, a small airplane buzzed overhead, following the course of the road. The two of them reflexively ducked their heads as the craft passed them and disappeared into the distance. Colling silently congratulated himself on having the foresight to use the pine branch to brush out evidence of their having crossed from one side of the woods to the other.

The reconnaissance plane did not return, which Colling took as a hopeful sign. The hours passed, and when it was fully dark,

Grau tugged at his sleeve, and after picking up the rucksack that he had been carrying, they made their way to where the others were waiting.

As they came out of the trees, Caldwell called quietly to his men, and they came to gather around. The Air Force captain did not recognize Grau in the dim light until Colling and the German were face-to-face with him. When Caldwell saw the uniform and who was wearing it, he exclaimed, "Jesus Christ! It's the Kraut lieutenant!"

Colling cautioned all of them to keep their voices low, and said, "Lieutenant Grau here helped us get out of the camp. He's going with us, and you can trust him."

"Yeah, sure," said Caldwell, "As soon as you explain why he was working with the Russians." This brought a murmur of agreement from the other American airmen.

"It's a long story, gentlemen," said Colling. "Suffice it to say that Lieutenant Grau was a POW, and didn't have much choice in what he was doing."

Hammerslee asked, "What did you say his name was?" This signaled Colling that Grau had probably not introduced himself to the Americans, and speaking German, he inquired of the *Luftwaffe* officer if this were indeed true. Grau answered in English, "It has been my custom to say that my name is Strauss when questioning. It has always been better to use a mild name, such as Strauss, and wiser that my true name not be known. This is, of course, for security purposes."

"So what is his real name?" Hammerslee persisted.

"Grau," said Colling and the German simultaneously. Colling continued, "The lieutenant here is a former *Luftwaffe* fighter pilot. Shot down and wounded. He was assigned to questioning POW's because he spoke English. When the war ended, he was captured by the Russians. He spent two years in one of their camps until they pulled him out and brought him here to question prisoners that the Russians were holding.

"When he learned I was arranging for your escape, instead of turning me in, he asked to help and to go along with us. So far, he's done what he said he would. If it wasn't for him, we wouldn't be where we are. So all of you calm down, and let's figure out how to get out of here in one piece."

As Colling was speaking, the initial hostility of the airmen seemed to subside in favor of a cautious tolerance of Grau. To further relieve the tension, Colling, suggested that they open the cans of Spam that had been among the rations in the cottage, and eat their supper. He reminded them that the compressed meat could be eaten cold, without the need to start a fire.

When Colling had finished his own portion, he pulled Grau aside, and speaking German, asked him in a low voice what his plan was to get to the American Zone. The *Luftwaffe* officer replied that he really did not have a definite plan, but in reaction to the expression on Colling's face, went on to say that he thought they might be able to obtain transportation at a place that he knew. They would have to cover somewhat more than ten kilometers in the dark, heading northeastwards. Then he emphasized his proposal by showing Colling the compass that Colling had had among his belongings when he reached *Stalag S-1*. When Colling recognized it, Grau smiled and reminded Colling that he had been promised that his things would be kept safe when he had arrived in *Stalag S-1*.

They set off in a file, Grau in the lead and Colling bringing up the rear. The October chill that had prevailed during the day soon settled into cold, and Colling was forced to pull the old suit coat he was wearing close to his chest. There was no clear path through the forest, and Colling flinched every time he heard the sound of someone stumbling ahead of him. He assumed that Grau was using the compass, at the same time feeling less and less confident that the German knew where he was taking them. The cloud cover obscuring the moon afforded them a mixed blessing, making it more difficult for any pursuers to see them, but at the same time rendering it equally difficult for them to find their way. It was only intermittently that their surroundings were illuminated, and Colling hoped it was sufficient to permit Grau to get his bearings.

Colling's nervousness was not relieved by their having, on more than one occasion, to cross open fields, and to skirt farm buildings that seemed to Colling to suddenly appear out of nowhere.

Only two of the farmhouses that they passed were showing lights in their windows. In Colling's mind, it was a toss-up as to whether the absence of illumination was due to a shortage of lamp fuel, a failure to restore electrical service, or just plain miserliness on the part of the local farmers.

If the aching in his legs was any indication, Colling would have sworn that they had been traveling for hours. He had estimated that it would take at most four hours, perhaps five, to cover the ten kilometers Grau had mentioned, making allowances for avoiding inhabited areas, and the inability to move entirely in a straight line. By Colling's calculation, he had thought they would be at Grau's destination by midnight at the latest. He had noticed nothing that would lead him to believe that the German lieutenant was lead- ing them in circles. Nevertheless, he was on the verge of sending a message up the line to ask Grau for a halt when he almost ran into Roberts, who was immediately in front of him, and who had stopped and dropped into a crouch.

Before Colling could ask the reason for the halt, Roberts repeated a whispered instruction that they were to all come forward slowly. Colling followed at the lieutenant's back until they reached a small clearing surrounded by hedge-like undergrowth that provided a concealed refuge. Colling sought out Grau, who was seated on the ground, unrolling the blanket that he had been carrying slung over his back. Colling asked, "Is this the place you spoke of?"

"Yes, I think so," said Grau. "We shall have to await the sun's rising to be certain. You must realize that I have not been to this place before, and I have come only on the word of someone else. Once it is light, we will know if we have come to the right location."

"And if we have not?" asked Colling.

"Then we shall be walking when night falls again," said Grau. "I would suggest we sleep while the chance to do so exists."

Colling relayed the German's words to the airmen, who heeded his advice and shook out their own blanket-rolls, and then settled down for the night. Colling had been more concerned with shep- herding the men into the woods when they had fled the cottage, and had failed to pick up a blanket for himself, leading him to volunteer to stand first watch, after which he would have the use of his relief's covering.

Colling's anticipation that he would be able to wrap himself so as to find some warmth that would permit him to sleep did not become reality. He had remained shivering and chilled, unable to doze off, long after Wilmont gave him his blanket on taking over the second round of standing watch. Colling was almost relieved when he opened his eyes to find that daylight had arrived. Grau and Caldwell were tending a small fire, over which they were heating open cans of C-Rations. When Grau noticed that Colling was awake, he said, in a low voice, "It is important to have hot food, and the Russkies are not, I think, looking for us here."

Colling was huddled next to the fire, warming his hands, feeling his stomach rumble at the smell of the pork and beans, when Roberts appeared, carrying the Spam tins that they had emptied the previous day. They were filled with water, which the lieutenant announced he had fetched from a nearby stream. Colling silently cursed himself for not thinking to keep the empty cans for just such a purpose, while at the same time giving thanks that one of his companions had had the foresight to do so.

Heating enough food for everyone, and the time taken up in making a number of trips to refill the Spam containers with water, meant that the sun was fully up before all of them had eaten and drunk their fill. Even though the beans were only partially warmed, and the water tasted greasy, Colling would have rated the breakfast among one of the more appreciated in his experience.

Grau had left their hiding place before Colling received his share of the C-rations, and returned only as Colling finished scooping up the last of his pork and beans with his fingers. The *Luftwaffe* officer crouched beside Colling as he was licking his fingers clean, and said, "This is the place. When you have completed your meal, come with me and I will show you."

Grau led Colling about a hundred meters through the forest before holding up his arm to stop them behind the trees at the edge of a large open grassy area. They crept forward until they had a view of the entire field. To their left and within 50 meters of their position was a tangled mound of scrap composed of the remains of a aircraft. Nearby were the carcasses of other planes. . A group of four men were engaged in what Colling guessed to be salvage efforts, as they were sorting the discarded items into piles. About a hundred yards from where they were concealed was a line of a half-dozen aircraft that appeared to be intact.

There was no one working near the planes that appeared serviceable. Based on having spent considerable time during his high school years poring over the illustrations of warplanes in *Life* magazine, Colling recognized the aircraft to be German. There were Dornier and Heinkel bombers, and a Focke Wulf fighter, their black crosses and swastika markings obliterated by swaths of gray paint.

Colling turned to Grau and remarked, "Does this bring back to you some memories? You have flown these, yes?"

"*Ja*," said Grau, "The He-111, but only after I was recalled to flying service. From 1939, I was in 109's, and there are none here. The Focke Wulf that you see there, I have never flown."

While watching the workers pick through the scrap material and toss their finds into piles, Colling had noticed a tank truck parked at the edge of the forest, prompting him to ask, "Is that to be the transportation of which you spoke?"

"Nay," replied Grau, "We go by first class, in the air."

"But do you know that these planes will even fly?" asked Colling.

"We shall find out. Wait here, and I will speak with these fellows."

Grau stood up and walked directly towards the group of laborers, raising his hand and calling out a friendly greeting. The men gathered around, apparently curious to find out what this stranger in German uniform wanted. After handshakes all around, an animated conversation ensued, and Colling guessed that Grau was asking for work, and emphasizing his experience in the *Luftwaffe*. After a few minutes, Grau motioned in Colling's direction for him to come forward.

When he reached Grau and the workers, Colling greeted them in

German and shook each of their hands in turn, introducing himself as Robert Pretzmann, also a German Air Force veteran. Grau mentioned to Colling in an off-handed way, that the aircraft parked near the edge of the forest had been there when the Red Army arrived. The four men who were engaged in salvage work were Germans from the nearby village.

A company of Russians was quartered there. They usually provided a pair of guards for the field, but they had been arriving later and later each day as the months of occupation passed. The foreman of the group, whose name was Garmacher, warned that the two Red Army men might arrive at any time.

Colling asked by what means the men traveled from their homes to the airfield, and was told that they walked the four kilometers, except for Garmacher, who had been authorized to possess a bicycle by the Russians. Garmacher added that he was supposed to use the bike to go for help should the need arise.

When Colling inquired about how the scrap materials were removed, one of the workers nervously responded that trucks came to take away the salvaged metals whenever a full load had been accumulated. In what Colling guessed was an attempt to dissuade Grau and himself from remaining, the man added that the next one would not come for several days.

All of the German workers were becoming increasingly nervous as the likelihood of the arrival of the Russian soldiers increased. It was obvious that Grau had not disclosed the existence of the Americans, and Colling joined in the charade of their being desperate to find employment. The sound of a truck approaching caused the Germans to scatter back to what they had been doing before the two strangers had arrived, and Grau and Colling ran back into the forest.

Lying flat on their stomachs, Colling and Grau tried to catch a glimpse of the Russian vehicle, but it had apparently stopped before driving onto the airfield. They could hear it being backed and turned, and then its engine fading away. Colling raised up in an effort to spot the Russians, and saw two men in brown uniforms reclining against the trunks of two pines near where a road emerged from the woods. Their rifles were propped beside them, and as Colling watched, one of them pulled his cap down over his eyes while the other took out his canteen and drank deeply from it before leaning back against the tree.

Colling turned his attention to the German salvage crew. None of them acknowledged the presence of the sentries, and they continued to be engaged in their work as they had prior to the arrival of Grau and himself.

"Do you have any ideas?" whispered Colling.

"Yes. We must overpower the Russians, and the others if they oppose us, and take one of the planes," said Grau.

"How are we to do that?" said Colling, in his own mind considering the possibilities open to them, and the difficulties interposed to their success.

"Return to the Americans. Explain what is to happen. We have my pistol and two Lugers, and that knife you seem to cherish. With some luck, we can accomplish this."

Caldwell was the first to ask where Colling had been when he reached their hiding place. Colling rapidly explained the situation. He outlined a plan of his own devising, wondering while he did so whether it would prove consistent with Grau's thoughts on the subject. His strategy called for Grau and himself to circle behind the Russian soldiers and try to take them by surprise. Caldwell would use his pistol to intimidate the four Germans and keep them from resisting. If there were any shooting, Caldwell would have to join in to eliminate one or both of the sentries. They would tie up the workers, making sure that none of them would appear to have provided any assistance in their escape. That accomplished, Grau would pilot one of the planes, with everyone aboard, to American territory.

It sounded simple as he outlined it, but Colling had serious doubts that it would succeed. He was particularly concerned that should Grau be injured or killed, that Caldwell or Hammerslee would not be capable of flying one of the German aircraft. There was also the question of fueling and preparing a plane for flight. Colling had no idea how long such a procedure would take, and whether or not the tanker that was on the field held enough gasoline for their purposes.

Colling led his companions to where Grau was waiting. A few meters behind the German officer's position, he instructed them to halt, and he crept forward on his own. Grau was still watching the activity on the field. As far as Colling could discern, the two Russians had not moved since he had last seen them.

Colling repeated the plan of action he had conveyed to the airmen, and Grau murmured his assent. A few moments later, Colling had summoned Caldwell and his crewmen forward. After admonishing them not to fire their weapons unless it was absolutely necessary, he handed his Luger to Hammerslee, and then he and Grau set out through the forest to take the Russians from behind.

Colling volunteered to take on the sentry farthest from them, and once he and Grau had crossed the narrow track leading to the airfield from the main road, Colling moved off in a wider circle so that he would approach his Russian on the man's right side, where he would have full use of his own right arm across the sentry's neck.

Colling was uncertain about what he would do with the knife in his hand, whether he would kill the soldier or simply threaten him, but he suspected that the German lieutenant would use his own pistol only as a last resort. Colling decided that he would attempt to subdue the man first, and then if that failed, use the blade.

The Russian was actually snoring when Colling came up behind him. Grau was in sight behind his man, and they exchanged nods and then simultaneously made their moves.

When the point of the butcher knife pressed into his throat, the soldier woke with a start. Colling pushed him forward and wrapped his left arm around the Russian's chest, increasing the pressure of the knife's edge, and with a silent hope that the man understood German, Colling whispered in his ear that he was to remain still or die. The man became motionless, and Colling sensed that there was to be no resistance. Nevertheless, he maintained his hold and continued to keep the blade tight against the soldier's throat.

A few meters away, Grau was standing over the other Russian, who was laying face-down in the turf. Colling wrestled his man up and marched him to where his companion was spread out, then pushed him to the ground. He looked over his shoulder to see Wilmont running towards him, his hands filled with strands of salvaged cable. With Grau pointing his pistol at their heads, the soldiers offered no resistance as Colling and Wilmont bound their hands behind their backs.

Caldwell came trotting over to them and asked which plane they would be using, and Grau pointed out one of the two-engine bombers. He shouted for someone to drive the tanker to the plane, and then ran to the aircraft, and clambered up through a hatch in its belly and into the cockpit.

As he headed towards the truck, Colling glanced over to see what was happening with the four German workers, and saw that they were seated in a circle on the ground amidst the piles of scrap, their arms in the air. Hammerslee was aiming the Luger at them while Tunsholder was busy wrapping their wrists with the wire.

Colling found Roberts had beat him to the fuel tanker. The lieutenant was at its wheel, trying to figure out how to start the engine of the German vehicle. Colling asked him to move aside, and looked over the dashboard. A moment later, he had the truck bumping across the field towards the bomber. As they approached the airplane, Roberts identified it as a Heinkel-111, expressing his amazement that it had survived the war.

Grau leaned from the cockpit hatch, pointing out the intakes for the gasoline. The tanker was equipped with a mechanical pump, requiring Colling to manually turn its handle while Roberts held the hose nozzle in the Heinkel's fuel ports. Grau left the cockpit and came to stand beside Colling, telling him that he would take over the pumping. The German lieutenant told Colling to go release one of the German workers. He explained that if someone were not permitted to go for assistance, it was likely that the Reds would execute everyone at the field. If the alarm were sounded, however, there was a chance that they might be allowed to live. Grau offered his opinion that no matter what was done, the two Russian soldiers were doomed to be shot or sent to a labor camp.

Colling untwisted the wire holding Garmacher's hands, and told him to take his bicycle and ride to the Russian garrison for help. As the foreman ran off across the field, one of the other Germans asked

Colling if could hit him a few times where it would show. The other two chimed in with a similar request, and Colling obliged, punching each of them three or four times in the face.

Hammerslee had not understood the conversation, and there was a shocked expression on his face when Colling finished his handiwork. Hammerslee was doubly confused when each of the laborers said, "*Danke.*" He was still staring when Colling tugged at his arm and they set off in a run towards the Heinkel.

Roberts informed him that the fueling had been completed, and Colling jumped into the tanker and drove it away from the bomber. The propellers were slowly turning as he reached the plane, and he was pulled aboard by the outstretched hands of the airmen. Everyone was crouched in what Colling took to be the bomb bay, and he was about to join them when he heard Grau shouting over the coughing roar of the engines to join him in the cockpit. Caldwell was seated beside the *Luftwaffe* officer, and Colling slipped into the vacant seat behind Grau.

The left-side engine was periodically stuttering between moments of running smoothly. When Caldwell commented about it, Grau shrugged his shoulders, but said nothing. The German pilot taxied the plane onto the field, then into position so that they would be taking off into what little wind there was. He brought the engines to a roar, and they began moving slowly over the uneven turf of the field, then with greater speed, until Grau pulled back on the wheel, bringing the bomber's nose up, and Colling experienced a lifting sensation as the ground fell away below them. His heart jumped in his chest when he thought that they would not clear the trees at the far end of the air strip. At the last moment, Grau managed to gain just enough altitude to graze their tops, leaving Colling certain he had heard the undercarriage hit their upper branches just before the plane's wheels retracted with a thud.

They began a wide turn to their right, and when it appeared that the morning sun was in their faces, Colling silently questioned whether Grau was headed in the right direction. Colling's anxiety on that score diminished when the plane completed a full circle, and the sun was behind them.

As they crossed the road serving the airfield, Colling spotted a truck with about a dozen men in Russian uniform slam to a halt below them, followed instantly by the unleashing of a fusillade of rifle and sub-machinegun fire aimed at the plane. Colling was about to comment that the shots had scored no hits when there were a series of loud klinks, and he heard someone in the bomb bay say, "Shit."

Colling and Caldwell simultaneously shouted, "Anybody hit?"

A voice that Colling guessed belonged to Hammerslee replied, "Yeah. Tunsholder got nicked, but it doesn't look serious."

The sound of the left-hand engine that had been running roughly on take-off did not improve as Grau attempted to gain altitude. Colling spoke German, asking Grau if he knew where they could land, and the pilot said he did not. He told Colling to watch for the cleared ground, guard towers and fences that was the demarcation between the two zones. Caldwell had not understood what they were saying, and seemed to be confident that the *Luftwaffe* pilot would deliver them safely to the American Zone.

Colling was intently scanning the terrain below for the deforested strip of land that would indicate the border between the zones, when the Heinkel was rocked sharply, and he looked up to see that another aircraft had come from behind them and was pulling rapidly upwards and banking away as it passed the Heinkel. Colling could see large red stars on the sides of its fuselage and on its wings. Grau, almost casually, remarked that it was a Yak-9d fighter, and immediately afterward, a second plane of the same design passed close overhead, causing the bomber to again shudder and vibrate violently.

For no apparent reason that Colling could discern, Grau suddenly pulled the stick to his left, and the Heinkel dropped and slid to one side just as a stream of bright lights passed by on their right, and the first Yak streaked past them. Grau repeated the leftward maneuver, and then quickly pulled sharply in the opposite direction. This time, the tracers went by on their left. The German pilot continued jinking the bomber from side to side, while losing altitude. He was successful in avoiding the second pass made by the first Yak, but its wingman anticipated Grau's next evasive movement, and the right wing of the Heinkel was stitched by a burst from the fighter's guns. A moment later, the right-side engine began to cough more roughly than its twin on the other side.

They were soon at tree-top level, and the Russian fighters continued to fly past overhead, but with the Heinkel below them, and moving at slower speed, they were having difficulty bringing their guns to bear. This was of small comfort to Colling, however, as smoke and flames had begun to spout from the right-side engine, and he wondered how much longer Grau could keep them in the air.

Colling was looking back over his shoulder in the direction from which their attackers had been coming when something large, silver and very loud passed over the cockpit canopy, momentarily darkening the inside of their plane with its shadow, startling Colling so that he felt as if he had almost jumped out of his skin. The Heinkel was rocked by its passage, and Caldwell was shouting something and Grau was laughing as Colling fought to recover his composure.

"Never have I thought I would be happy to see one of your 'Mustangs,'" screamed Grau while Caldwell whooped his pleasure at the sight of the American fighter and another that had joined it, chasing off their Russian pursuers.

Colling had been so concerned with the attack that he had neglected to watch the ground, but the presence of U.S. planes suggested that they must be over friendly territory. Grau spotted an open meadow below them, and after making a low pass to chase away the cows grazing on it, he brought the bomber down to a bumpy landing. The fire had spread slowly while they were in the air, but as they rolled to a stop, it seem to flare dramatically over the wing and towards the fuselage.

Grau and Caldwell were shouting for everyone to get out of the plane, and Colling felt himself being pushed out of the canopy hatch and rolling down the wing. He stumbled as he hit the ground, and he saw Hammerslee extending his hand to help him to his feet, and then he ran panting beside the Air Force lieutenant until he was thrown face-down on the ground by the concussion wave that came from the Heinkel as it exploded.

As Colling rolled over and tried to sit up, he saw Caldwell's lips moving, but he could not hear what the man was saying. Colling shook his head, trying to rid himself of the ringing in his ears. He gradually heard voices, then the crackling of the burning plane. He surveyed his surroundings, and as he did so, he decided he probably should count the men sprawled around him. He was relieved to see that everyone seemed to have been able to escape from the Heinkel. Tunsholder had his hand clamped on his upper arm, smears of blood showing between his fingers.

Colling was trying to focus his thoughts on what he should do next when he became aware of the sound of an approaching vehicle, which turned out to be a jeep that came to a halt only a few meters from his outstretched feet. Three men in American uniform alighted from it, and Colling realized that one of them was pointing a Tommy gun at him and his companions. A fourth man remained in the rear of the vehicle, standing and holding the grips of a .50 caliber machine gun, while scanning the sky.

Another was standing over Colling with the sun behind him, and it took a moment for Colling to see that he was wearing the silver bars of a first lieutenant. Before Colling could say anything, Caldwell scrambled to his feet and exclaimed, "Lieutenant, are we glad to see you guys! We just managed to bust out of a Russian concentration camp."

It seemed to Colling that the lieutenant was having a hard time taking in what the Air Force captain had said, which did not surprise Colling, given that all of them except Grau were wearing tattered, dirty German civilian clothing that left them looking like tramps. The newcomers also did not seem to be put at ease by the rumpled *Wehrmacht* uniform that the *Luftwaffe* officer was wearing.

Colling rose to his feet and confronted the officer, who moved his hand closer to his holster flap. Simultaneously, the man with the Thompson sub-machine gun narrowed his gaze and pointed the weapon directly at Colling. Colling raised his hands above his head, and said, "Sir, if you would contact Lieutenant Colonel Andrew Quarles in Heidelberg, he can explain what's going on. These men are American flyers who were imprisoned by the Russians. They just escaped. I know we look like hell, but we had to dress like this to get away."

"What's your name?" asked the lieutenant.

"Colonel Quarles knows me as 'Jan Woznica,'" replied Colling, using the pseudonym that he had traveled under when he had been in Poland.

"Sounds like a Polack name," said the lieutenant.

"It is," said Colling.

"Well, that's okay. Mine's Wilanowski. Tell your guys to get over there and stay together," then the lieutenant shouted at the jeep, "Corporal, get on the radio and tell 'em to get a truck out here. And one of these guys has been hit, so send an aidman."

CHAPTER 13

OCTOBER - NOVEMBER, 1947

By the time that the Army deuce-and-a-half that Lieutenant Wilanowski had ordered showed up, a battered truck bearing the local German fire brigade, a U.S. field ambulance and a second jeep bearing four more soldiers had already arrived in the meadow. The wound in Tunsholder's upper arm was cleaned and bandaged, and Wilanowski gave orders that he was to be taken to a medical facility to see a doctor. The firemen extinguished the burning Heinkel, and a farmer appeared seemingly out of nowhere to excitedly present his case for compensation to Wilanowski on account of the death of one of his cows. Colling was unable to discern from the shouting whether the poor creature had died of fright, or had been struck by a piece of debris thrown from the exploding airplane.

As Colling and his companions climbed into the deuce-and-a-half, a sergeant stood at the tailgate, recording the names, ranks and serial numbers of the Air Force men. Grau told them he was a discharged *Luftwaffe Oberleutnant*, and he was not asked for more detail. Colling repeated what he had told Wilanowski, and gave his name as "Jan Woznicka," saying he was a civilian working for Lieutenant Colonel Quarles.

They were driven to a cluster of prefabricated plywood barracks surrounded by a barbed-wire fence. A sign over the gate said it was occupied by the 19th Squadron, United States Constabulary. Colling recalled hearing that the Constabulary was created to serve as a heavily-armed, mobile paramilitary police force capable of dealing with serious disorder or insurrection in the American Zone. While he had seen men wearing the organization's shoulder patch, a "C" with a lightning bolt superimposed on it, on the streets of Munich, this was Colling's first close contact with any of its members.

They were conducted under guard to the second floor of what appeared to be the camp's headquarters, and into a large room that bore an eerie resemblance to the quarters in which they had been confined at *Stalag S-1*. Lieutenant Wilanowski advised them that this was the "holding area," where they would remain until they had been "processed out." The Air Force men seemed to take this in stride, and Hammerslee, Roberts and Wilmont appropriated cots for themselves and stretched out. Grau appeared anxious. Colling was tempted to take him aside and try to reassure him, but decided not to do so in the presence of the airmen.

Tunsholder was ushered in, his arm bandaged, and a moment later, Caldwell's name was called, and he was taken away by a pair of military policemen. In thirty minutes, he came back, pink-faced, wearing a fresh set of khakis and a black sweater. He happily informed everyone that he had been allowed to shower and shave, and that the Constabulary officers were letting them borrow their summer uniforms. The sweater was not regulation, but Caldwell added that it was also on loan, and that there were a couple of more like it and some field jackets from which the rest of them could choose. The guards who had brought Caldwell asked for the next man to accompany them.

Colling deferred his turn in the shower until everyone else had taken theirs. The cascade of hot water was overwhelming when he finally did find himself under its spray. The *Stalag* shower rooms had provided only cold water for both the camp staff and prisoners on a weekly basis. A daily shave had been required when Colling was a member of the camp's personnel, but after he had been assigned to act out his role as Roper, a weekly shave under close supervision had been all that was permitted. In either case, the German razor blades had been well-used, so that the new Gillette Blue Blade that he was given by the Constabulary guard glided over his face in comparison.

There were several shirts and pairs of trousers from which he could chose, and he found a uniform in his size. He had to make do with the shoes he had been issued when he was first outfitted in the prison camp. There was one field jacket remaining, a bit too large, but welcome after the worn civilian suit-coat that provided little relief from the chilly fall weather.

He returned to their quarters to find his companions seated around the table in the center of the room, concentrating on a meal that had been brought to them. Two Constabulary men were standing near the door, clearly there to prevent anyone from leaving. An empty metal mess-tray indicated where a place had been left for Colling, and large square pans holding their food were arrayed in the center of the table. He sat down and proceeded to help himself to some of the mashed potatoes, several thick slices of Spam, spoonfuls of green peas, and a few slices of white bread.

There was plenty of butter, and someone poured Colling a heavy mug of coffee. He added generously to the steaming brew from the bowl of sugar and the can of condensed milk that Tunsholder pushed in his direction.

The potatoes were reconstituted, the peas had been dried before they were boiled to make them edible, the bread tasted bland after so many weeks of German black bread, the butter was margarine, and the Spam was Spam, but Colling, like everyone else seated around him, shoveled in the food, praising Uncle Sam between mouthfuls. Colling refilled his tray only once, but noticed that Grau, Wilmont and Tunsholder did so twice.

When the last of them had finished eating, the two attendants cleared the table, and one of the soldiers who was standing guard slapped a carton of Lucky Strikes on the table. As the airmen expressed their thanks, the cigarettes were distributed. The only ones not to light up were Wilmont and Colling. When Colling looked quizzically at the Air Force lieutenant, he said, "I'm Mormon,"

"Never did start," said Colling in reply.

Grau was blowing smoke towards the ceiling, an expression of pure bliss on his face. He was seated next to Colling, and he turned and said, "*Mein Gott!* Nothing in the world is like American tobacco. *Wunderbar, ach, wunderbar.*"

Colling's attention was caught by the arrival of a Constabulary master sergeant, who asked for their attention, then ordered the Air Force men to come with him, and for Colling and Grau to remain.

"Now it is that they will be questioned by your people," said

Grau in German, tapping the ash from the fourth cigarette that Colling had watched him light.

"True enough," said Colling, also speaking German. "I have wondered often whether they in truth possessed this knowledge of the A-bomb, as the Reds believed."

Grau laughed, "Ach, Pretzmann...or is it Woznica? Do you really believe that all was as it seemed?"

Colling responded, "What do you mean? And it is good enough, by the way, that you call me Pretzmann, or Roper, if you wish. But what is this you say?"

"You must be an American, to possess such naiveté," said Grau. "Did you never question why the Russians were seeking information that their many spies in England and American must have the ability to easily provide?"

"It was my thought, on more than one occasion, that Lindsey would have had the ability to discover how many atomic bombs the Americans had based in England, and the number of B-29's that had been brought to that island."

"You have knowledge, my friend, that the American plane had a piece of equipment on board that pertained to the atomic bomb?"

"I have heard this," said Colling

"And did you also know that the equipment was armed with an explosive charge to prevent its being removed?"

"This, also, I have heard," admitted Colling.

"Did your superiors tell you that the American bomber was destroyed by that explosive charge a day or two after it was taken by the Soviets?"

Colling did not respond, and Grau continued, "Your silence speaks to me that you were not told, but no matter. Our superiors often do not tell us everything."

Colling said, "Go on, my friend. It is clear that you itch to tell me more."

"Ach, true enough, if only to watch the expression on your face," laughed Grau. He continued, "The MVD, that is what they call the NKVD these days, had learned of the Americans' use of the explosive charge when they captured another B-29. This one had landed in

Manchuria or Siberia, I am not certain which, but it had flown from a base in Japan. Ever eager, the Reds attempted to remove this thing, the bomb device, and there was an explosion, which unfortunately, or fortunately, depending on your point of view, killed an MVD general and two of his aides, and two scientific technicians that the Soviets find it very hard to replace. This method of learning about the explosive charge was, of course, quite impressive, and moreover, unpleasant.

"Plans were made at the highest levels, perhaps by Beria or Stalin personally, to capture another American B-29. At this point, Kremlin politics came into play. Those in charge of the GRU, the Red Army intelligence agency, were in the most recent of many struggles with the State Security Service, the MVD, for control of intelligence activities. It was important to the army people that they be seen as a respected Soviet intelligence service in the eyes of Stalin and the Politburo.

"A certain general of the GRU was chosen by his peers to suggest to Stalin that the harsh methods of the MVD were certain to result in further disaster, and that calmer, more psychological approaches to extracting information from American prisoners would be more effective. The example of *Luftwaffe* intelligence was put forth, and hence my release from the labor camp. Kottbach and the SS guards were brought in to complete the 'German' method, but more likely, to serve as scapegoats if failure were to result."

Colling raised his hand, causing the German to pause in his narrative, and interjected, "But I thought that the second B-29 was also destroyed?"

"True enough," said Grau, "The MVD had not heeded the GRU, and applied its usual methods to the American technicians responsible for the A-bomb device. One of them, a major, must have decided that it was a better choice to vaporize himself and his fellow technicians, as well as some Russians, and he must have set the charge off, rather than disarming it. Fortunately for the MVD, this time only some low ranking MVD soldiers and two less-learned Soviet scientists were killed in the blast."

"But why then bring the rest of the crew to *Stalag S-1*?" asked

Colling.

"Ah, to play out the rest of the political struggle, my friend. The GRU had committed itself to its position by asserting that the new approach to interrogation was superior. The MVD, knowing that the main prize of the device from the plane was no longer at stake, speculated, with some confidence, that there would be a failure by Red Army intelligence to glean anything useful from the remaining crewmen of the B-29. This would, of course, mean that Beria could paint the generals as wild-eyed 'revisionists' who lacked the strong will of State Security to get things done."

Colling commented, "And now heads will roll, as that is, in truth, what happened."

"Ach, *ja*, my friend. That is what happened. What had not been anticipated was your entry into the game. The MVD will be even more pleased that the GRU permitted the Americans to escape, not to mention that myself and others were given the opportunity to defect."

"And what would have happened to the crewmen otherwise?" asked Colling, searching for something to offset the realization that his efforts had been of benefit to the MVD.

"They would have been liquidated, of course, when it was clear that the experiment was a failure. The fact that they indeed know nothing of value would be overlooked."

"So perhaps, at least, some lives were saved," said Colling.

"Ach, so, my friend. And my own, as well, for which I heartily thank you. Even if it is that I am returned to the Soviets," said Grau.

Colling assured the *Luftwaffe* lieutenant that he was confident that he would not be sent back to the Soviet Zone.

Further conversation was interrupted by the Constabulary master sergeant's return. The NCO informed them that the Air Force men were all being transferred to an airbase, which he did not name, and that Colling and Grau would have the place to themselves for the time being.

Colling inquired whether anyone had been able to contact Quarles, and the sergeant replied that he knew nothing about that.

Colling asked how long they would be held and was told, "Can't say. Just sit tight."

Colling decided to see if he could get some sleep, selecting one of the cots and wrapping himself in a blanket. He was awakened by the mess attendants bringing their supper. This time the menu consisted of baked beans, boiled cabbage, and canned roast beef. As with lunch, there was a loaf of white bread on the table and a block of margarine. As Colling began to eat, one of the mess men set a dish of chocolate pudding next to his tray.

Grau was taking a second helping of everything when he said, "You Americans do not know how fortunate you are. Napoleon said that an army marches on its stomach, and with food like this, it is no wonder that you won the war."

"True enough," said Colling, "But tanks and planes in great quantities also helped, as well as the ability of American soldiers to learn to fight as well as Germans and Japanese."

"With that I must agree," said Grau, through a mouthful of beef.

The master sergeant brought them a radio after the table had been cleared, and showed Colling how to tune it to Armed Forces Radio. The news came on, and the announcer let them know that the Communists were making political gains in France and Italy, as evidenced by the rioting in the streets. On the other hand, the Greek army had had some successes against the Reds in the northern mountains. Following the newscast, they listened to *The Shadow* and *The Jack Benny Show*, the gist of which Colling had to explain to Grau. By 2200 hours, they were both asleep.

Two more days went by without any change in this routine, although after Colling found a dog-eared deck of cards in a wall locker, they spent a considerable amount of time playing cards. Grau taught Colling the finer points of Skat, using a dummy hand as the third player. Colling had some familiarity with the game, having watched his father and his friends play at the Bel Cors German-American Club. In turn, Colling showed Grau how gin rummy was played.

Colling had repeatedly asked the Constabulary NCO's who seemed to be in charge of their confinement, if contact with Quarles had been successful, but all of the American soldiers denied any knowledge of the intelligence officer. Colling was becoming increasingly concerned, to the point that he began to speculate that perhaps they had not escaped into the American Zone, and all that they had experienced was an elaborate charade concocted by the Soviets. He was considering whether to share such wild thoughts with Grau when Quarles arrived.

The lieutenant colonel greeted him warmly, slapping him on the shoulder and pumping his hand. Before Quarles could say anything that would disclose his real name, Colling introduced him to Grau, and speaking German, said, "Sir, I am surprised that you have allowed Jan to languish in this place. You will have my Polish temper up."

"Ah, yes, Jan," replied Quarles, taking Colling's cue. "It was required that a message be sent to me. I was elsewhere. The Constabulary commander of this place tells me that *Oberleutnant* Grau here piloted the airplane that spirited you away from the Soviets."

"True enough, sir. He is a remarkable person. He wishes to remain in the West. A return behind the Iron Curtain would spell his doom."

"Understandable, my friend. I guarantee that he will remain on this side of the line."

Grau breathed an audible sigh of relief, and grasping Quarles' hand, thanked him profusely.

Quarles indicated that the *Luftwaffe* officer should go with the Constabulary sergeant who was standing by the door, and that he would speak to him privately in a few minutes.

With Grau out of the room, Quarles' demeanor was even more exuberant, "You sure and hell did it, Jim!"

"I had lots of help, sir. And a lot of luck. Without Grau, we never would have made it. You need to see that he gets to the States, if he wants," said Colling.

"I take it he was the interrogation expert from the *Luftwaffe that we heard was involved?*"

"Right. And also, sir, Vogelsang is playing both sides of the fence. Grau says he provided a diversion to cover our escape, but I met him in the camp when he thought I was one of the guards. He admitted he was working for the Reds while receiving support from our side. It was common knowledge among the camp personnel."

"No surprise, Jim," said Quarles, "We knew he had a brother who was a POW in Russia, so they had some leverage with him. If he helped you get away, maybe something happened to change his attitude."

"And something else, sir," said Colling, "The major who was in charge of the technical staff on board the B-29 apparently set off the explosive charge. It looks like he and the other two officers in his detail were all killed, along with some Russians. The device was destroyed. It happened only a couple of days after they were forced down.

"Grau also says that Caldwell and his men were brought to Germany as part of some kind of rivalry between the GRU and the MVD. It looks like the escape embarrassed the GRU types, and helped the MVD. I don't feel real good about that."

Quarles listened thoughtfully as Colling was speaking, and when he concluded, said, "Don't let it bother you, Jim. You did get five guys out, and that's what counts. When I asked you to do this, I didn't expect Major Evans to touch off the booby-trap. But even if I had, I would have asked you anyway."

Colling did not respond, and Quarles continued, "I was wondering why Evans, Abrams and Lomax weren't among the guys you brought out. That explains it. But what happened to Sergeant Lindsey?"

"He was a Soviet plant. He did something to sabotage the plane, then acted as an informant once they were in custody."

"I guess he stayed with the Russians?" asked Quarles.

"He's dead."

"You?"

"Yessir," admitted Colling.

"No matter, Jim. I'm sure it was you or him, and he probably got what he deserved," said Quarles. "I have a car downstairs. After I get done talking with the German...Grau, is it?...I'll take you to a place near Munich where you can get back in uniform and back to your outfit."

The staff car was a well-polished black Packard, prompting Colling to wonder how Quarles had managed to obtain the use of a vehicle usually reserved for generals or civilian VIP's. The commander of the Constabulary Squadron had provided a second automobile, an olive-drab Plymouth, to take Grau to another destination chosen by Quarles. A pair of Constabulary jeeps escorted them, front and back, until they reached the autobahn, where the Plymouth and one jeep headed north, while the Buick and the second armed escort went south, towards Munich.

Colling relayed his impressions of *Stalag S-1*, providing as much information as he was able, while Quarles made notes. Colling omitted any mention of how he had gained entry to the camp, or the identities, other than Pretzmann, that he had used in doing so. When Quarles casually inquired about his preparations for the mission, Colling bluntly told him that he wanted to keep that information to himself.

Colling concluded by mentioning that he had seen a dossier regarding Elizabeth Hamilton's husband, Brian Moorehouse. This seemed to arouse Quarles' interest, and Colling theorized that Moorehouse was probably dead, based upon all of the man's personal effects having been in the file. Quarles thought for a moment before remarking, "More likely the file was intended as bait for someone like you. Elizabeth admitted that she had been unable to hold back anything when the Reds had her in Poland last year. They put her through the mill."

"I got her out, remember?" said Colling, sharpness in his voice, "I know damned well what she went through."

Quarles continued, "They knew she was one of our agents, and they knew Moorehouse was her husband. I'm reasonably certain they've figured out by now that she's still alive. How did you react when you realized that the file was Moorehouse's?"

"I made a dirty joke about it. Her picture was in the file, and that's how I made the connection. I never knew her husband's last name. When I said she would be good lay, that was the last I heard about it," said Colling.

"Jim, I need to warn you. Watch your back. The Soviets are not a bit happy with what we did over there last year. As far as I know, they don't know who you are, but if they find out, you'll be a target. The word is, they think the guy who pulled off the extraction of the Polish scientists was a Pole. In fact, that's what they're calling you, 'The Pole.' Which is fine, because it means they're off the track. They're probably going to figure out how Elizabeth escaped, and maybe even that you were in on this latest caper. That will make them really interested in getting their hands on you, or if they can't do that, knock you off."

"Do they have any idea that 'The Pole' is connected to you?" asked Colling.

"I wouldn't doubt it. I would guess that they know that you've used the name 'Jan Woznicka'."

"And because I used that name with the Constabulary, there's a good chance that the Reds will make the connection to the escape of Caldwell and company."

Quarles nodded his head affirmatively, leaving Colling absorbed in his own thoughts about what steps he would have to take to protect himself and those close to him, now that he was aware that he might be a target for retaliation.

The two of them said little during remainder of the drive to Munich, and what conversation there was consisted of Quarles first speculating about which teams would be going to Pasadena to play in the Rose Bowl, and afterwards, his commentary about landmarks and scenery that they were passing.

The place that Quarles described as one of his "establishments" turned out to be a large house behind a high brick wall, situated several kilometers off the Autobahn. An armed guard wearing an MP brassard opened the wrought-iron gate to admit the Buick, and the car drove through and stopped at the mansion's front steps. As Colling emerged from his side of the vehicle, another MP was immediately at his side, and remained close behind him as he followed Quarles into the house.

The lieutenant colonel led Colling to a bedroom on the second floor, pointed out the adjacent bathroom, and to a large wardrobe, telling him he would find a uniform there. Before he left, Quarles added that he was free to clean up, after which he should come with the MP, who would be waiting outside the door. Colling decided to take his time when he found that there was a shower over the tub in the bathroom. He treated himself to a long hot shower, then a shave. When he finally looked in the wardrobe, he discovered that the Army uniform fit him perfectly. The Ike jacket bore his tech-four chevrons, Medical Corps lapel insignia, and service ribbons. Someone had polished the brass and spit-shined the shoes.

The military policeman ushered him downstairs and into a room that Colling guessed had been the former owner's study. Quarles was seated at an ornate walnut desk, writing, and Colling speculated that the officer was using his notes to compose a more detailed version of his debriefing.

Quarles glanced up and said, "Ready to leave?"

"Seems like it. Did you have someone swipe my uniform and bring it here?"

"Nope. My secretary guessed at your sizes. She's good at that. Used to work in a Penney's in Idaho," replied Quarles. The lieutenant colonel opened the desk drawer and brought out an envelope, which he handed to Colling. "Here's your five grand, less the five hundred I advanced you for expenses. Uncle Sam is getting to be stingier than in the past."

"Figures," said Colling, thumbing through the cash in the envelope. "How do I get to Munich?"

"You won't be using the Buick. The man outside the door will take you in one of the weapons carriers. It should look like you hitched a ride when he drops you off."

"How do I get in touch if I need to?" asked Colling.

"Use the APO address I gave you," replied Quarles, "And oh, yeah, I almost forgot, you might want to read this on your way to Munich," said the intelligence officer as he tossed a tan-colored paperback to Colling.

The book was an Army Medical Corps publication titled *Manual of Tropical Diseases*. Its worn appearance suggested to Colling that it had served some student of the subject well in the past. Tucked among its pages was a tourists' brochure for Casablanca, equally well-used.

Colling came to attention and saluted, and Quarles reciprocated, after which Colling did a crisp about-face. The MP who had conducted him to the lieutenant colonel's office was gone, but a sergeant who introduced himself as Mike Kelly was waiting for him.

Rather than ride with Kelly in the cab of the truck, Colling chose to climb into the back. He discovered that the sergeant must be making a laundry-run, as the rear was piled with soft canvas bags. Thankful for the cushioning, Colling pushed the tarp covering the truck bed up a few inches to give himself enough light in which to read, then settled back and began learning what he could about malaria, sprue and schistosomiasis.

When they reached the outskirts of Munich, Kelly stopped the truck and leaned out his window, asking Colling where he wanted to be dropped. Colling climbed over the tailgate and joined the sergeant in the cab, telling him to let him off close to a streetcar stop. He was carrying no luggage, and the *Strassenbahn* seemed to be the easiest way to return to the 511th. He would have to arrange with Meltzer to recover the bags that he had entrusted to the German. After all, one of them held the remaining expense money that Quarles had given him.

Before Colling parted ways with Kelly, he asked if the sergeant had some marks that he could lend for trolley fare. Kelly groaned, and then handed over a 20-mark occupation currency note. Colling promised him he would replace it as soon as he received his pay.

The female streetcar attendant gave him a sour look when she had to make change for the bill, which changed to a smirk as she handed him thirty-nine half-mark notes.

Colling had not expected to experience as comfortable a feeling of homecoming as he did when he walked through the hospital gates. He did not recognize the MP manning the gate, but the man made no move to stop him or question his presence, and Colling strolled first to hospital headquarters, where he asked the PFC manning the orderly room desk for Sergeant Gayle. He heard the master sergeant's voice from his office, asking who wanted to see him, and Colling called out, "T-Four Colling, Sergeant, reporting in from TDY."

Gayle appeared, looked Colling up and down, and told the clerk to note Colling in on the personnel roster. The sergeant asked him how he liked Morocco, and after Colling had lamely answered with a reference to rocks and sand, Gayle told him to change into his work uniform and report to Major Elliott.

The nurse was happy to see him, and asked questions about the tropical disease school, which Colling tried to answer with as much plausibility as he could. She appeared satisfied with his responses, but at one point, she commented that he did not have much of a tan. Colling replied that he had done his best to stay out of the sun. He modestly minimized the extent to which he had learned anything about tropical diseases, instead repeatedly asserting that he had spent most of his time becoming skilled at killing various insects and avoiding contact with the parasites found in African food and water.

Fortunately, Colling's arrival in late afternoon spared him from further conversation about his sojourn in North Africa. The medic who had taken his place in the clinic interrupted to remind the major it was 1700 hours, and to ask if he should close up for the day. Colling realized that he had had nothing to eat since breakfast, and after telling Major Elliott he would see her in the morning, he headed for the mess hall, where he was pleased to see that C-ration chicken and noodles, a relative rarity, was being served.

Colling debated whether he should try and see Veronika that evening. Because he had not asked the major for a pass, he opted to telephone instead. Because the call would have had to go through the hospital switchboard, he ruled out using the key he had bought from Willoughby to enter the hospital headquarters offices and use one of the telephones there. Instead, he bought some tokens at the small hospital PX and called from the pay phone in the hallway.

Annelise, the maid, answered, and when he told her who was calling and asked for *Fräulein* Schönenberg, he heard her set down the receiver and excitedly run off to find Veronika. A few seconds later, Colling heard Veronika exclaim, "Jim, you are returned!"

"Yes, at last. It is so good to hear you," said Colling.

"It is wonderful! I have missed you. Will you come to my house tomorrow?"

Colling realized that he had lost all track of the calendar, "What day will tomorrow be?"

"Saturday, of course. Has the sun in Africa affected your knowing the day of the week?" she asked, a smile in her voice.

"Neh, I have been traveling, and one day is like another when one is on board a ship."

"I cannot use the telephone for long, Jim. *Frau* Barrowsmith is so kind, but I do not wish to impose. Will you be here at the usual time?"

"Yes, after inspection. At noon. We must find a place to have our midday meal."

"Of course. I have missed you, Jim. Until I see you," she said, and as soon as he replied in kind, he heard the click of her hanging up.

Chapter 14

November, 1947

On his arrival at the Schönenberg residence, Colling discreetly went to the rear cellar entrance and knocked. Veronika must have been waiting for him, because she opened the door immediately, gave a delighted little cry and threw her arms around his neck, kissing him enthusiastically. He matched her embrace with his own, relishing the warmth and softness of her body close to his. When at last they relaxed against one another, he tried to find the words in German to express himself, but was only able to say, "My treasure, my own," while stroking her back. He heard her murmuring her own endearments against his chest, reminding him more than anything of the purring of a cat.

Approaching footsteps caused them to break apart, and Hilde, the Schönenberg's middle-aged cook, came into the kitchen. Colling greeted her heartily, "*Guten Tag, Gnädige Frau. Wie geht es?*" and she responded with "*Sehr gut, Herr* Colling," accompanied by a broad smile.

"Jim," said Veronika, "Do you wish to eat? I have found a place much better than before."

Colling replied that he was famished. While Veronika retrieved her coat, Colling teased Hilde about her looking to have gained weight on the Barrowsmith's commissary provisions. The cook responded with a great deal of red-faced giggling.

The restaurant chosen by Veronika was some distance into the outskirts of Pasing, almost a kilometer beyond the end of the streetcar line. During their ride to the restaurant, Veronika told him that Colonel Barrowsmith had arranged for her employment in the hospital laundry. Not only was she earning 300 marks a month, she was permitted two meals in the mess hall every day when she worked. Of course, the Germans were allowed to eat only after all the Americans had finished.

The other women in the laundry were pleasant enough, although she had overheard some of them comment that she was too "refined" for such work. For her own part, Veronika did her best to fit in, avoiding any mention of her former situation in life. At first, she was unaccustomed to the physical labor involved, and having to work in the heat, but after a week or so, like many other unpleasant experiences that the war had brought, it became routine. She conceded to Colling that she had become used to getting by on little, and harbored no optimism that her father would ever regain his business, or the money that had come with it.

When she changed the subject and asked him about Morocco, he kept his answers as brief as possible, while trying to make it appear as if he had actually been to North Africa. She seemed to accept what he told her, although at one point, she asked him why he did not have a tan. Colling gave her the same response about avoiding the sun that he had given to Major Elliott.

The place Veronika had recommended was called the *Apfelbaum*, and it appeared to Colling as if it had once been a faux hunting lodge meant to provide some wealthy *Münchener* with the trappings of country living while remaining close to the city. It was constructed to look like a large log house, but inside, there were polished hardwood floors and plastered walls. Stuffed animal heads and sets of antlers were everywhere. Colling had noticed that there were a number of automobiles parked outside, so he was not surprised to see that most of the restaurant's tables were occupied, many by American officers and their female companions. Colling's NCO stripes caused a few stares as he and Veronika were seated, and he was conscious that the Apfefbaum was probably not patronized with any regularity by enlisted personnel.

Speaking softly in German, Colling informed the waiter that he would be paying in American dollars, and that he trusted that the food and service would meet his expectations. This engendered solicitousness on the part of the man that Colling anticipated would be conveyed to the kitchen staff in the preparation of their food.

With Veronika's consent, Colling selected venison steaks from the menu. The waiter took their order, bowing as he left their table.

The venison, served with steamed fresh vegetables and seasoned potatoes, turned out to be delicious. Colling could not help but wonder to what extent the game had been poached from someone's private preserve. Feeling well-satisfied after having finished his meal, Colling ordered an after-dinner *café au lait,* while Veronika selected a piece of chocolate cake from the tray that the waiter brought to their table.

They were walking to their streetcar stop when Colling suddenly asked Veronika in English if she had picked up any of the language.

"Yes, Jim. I am learning a little bit," was her reply.

"Very good," said Colling, "I'll be glad to help you learn more. From now on, let's use English whenever we can."

True to his request, they continued their conversation, Colling asking questions, and Veronika hesitantly putting English sentences together. Colling readily assisted by supplying correct words and phrases. By the time they were strolling up Kleberstrasse, Colling had decided that Veronika's command of the language was only slightly inferior to that of his grandmother, whose avoidance of speaking anything but German, despite having lived in Wisconsin for forty years, had so frustrated his father.

One piece of information from Veronika that did make an impression on Colling was that Staff Sergeant Bernie Wilson thought it amusing to teach American profanity to the new additions to the female laundry help who had little or no English. Veronika assured Colling that the other women had warned her about Wilson, and besides, he had not used any word that she had not already heard before. Colling was about to ask whether the sergeant had ever made any advances, but thought better of it.

On their return to the Schönenberg house, they discovered that they had been left alone in the big cellar kitchen, and Veronika led him to a cushioned bench in an alcove to one side of the room, where they began necking. She was as enthusiastic as she had been earlier, but when Colling tried to increase the intimacy of his caresses, she pulled away, out of breath, but able to tell him he should not go further. He settled for what she would permit, resigned to biding his time, but determined to take things as far as they would go.

Eventually, they were interrupted by Hilde, who seemed embarrassed to have caught them in one another's arms. They separated, and Colling was about to say that he had to return to the hospital when Veronika asked if he would help her learn to read and write English. She went to one of the cupboards and returned with an elementary schoolbook which Colling recognized as similar to one he had used in First Grade. Veronika informed him that Mrs. Barrowsmith had had it sent from the States when Veronika told her she wished to learn to read and write English.

While Hilde prepared the evening meal for the household, Colling and Veronika sat at the kitchen table, he the teacher and she the pupil. At Colling's suggestion, she produced a tablet, and studiously copied from the textbook, then read back what she had written. After an hour or so, Veronika had mastered half the slim volume's pages.

Annelise arrived and Hilde helped her set up a tray with food for *Herr* and *Frau* Schönenberg. Veronika offered to take it to her parents, and asked Colling to come with her. He was surprised when he found that the back stairway had been fitted with a mechanical chair lift. Veronika excitedly informed him that the Barrowsmiths had had the contraption shipped from America. It permitted her father to ride from the first floor to the second floor without being carried. Her father and mother were now occupying an upstairs rear bedroom instead of the library, which Colonel Barrowsmith had taken for his own use as a study and office.

The Schönenbergs greeted Colling warmly, asking him about Morocco, and he responded with the same general description of North Africa that he had been using with others. He was relieved that neither of them asked about his not having a tan.

When Veronika finished setting out the contents of the tray for her parents, she asked if Colling wished to have supper with her. When he said that he would like that very much, she told her parents she would be eating in the kitchen with Hilde and Annelise, as soon as the Barrowsmiths had been served.

The meal that Hilde set in front of him was immeasurably improved from when he had first eaten in the cellar kitchen. Half a roasted pork loin was on a platter in the center of the table, along with bowls of potatoes, carrots and sauerkraut. Hilde seemed very proud when she placed a plate holding a loaf of American white bread and a slab of margarine beside the meat. As they ate, Veronika explained in English that Mrs. Barrowsmith purchased enough from the commissary to permit everyone else in the house to have a share. Only one of her brother's comrades remained living over the garage, but even he received his portion.

It was dark when they finished eating, and Colling took Veronika by the hand, leading her outside to say goodbye. They were in each other's arms for a long time, until finally, Colling said he had to return to the hospital. He asked her if he could see her the following day, and she invited him to come with her to Mass. Colling recalled his mother's repeated admonitions regarding church attendance, and that he had generally ignored that advice. The last time he had taken Communion had been while traveling behind the Iron Curtain, when to do otherwise would have engendered suspicion that he was not the Polish peasant he was supposed to be. He inquired as to the hour and place that she normally attended, and was told that the church was close by, and her family attended the nine o'clock service. He told Veronika that he would be at her door a half-hour earlier.

As was his usual experience, Colling found the Mass comforting, but not necessarily inspiring. Veronika introduced him to the priest, who seemed pleased that Colling was able to carry on a conversation in the cleric's native language. Afterwards, he and Veronika parted company with her parents, leaving Hilde pushing her father's wheelchair homeward, with *Frau* Schönenberg and Annelise following.

Colling and Veronika went for customary stroll through the Nymphenburg neighborhood, albeit the day's overcast skies and chill of November made it a less pleasant pass-time than it had been during the summer. As a consequence, they returned to the house sooner than they had intended, whereupon Veronika invited him to lunch. Hilde served another hearty meal, courtesy of the Barrowsmiths, after which Colling excused himself, explaining that he had to unpack and make sure that all his clothing and equipment were adequately arranged to satisfy his master sergeant. When he parted company with Veronika, he promised that he would try to see her at the hospital.

Hardesty was sprawled on his bunk, reading, when Colling returned to his quarters. While Colling was making sure his gear was all where it should be, his room-mate put aside the paperback and launched a stream of questions at Colling about Morocco and the tropical diseases course. Colling provided the now-familiar responses, and when Hardesty eagerly asked about North African women, Colling provided a negative opinion, saying he found them to be unattractive and unfamiliar with modern hygienic practices.

When he woke on Monday morning, Colling found himself actually looking forward to returning to the clinic. The number of patients reporting on sick call had not diminished, and he was able to easily readapt to the routine of seeing patients and working with Major Elliott. Between cases, he was called upon repeatedly by his fellow medics to recount his experiences while at the tropical disease course. He had to be more inventive, however, when one of the physicians asked some pointed questions about the instructors and the curriculum. Colling came up with descriptions of the teaching staff, emphasizing that they were all French, relying in part on his memory of movie characters from films about French Colonial Africa. He based his responses to the inquiry about the training course's content on the manual that Quarles had given him. The doctor seemed impressed, and even went so far as to congratulate Colling on his grasp of the subject.

The clinic's workload had not changed, permitting a few minutes in mid-afternoon each day for Colling to slip away and find Veronika when she was in the mess hall, taking lunch with the other laundry workers. They were limited to simply greeting one another, but his presence always seemed to be a source of amusement for Veronika's companions.

Meltzer brought him the duffel bag he had been holding for him, and when he did so, he informed Colling that Sergeant Wilson had made suggestive remarks to Veronika, and that Colling needed to know that the advances had been rebuffed. Meltzer added that Veronika was a woman of the upper class, who should not have to work in a laundry, and Colling sensed that the German was hinting that he should feel himself obligated to do something about it.

Meltzer's comments, coupled with Veronika's remarks about Wilson, reminded Colling that a score remained to be settled with the staff sergeant. He had already learned from Meltzer that the staff sergeant arrived at his work early and stayed after everyone else had gone. First Lieutenant Pennington, the CO of the ambulance company attached to the hospital, devoted most of his time to overseeing his men's appearance and performance, and left administrative details concerning the company's vehicles to Wilson.

Aware that late night would be the best time to see what he could find out about Wilson's activities in the motor pool, Colling waited until after lights out to slip out of his quarters and go quietly to the hospital garage. It was deserted, and he used the skeleton key that he had obtained from Willoughby to enter Wilson's office.

Colling started by going through the office's single file cabinet until he found the trip records for the hospital vehicles. While a number of them were assigned to the five outlying dispensaries for which the 511th had responsibility, all of them used the hospital motor pool to refuel. Colling knew that access to Army gasoline was a temptation for many NCO's assigned to unit motor pool duties, and suspected that Wilson was no exception.

Colling began comparing the recorded mileage, all of which, he noted, was in Wilson's handwriting, with the distances Colling himself estimated were required to be traveled to the listed destinations. As he made his own mental calculations, Colling realized that the commonly-used vehicles were being charged for additional mileage as a matter of course. That would naturally permit Wilson to divert fuel, which he presumably had some method of storing separately; but the odometers on the vehicles would have to be adjusted to match the trip tickets.

Fortunately for Colling, he was able to gain access to the sergeant's locked desk by finding a screwdriver in one of the repair bays, and using it to remove the screws that held the desk's top in place.

Colling had a distant cousin who owned a used-car lot in Chippewa Falls, so that within minutes, he recognized the tool used to adjust odometers. Among the other articles in the desk's top drawer was one of the small boxes of matches given away by German businesses. The label on its top displayed a small figure of a blue rabbit and the name and address of *Der Blauer Hase*, a Munich bar that Colling had heard of, but never patronized. On the reverse of the box was a penciled name, Karl Schreckler. Colling made an educated guess that *Herr* Schreckler was Wilson's black market contact. Colling copied the information from the matchbox onto a slip of paper that he tucked into his shirt pocket.

He carefully replaced everything, remounting the desk top and replacing everything he had removed from its surface, and then took one last look around to make sure all was as he had found it, before locking the office door behind him. On an impulse, he walked to the rear of the garage to where a row of fuel drums were stored. He began tapping on their sides, and it did not take him long before he heard the hollow sound that indicated two empties among those that were full. It looked as if Wilson were setting aside the gasoline surplus his paperwork was creating, and then having someone haul it away and bring back the empty drums for refilling.

Colling estimated that Wilson must be purloining ten to twenty gallons of Army gasoline a week. The German black market charged upwards of a dollar a gallon, so that Wilson was bringing in perhaps fifty dollars or more a month as a wholesaler. Small potatoes, but over time, the NCO would have accumulated a considerable sum to take home when he returned to the States. If Schreckler were Wilson's distributor, he must be big enough to be able to pay in dollars, and to handle transportation of the fuel.

Now that he possessed this information about Wilson, Colling was left to consider how to best use it to the sergeant's disadvantage. He could just turn him in, but to do so would require that he disclose that he had learned the technique Wilson was using to steal Army gasoline, and how he had come into possession of that information. If he tipped off the authorities anonymously, he would have to convey only a brief message that the NCO was diverting fuel. In the absence of an explanation of how it was being done, it was likely that it could all come to nothing, as a cursory examination of the trip records and the odometers would undoubtedly find that they coincided. In either case, Colling would be running the risk that there could be some unpleasant retaliation against himself, not only from Wilson, but from the sergeant's black market friends, as well.

Colling continued to see Veronika on weekends, and began using Saturdays to introduce her to the American movies being shown in the Army theaters in Munich. While she was attaining increasing proficiency with English, she often whispered for him to explain portions of the films. After they had seen a few of them, she expressed her opinion that the American motion pictures were superior entertainment to German ones.

In an effort to please Veronika, Colling reacquainted himself with regularly attending Mass, and found that he was taking pleasure from the obvious happiness she was deriving from his being there beside her.

Another source of accomplishment was the satisfaction he took from his work treating patients in the clinic. Major Elliott continued to trust his competence, and did not hesitate to ask his opinion from time to time. Colling often wondered why the woman had not demonstrated any romantic interest in any of the single male officers she knew. He was aware that she attended the weekly social affairs at the officer's clubs in the area, but had heard no gossip about her involvement with anyone.

Accordingly, he was surprised when he returned from his daily excursion to say hello to Veronika in the mess hall to find the nurse engaged in conversation with a tall, dark-haired major wearing a Constabulary shoulder patch. When Colling walked in on them, they were unaware of his presence for a moment, and she was almost girlish, displaying flirtatiousness that Colling had never seen before. He hesitated as he entered, causing the couple to cut short their tête-a-tête, and Major Elliott introduced Colling to Major Frank Kinney. The Constabulary officer acknowledged Colling with a muttered, "Lucille here has told me a lot about you, Sergeant."

"All good, I hope, sir," said Colling.

Without responding, Kinney told Major Elliott that he had to run, and after a barely-noticeable nod in Colling's direction, he was gone. As soon as Kinney departed, as if speaking to herself, the nurse said, "He's very sweet, you know."

"Yes, ma'am," was all that Colling could think of to say.

"He's been in twice now to check on one of his men who was injured. Very thoughtful."

Colling impulsively said, "More likely he came to see you, ma'am," then regretted having voiced his thoughts. He almost let out a sigh of relief when she laughed and said, "I hope so, Colling. I really hope so."

Changing the subject, Major Elliott informed Colling that the hospital was extremely short-handed, and as a result, she had been informed that he would have to pull duty on one of the wards for a few days from 1500 until 2300. Unfortunately, he would have to continue to assist her in the clinic from 0700 until it was time to go to his inpatient assignment. She expressed her understanding that it would mean long hours, but assured him that she had insisted that he continue to have Saturday afternoons and Sundays off. And replacements were expected, so that the situation would last for not more than a couple of weeks. Colling readily accepted, but asked if she would be able to manage the clinic on her own for the last half-hour or so of the day, so that he would be able to pay his customary visit to Veronika. The major smiled and told him that that would present no problem.

The ward to which Colling was assigned was designated for

medical cases, as opposed to the much busier surgical wards. Most of the 511th's patients were there because of injuries received in accidents of one sort or another, and if a soldier were hospitalized, it was because surgical intervention was required to treat his wounds. Medical cases, on the other hand, were less common, and consisted of serious infections, or cardiac or circulatory problems. The latter were rarely found in a population of generally young men fit for military service.

Colling found that he would be assisting Lieutenant Kate Manderlee, the charge nurse for the ward. He had seen the attractive brunette in the hospital hallways, and had heard that she was romantically involved with a captain in a Civil Affairs outfit. He reported to her, explaining that he would be her medic for the three to eleven shift. She reviewed the ward's patients with him: Three strep throats in isolation, an eighteen-year-old recruit with measles, a jaundice case, and a middle-aged chief warrant officer who had had some chest pain, and was in for observation. The warrant officer's EKG was inconclusive, and he had not had a recurrence of angina. The lieutenant expressed her hope that the night would be a quiet one, since there were only the two of them on duty.

One of the German mess hall workers brought a cart with the meal trays at 1645. Colling put on a surgical mask and gloves and delivered three trays to the men in isolation. None of them appeared very ill, and Colling once again gave silent thanks for the discovery of penicillin.

The patient with jaundice was as yellow as Colling had seen. The man attributed his condition to an infection he had contracted in the South Pacific, and morosely speculated that this attack would mean an end to any further service in the Army, which he had intended to make a career when he enlisted in 1940.

The young soldier with measles was in the infection's early stages, and was miserable. Colling made certain that the curtains were drawn so that the room would remain as dark as possible, and while doing so, reminded the man that he had to protect his eyes from bright light until his spots disappeared.

The warrant officer was assigned to a private room at the end of the hall. He was in the water closet when Colling brought in his tray and set it on the white enameled over-bed table. Colling waited until the man emerged, and introduced himself. The warrant officer told Colling his name was Chief Owen Corneille, saying, "Been in since '17, son. Enlisted as a private, stayed in, and worked my way up. Don't stand on ceremony unless there's officers around. I was a non-com for too many years. Can't get used to being a 'Mister'."

As Corneille began to eat, he asked Colling to stay for a moment, curious about Colling's military service, and after Colling's brief narrative, the warrant officer asked Colling not to tell his doctor or the nurse that he was continuing to work while he was in the hospital. Colling inquired what branch Corneille was attached to, and the warrant officer responded that he was in Ordnance, and having a hell of a time making sure gasoline supplies got where they were supposed to go. He pointed with his fork to a pile of file folders and papers on the foot of his bed. Colling assured him he would tell no one, but advised that the warrant officer cover up the paperwork or hide it when he expected a visit from his physician.

Chief Corneille's friendly demeanor, coupled with his being a gasoline supply officer, caused Colling to consider whether to disclose to him what he knew of Wilson's activities. He would have done so the next day, if he had not walked in on the chief warrant officer speaking on the telephone, "Dammit! You need to get that tank car out of there right now! I don't care if you can't find a locomotive. There's 10,000 gallons of gasoline just sitting out there with nobody around. All's you have to do is go get it. The Kraut railroad people gave me a map showing where it is. It'll be somebody's ass if it turns up missing!"

The warrant officer noticed Colling standing with his dinner tray and motioned for him to put it down. Corneille said some final words of warning to the party on the other end of the line, and then shook his head in dismay. "Who in hell could lose a tank car full of gasoline? The damn German railroad, that's who! No wonder I got pains in my chest."

"Try and calm down, sir. You don't want to have 'em come back," advised Colling.

"Yeah, yeah," said Corneille, picking up his fork and knife and cutting into the ham that had been brought to him. "Listen, son, I want to take a shower. Can you come back after I eat and get me down the hall to the latrine?"

"Sure, sir," said Colling, and true to his word, an hour later he escorted Corneille to the shower-room, then returned to the warrant officer's room. The second manila folder that Colling opened had a hand-drawn map with directions for location of the railway tank car. Colling rapidly copied it on the back of a vital signs form he had taken from the nurse's station, making sure that he had included everything on the page. When he was finished, he replaced the map where he had found it and pocketed his own copy. Then he quietly returned to the hallway outside the ward bathroom, and stood waiting until the warrant officer indicated he was finished with his shower and was ready to return to his room.

Knowing where $10,000 worth of Army gasoline was sitting unattended was a gigantic temptation for Colling. According to Corneille's map, the tanker was nearby, just outside Munich, on a siding at a place called Kestner Forst. Colling was not pleased, however, with the prospect of having to take on Wilson as an accomplice, but it seemed unavoidable. After all, the staff sergeant did have the contacts to take the fuel off their hands. Colling was not looking forward to having to negotiate how the profits would be divided, certain that Wilson would want more than half.

It was Major Elliott who spared him the trouble. Intending to gently tease her, he casually asked her if Major Kinney had dropped by again, and when she admitted that he had, he said, "See, ma'am, I told you so. He's coming by to see you. The guy from his outfit went home yesterday, so it must be you he's coming to see."

"Well, possibly," she said, "But I think I'm second fiddle. I found out he's also been visiting that warrant officer who's here, supposedly with chest pains. Grace Farber, who's charge on the day shift, told me that Frank comes to see the chief every day. She overheard them talking, and they're setting up some kind of trap for Frank's men to catch black marketeers."

Colling had to suppress a reflexive reaction to this news, and thinking quickly, he responded that the news was interesting, adding that he had spoken to the warrant officer, whose name was Corneille, and he seemed a nice enough fellow; long-term service, since the First War.

When the beating of his heart had returned to normal, Colling realized that Kinney must see him as a suspect, and had some confidence about his involvement in black marketeering. Colling was dismayed when he reflected on the reason for his being assigned to extra duty on the medical floor, and that it might be possible that Major Elliott also thought that he was engaged in black marketeering. But she had given no indication that she viewed him as a suspect, and, in fact, had inadvertently let him know that a trap was being laid. But someone in the hospital hierarchy must have such an opinion, making sure that he would have an assignment where he would be caring for Corneille, and where he would have the opportunity to learn about the fuel tanker. Colling did not want to think about Colonel Barrowsmith's role in the scheme.

With his newly-acquired knowledge, Colling's good sense told him to just do nothing, but then the pieces of a plan of action began forming. He would have liked to disregard the direction his thoughts were taking, but it was too good to let it pass. Not only did he foresee that he might gain some personal financial benefit, but the opportunity had arisen to arrange for Staff Sergeant Bernie Wilson to be the recipient of what Colling was convinced he so richly deserved.

At his first opportunity, Colling asked Meltzer if he could relay a message to the German working in the hospital who was closest to Wilson. With an expression of distaste, Meltzer said that Hans Kolber was the man. Colling said, "My friend, you must let this Kolber know, appearing to do so innocently, that your American friend, Colling, has embarked on an enterprise involving a great deal of *Benzin*, but he is having difficulty negotiating a decent price with his French contacts. Can you do this?"

"For certain, Colling. I know just how to say this that he will immediately carry it to Wilson."

Colling was surprised at how fast the news traveled. He had asked Major Elliott for a few minutes to go to the small snack bar in the hospital PX, and he was only half-way through the hot fudge sundae he had ordered when he saw Wilson at the door, scanning the place. Without any hesitation, the staff sergeant walked in and sat down across the table.

Leaning forward, Wilson said in a low voice, "I hear you got something goin' with gasoline."

Colling sat back, slowly licking chocolate syrup from his spoon, and replied, "Could be. What's it to you?"

"I got some contacts who can move it for you."

"Yeah," said Colling, "What if I say I got my own contacts."

"I heard tell they're Frenchies. That means you probably have to get the goods across the border into France. I ain't heard of any Frenchy who'll risk trying to smuggle anything out of Germany. Besides, they ain't gonna give you as good a price as my guys can. Gas may still be in short supply in France, but it don't cost as much, and it ain't rationed."

Colling pretended to be mulling over what Wilson had said. After a moment or two, he admitted, "My contact says he'll pay five francs a liter. But you're right, it has to be delivered in France. I haven't got that part of the deal sewed up yet."

"Jeez!" said Wilson, "Five francs a liter is only fifty cents a gallon. I can get you eighty at least, depending on how much you got."

"A lot," replied Colling.

"Where is it?" asked the staff sergeant eagerly.

"Safe," said Colling. "Listen, give me a chance to think this over. I need to know exactly what the deal is. Say, for instance, I got more than 5,000 gallons, and let me know what you can get for it," Colling dropped his spoon noisily into the sundae dish, and added, "Tomorrow night, in your office, at 2000," before getting up and walking away.

As he had anticipated, when he returned to the clinic, Major Elliott informed Colling that the replacements had arrived, and he was relieved from duty on the ward, effective immediately. Kinney apparently thought his trap had been set. Colling decided not to disappoint him.

Wilson was in his darkened office, seated at his desk in a circle of light, when Colling arrived as promised. The staff sergeant stood and offered his hand while expressing the usual insincere pleasantries involved in one criminal conspiring with another.

"What can you do?" asked Colling.

"Depends. If you got 5,000 gallons, my guy can go seventy-five cents per."

"And if I got ten?" said Colling.

Wilson whistled through his teeth. "Okay, I think if you got ten, he'll go eighty."

"That's net?" asked Colling.

"Yeah. Let's see, 10,000 at eighty is eight grand."

"U.S. dollars?"

"Sure. It might take him awhile to come up with that bigga' wad, but he can swing it."

"When do I get paid?"

"Well, Jim-bo, this is the thing...you and me are in this together, so it's a matter of *us* gettin' paid."

"I figured you'd want a commission for steering me," said Colling. "Ten percent seems fair. That's eight hundred for doing nothing."

"Hey, hey! Let's not get hostile, here. Without me, you got nothin'. I figure the ten percent for the steer, then half of the rest because we're partners."

Colling stared at Wilson steadily, prolonging the silence, watching the sergeant's face. Wilson was unable to cope for long with the absence of a response on Colling's part, and finally whined, "Hey, Jim, you know, you got no choice. Obviously, you stumbled onto something. I got to take all the risks, dealin' with a bunch of German gangsters and all. Why shouldn't I get a little more than you? You still got thirty-six hundred out of the deal, and if anybody's gettin' paid for doin' nothin', it's you."

Once again, Colling held back any reaction, continuing to

look directly at Wilson, then he said, "Okay. We got a deal..," and as a broad smile broke across the sergeant's face, he completed the sentence, "...Except, I got to have some money up front to prove your guy is good for it."

Wilson's face fell. "Jim, he ain't gonna advance anything. He has to have the goods before he pays. That's the way it's done."

"You should have some cash. Pay me and get it back out of the pay-off."

"How much?"

Colling thought for a moment, and then said, "Five hundred, U.S. currency. No military payment scrip."

Wilson was hesitant, but when Colling shrugged his shoulders as if to indicate he was about to leave, he said, "Okay, okay. But when I give you the five hundred, I need to know where the gasoline is."

"Fair enough," said Colling. "Bring me the money tomorrow, and I'll tell you all about it."

"Where?"

"Catch me outside the mess hall at about three. I go there to see my girlfriend. She's the good-looking dark-haired one. You ever see her?"

"Nah, I never pay any attention to them Kraut girls," was Wilson's reply.

Veronika was pleased to see Colling, as usual. He told her he would visit on Saturday afternoon, and squeezed her hand before leaving. Wilson was waiting in the hallway, and handed him an envelope. Colling stepped to one side, and rapidly counted the cash that it contained. Satisfied that the five hundred dollars was there, he told Wilson that the gasoline was in a railway tanker on an isolated siding about twenty kilometers west of Munich.

"I got to have an exact location, Jim," said Wilson.

"Don't worry. I got a map that shows right where it is," replied Colling.

"Yeah, so where is this map?"

"In a safe place, don't worry. I'll give it to your guy as soon as you introduce me to him," said Colling.

"I gave you the five hundred, Jim-boy. You got to tell me where you got the map hid."

"It's in the clinic narcotics cabinet. It's locked all the time, and only Major Elliott and me have a key. Like I said, when you set up a meeting with your guy, I'll turn it over."

Wilson was reluctant, but accepted what Colling told him and walked away, promising to arrange for a meeting with his contact.

Colling returned to the clinic and began cleaning and restocking for the next day's sick call. Major Elliott left, telling him to be sure and lock up when he was through. As soon as she was gone, Colling put the map in the back of the first shelf of the small locker where the clinic's supply of narcotics was stored, making sure that it remained visible, and that the cabinet was left unlocked. Using a trick he had learned from Elizabeth so long ago in Poland, he took a tiny piece of adhesive tape and placed it on the top of the cabinet where it could not be seen, but where it would be loosened if the door to the locker were opened. When he departed, he neglected to lock the clinic.

Afterwards, he strolled to the mess hall to have supper, and then went to his quarters, where he discussed with Hardesty the relative merits of Betty Grable, Rita Hayworth, and other female Hollywood stars for some time, until both of them decided it was a better use of their time to read. After lights out, he slipped out of bed, dressed, and went to the clinic. As he had expected, the adhesive tape was loose, indicating that the door to the narcotics locker had been opened. The map was still there, but it did not appear to be in the same position he had left it. He surmised that Wilson had copied it, and when he held each of the clinic's medical record clipboards angled to the light, his assumption was confirmed. The faint indentation of a hand-drawn diagram in the top sheet of one pad could be seen. Colling struck a match and used it to set fire to both his own map, and the top two forms of the pad that Wilson had used, and flushed the charred remnants down the commode.

Major Elliott was engrossed in competing reports the following afternoon when Colling reminded her that it was necessary to replenish the supply of "Off Duty - Sick" forms that were used to authorize the men they had treated to remain off duty for a day or two. One of Colling's responsibilities was to periodically run off a number of mimeographed sheets of the forms, then cut them apart for use. He advised the major that the stencil had worn out, and he that would have to obtain a new one from the administrative office. Without looking up, she told him to do so.

The corporal at the orderly desk gave Colling a handful of fresh mimeograph stencils, and Colling returned to the clinic and began typing, working slowly and carefully, so as to avoid any errors. He was still tapping away when Major Elliott laid down her pen and straightening the sheaf of papers on which she had been concentrating. She announced that she was through for the day. Colling replied that his work was far from complete, and he would be required to continue on duty for awhile.

After Major Elliott had departed, Colling rolled a blank stencil into the typewriter and began work on another document. Using his prior experience as a battalion clerk, he was able to create the correct heading, and official jargon, as well as cite what looked like correct portions of Army Regulations. When he was done, he held up the finished stencil to the light and re-read it. To his eye, it appeared genuine. It said that the United States Army in Europe, through its headquarters in Heidelberg, had bestowed a commendation on Staff Sergeant Bernard E. Wilson, on account of his assistance in the apprehension of German nationals engaged in attempting the theft of Government property, more particularly, a large supply of automotive gasoline, near Kestner Forst, Bavaria. Colling's final touch was to add a somewhat scrawled signature, under which was printed, "Major General, U.S.A.," without any printed name.

A few minutes before 1700, he returned to the headquarters office. As he had anticipated, the corporal was clearly displeased that Colling wanted to use the mimeograph machine at a time when he was about to go off duty. Colling assured the clerk he could leave, and that he would make sure that the door was locked after the printing was complete.

Colling printed fifty sheets of the off-duty forms for the clinic.

After he had finished that task, he ran off one copy of the commendation order, and then tore the stencil into small pieces which he
flushed down the commode. It had been some time since Colling
had written anything in German by hand, so that he made some
practice attempts to make sure that the script was correct before he
wrote the notation, "*Ihre Spitzel*" in the margin of Wilson's commendation. Having identified the staff sergeant as a stool pigeon,
he folded the order and placed it in the pocket of his white medic's
jacket. Another half-hour was spent using the office paper-cutter to
divide the sheets of forms, which he delivered to the clinic before
going to the mess hall for dinner.

Hardesty was out, so Colling had their quarters to himself. He
removed the cash that he had accumulated, which he estimated
amounted to over $14,000. Either superstition or fear of being
discovered in the act had kept him from counting it. He sealed
the money in an envelope, together with all of the false identity
documents that he had brought with him from Poland, and put
everything in the old suitcase containing Cousin Jerry's civilian
clothes. He replaced the case in its hiding place in the bottom of
his wall locker.

The following day was Saturday, and Colling slid the suitcase
into his empty duffel bag before heading to the Schönenberg house.
No one seemed to notice when he walked out the front gate of the
hospital, the heavy bag slung over his shoulder.

Veronika greeted him with a warm kiss when he arrived, which
he returned with equal enthusiasm. When they finally stepped
apart, she asked what was in the duffel bag. With a conspiratorial
air, Colling removed the suitcase, opened it and retrieved the envelope containing the currency and identification papers. Handing
it to her, he said, "Sweetheart, this contains a great deal of money,
American money. You must hide it somewhere that it will remain
safe, even if the house is searched. As far as the suitcase is concerned,
store it someplace. If it's found, just say that it belonged to one of
the refugees."

Veronika promised, "Of course, Jim, I can do this."

"Another thing," said Colling, "If anything happens to me, the money is yours. Burn the rest of the documents."

"But I could not do such a thing, my love," she replied.

"Then keep what you want, and send the rest to my family in the States. You have the address."

Veronika nodded her head, "Yes, Jim. But all of it will go to your family. Besides, what do you think might happen to you?"

"Probably nothing, Sweetheart, but it pays to be prepared. By the way, I need a mailing envelope and a German postage stamp."

Veronika left him for a few minutes, and then returned with a European-style envelope, into which he placed the spurious commendation order for Wilson. When Colling finished addressing it to Schreckler at the *Blauer Hase*, she handed him the stamp. After sealing the envelope and affixing the stamp, Colling gave her the envelope and requested that she hold it for him. He told her he would either ask her to give it back to him, or that he would let her know that she should drop it into the mail.

That evening, Colling took Veronika to see *Casablanca*, which was being re-played on the Army theater circuit. She was wiping away tears as the movie ended, and he was surprised, not so much at her reaction, but because she had been able to follow the dialogue without his translating for her. Afterwards, there was the usual necking on the bench in the cellar. On Sunday, they went to Mass, and then Colling joined the Schönenbergs and their servants around the kitchen table to partake of the remains of the meal enjoyed by the Barrowsmiths the evening before.

CHAPTER 15

NOVEMBER, 1947

Colling learned from Major Elliott that an attempt had been made to hijack the gasoline tanker when he reported for work on Monday morning. The nurse excitedly told him that on Saturday night, Kinney and his men had been involved in an actual gun battle with black marketeers somewhere in the woods outside of the city. Two of the major's detachment had been wounded, but the Germans whom the Americans had been trying to apprehend had fared far worse. Three were dead, and four others with gunshot wounds had been brought into the hospital's casualty ward. Two of the wounded Germans had been taken away to prison, and the others were under guard on the surgical ward. A few more of the black marketeers were under arrest, but not all of the criminals had been caught.

As Major Elliott neared the end of describing these events, Major Kinney walked into the clinic. He returned her greeting, then spoke to Colling, "We nailed a bunch of Kraut gangsters over the weekend, Colling. They were trying to run off with a tanker-full of gas. You happen to know anything about it?"

"Jeez, sir, why would I know anything about it?"

"Because you found out by searching Chief Corneille's papers that it was there."

Colling noticed that two Constabulary men had taken up positions outside the clinic entrance, and were standing at ease, observing the conversation. He said, "Sir, I swear, I don't know what you're talking about. I did take care of the Chief, but I sure and hell didn't search any of his things."

"It was a set-up, Colling. The Chief was a plant. We had word that someone in this hospital was marketing gas to the Germans, and figured we'd offer a little temptation for a big score."

Major Elliott seemed stunned by this exchange, but recovered enough to interject, "Wait, Frank, I heard there was something up from other staff members. I told Colling about Corneille's being part of a plan to catch gas marketeers. That was days ago. Why on earth would he be involved with this, knowing that it was a set-up?"

Kinney's facial expression betrayed that this news had disconcerted him to a considerable degree, but then he reached into his jacket and brought out a sheet of paper, and holding it in front of Colling's face, said, "You recognize this map, Soldier?"

"No, sir. Never saw it before."

"It's a copy of one that the Chief had," and then as the MP officer turned the paper over and held it up with its reverse facing Colling, he asked, "And how do you think it might have ended up being drawn on the back of a medical record form that's used in this clinic?"

"I have no idea, sir. Like I said, I never saw that piece of paper before."

"I've been easy on you so far, Colling. In fact, I haven't exactly followed the book by asking you questions here, in front of the Major. But I think it might be a good idea to place you under arrest and take you in for some *real* questioning."

Major Elliott interrupted once again, "Frank, could we talk privately?"

Kinney seemed embarrassed at her intervention, but agreed, and she led him off into the next room. Colling remained where he was, aware that the two military policemen were alertly watching him, and would probably welcome the chance to use force to subdue him.

A few moments later, the two officers emerged, and Kinney said, "Colling, you're off the hook for now, but I'm warning you, I'm going to be watching you, and if there's one misstep, you've had it."

Colling came to attention, "Yessir. You don't have anything to worry about, sir."

As the MP officer brushed past him, Colling relaxed, and once he had departed, his men following him, Colling asked Major Elliott, "Ma'am, what did you tell him? Whatever it was, thanks very much."

"I told him that those medical forms are used all over this hospital. A year ago, we got a shipment of about a hundred times more of them than we ordered, and everybody and his brother has been taking them to use for note paper and whatever. I told him he'd find pads of them everywhere, including the kitchen. I also told him that the writing on that map was not yours."

"Thanks, ma'am. I really had never seen that paper before."

"Clever choice of words, Jim. I won't ask whether you've ever seen the map itself before."

A quiet, "No, ma'am," was all that Colling could think of to say.

Major Elliott seemed to have allowed the whole affair to drop, mentioning nothing about it that afternoon when he requested her permission for some time to say hello to Veronika in the mess hall. When he spoke to Veronika, he told her to go ahead and mail the letter he had given her.

Colling took a few additional minutes to go to his quarters after his visit with Veronika. He found that his wall and foot lockers were open, the locks broken, and his belongings tossed onto the floor. His bunk had been pulled apart, and his stationery portfolio, together with the correspondence from his parents, was spread open on top of the bare mattress. There was a space where his wall locker had been moved in order to search behind it. He hastily made up his bunk and put everything else back into some semblance of order. Apparently Kinney had not entirely given up attempting to implicate him. Whether the Constabulary officer would go so far as to search the hospital commander's residence remained to be seen.

Colonel Barrowsmith and the Schönenbergs were left in peace, and Major Kinney actually continued to come to the clinic to see Major Elliott. Colling wanted to tell her that she could now be certain that the Constabulary officer's interest was in her, and not a mere adjunct to Kinney's professional duties; but he did not do so.

Surprisingly, Colling learned of Bernie Wilson's fate during a lunch-time conversation with his fellow medics. A tech-four named Langerman, who was assigned to the casualty ward, asked if the others at the table had heard about what happened to the staff sergeant, clearly having a difficult time restraining himself from instantly blurting out the news. Colling decided not to seem curious, but his companions were, and Langerman was eager to please, "He got the living hell beat out of him. Both arms broken, ribs cracked, and more bruises than you can shake a stick at."

"No shit?" said a motor pool corporal named Prentice, "He told me he was taking a week's furlough at Chiemsee. Where the hell was he when it happened?"

"Here in Munich, I guess," said Langerman, "The MPs called for an ambulance."

Prentice turned to Colling, "Hey, Colling, wasn't you and Wilson buddies?"

A couple of the other men laughed, and Colling said, "We had our moments."

This caused more laughter, but Prentice was serious, "No, I mean it. He was looking for you a few days ago, and he said he found you in the PX. He acted like you and him was pals."

"He wanted me to do some deal with him. He believed all the rumors about me having some extra cash. I couldn't help him."

Langerman interjected, "Well, jeez, if getting shit-kicked was part of the deal, it's a good thing you weren't in on it."

Someone asked Langerman what ward Wilson was on, and the tech-four said that the staff sergeant had been transferred to the hospital in Augsberg, and that the word was that he would be shipped home, probably with a medical discharge.

There were murmurs of sympathy for Wilson from some of the soldiers at the table, tempered with a couple of voiced opinions that the son-of-a-bitch finally got his. Colling made no comment one way or the other.

When Colling returned to the clinic from the mess hall, he found Major Kinney there, engaged in conversation with Major Elliott. Kinney broke off in the middle of a sentence to speak to him, "Colling, I hope you've been watching your step."

"Always, sir, always," said Colling, "Say, sir, since you mentioned this thing about gasoline, I asked around. I have a few of the German workers here in the hospital that I've gotten to know."

"I'm aware of that, Colling," said Kinney sourly, "Especially that little brunette who works in the laundry."

"Yessir, she's the daughter of the family that rents their house to the Colonel. That's how I met her. I think Colonel Barrowsmith helped get her the job here."

Kinney seemed to have been caught unawares by this revelation, and taking advantage of the officer's discomfiture, Colling pressed on, saying, "Sir, like I was saying, I've asked some of the Germans about who might be in the black-market gasoline business, and it might behoove you to check the motor pool. I just heard that Sergeant Wilson, who's the motor pool NCO, met with some misfortune last night, and it might be connected."

"What happened to him?" asked Kinney.

"He got beat up pretty bad, I hear. Rumor is, he was over-charging mileage and resetting the odometers on some of the hospital's vehicles to account for more fuel use, then selling the extra to some German gangster, who's supposed to be a real nasty number."

"Interesting you should know this, Colling. Who told you?"

"Can't say, sir. Just some rumors. The Germans are so scared that they'll clam up if they're asked about it."

"The first place we checked was the motor pool, right after we got a tip that someone in the hospital was involved," said the MP major, and then, as if thinking aloud, "But we only checked the records. If Wilson was resetting the odometers, that would explain why we didn't find any discrepancies."

Over Kinney's shoulder, Colling could see that Major Elliott was smiling, obviously pleased that her beau and Colling seemed to be getting along with one another. At the end of his discussion with the Constabulary major, Colling said that he was pleased to have possibly been of help, and that he held no hard feelings about the military police doing their job by searching his quarters.

Secretly, Colling had mixed feelings about Bernie Wilson. On one hand, he was happy to have exacted revenge for the man's obnoxious behavior, but on the other, if it had been within his power, he would not have chosen to inflict injuries of such severity.

While Colling wondered what the staff sergeant would have to say about him, if and when the military police questioned him, he had given careful consideration to all aspects of what he had engineered. To begin with, Colling was comfortable that he had covered his tracks, and that if Wilson did tell the MP's what had actually happened, without any substantiating evidence, it would sound like a desperate, fantastic fabrication. As far as the chance that Wilson might attempt his own retaliation, the staff sergeant would be in no condition for a long while to attempt to do so, especially from a hospital bed in the States. Colling also felt confident that Schreckler would have destroyed the fake commendation order, in order to eliminate any connection to Wilson, and would in any case, have no idea who James Colling was, although he might be curious to know who the German was who had betrayed Wilson.

Colling had put most of these thoughts aside before the weekend arrived, and he arrived to take Veronika to a matinee to see the new Gregory Peck film that was playing. After their usual embrace at the kitchen door, she took him by the hand and told him that there was someone that he must meet. His initial surprise when she led him towards the library was allayed when, as they passed through the entry hall, Veronika mentioned that Mrs. Barrowsmith had been kind enough to permit her parents to entertain their guest there, instead of climbing to their rooms on the second floor.

Herr Schönenberg was seated in his wheelchair, his wife on the sofa, in almost the same position as when Colling had first been introduced to them. Veronika was smiling, speaking English, as she introduced Colling to a tall, heavy-set man who stood to shake Colling's hand, "Jim, this is *Herr* Max Biedermann, a colleague of my father's from the old days. He has just come from America. *Herr* Biedermann, this is Sergeant James Colling."

Colling was trying to estimate how much the elegant double-breasted suit that Biedermann was wearing must have cost, so that his initial response was simply, "My pleasure, sir."

Biedermann smiled broadly, "So, this is the fine American that everyone speaks so well of. Veronika and her mother said you look like this Peck fellow, the Hollywood star, but he is much older than yourself. I would say, you are more like John Garfield."

Colling had never conceived that he bore a resemblance to any movie actor, and he said so, at the same time, taking notice that Veronika was blushing bright pink, obviously taken unawares by Biedermann's disclosure of her opinion about his appearance.

Biedermann continued, "You have seen action in the war, James?"

"No, sir. I came in, the middle of '45, and the A-bomb was dropped as I finished training. I was actually on a train here in Germany when we heard news of the surrender signing in Tokyo bay."

"I take it you were smart enough to wait to be drafted," said Biedermann.

Colling replied, "Sort of, I volunteered to be drafted, then requested to serve an additional year. In '45, the Army wasn't accepting enlistments."

"None of my boys were smart enough to wait. His mother and I could not believe it when Nathan, my youngest, enlists, right out of college, in the summer of 1941, before even we were in the war. And in the Army, no less. I told him he was crazy, he should go in the family business, but he had some notion he wanted to be in uniform. Then he says he has volunteered to jump out of airplanes, and then to go to the OCS, to be an officer. More craziness."

Despite the man's attempt to minimize what his son had chosen to do, Colling guessed that it was false modesty, and said, "You must be very proud of him. I trust he returned safe from the war?"

"Thanks to God, yes," said Biedermann, "But he had no right to have such good fortune. He was with the 82nd Airborne. In Normandy, in Holland. He came through without a scratch," and then after a solemn pause, "And God's blessings on those who did not."

Colling suspected that Nathan Biedermann probably had a chest full of ribbons, but he did not ask. While Biedermann was talking, Colling had noticed that Veronika was translating for her parents.

"It is fortunate that he has come back safe," said Veronika, to which Colling added his agreement. Colling then asked, "He's back in the family business?"

"Yes, but the war has made him too restless. Now he says he should go to Palestine," said Biedermann, "His mother and I have tried to talk him out of it, but he insists. Oh, well, may God be with him, whatever he decides."

"Did your other sons serve as well?" asked Colling.

Biedermann's face brightened, "Oh, yes. My oldest, a doctor, he joins the Navy after Pearl Harbor. I thought, a doctor, certain to be in a nice safe hospital on land, but he ends up on a ship, an aircraft carrier, can you believe? He comes home and tells us that these crazy Kamikaze's were as bad as they looked in the newsreels. And our middle son, he is the smartest. He goes with the Air Force, and has a nice job in the supply end of it. Never leaves the States, although he does have to be stationed in Texas."

"You are lucky, all safe and sound," said Colling.

"Not so for my friends, Albert and Marie," said Biedermann, speaking German, sadness evident in his voice, "They have lost one son, and two others remain unaccounted for. God willing they will return safe."

At these words, tears appeared in *Frau* Schönenberg's eyes, and her husband, stone-faced, leaned towards her and laid his hand on her arm, stroking it and whispering for her to be strong, that Willi and Friedrich would come back. Colling looked in Veronika's direction, and saw that she had turned away, wiping tears from her own eyes.

Biedermann was obviously upset with himself that his comment had caused such heartache, and he glanced at Colling, as if seeking his assistance to relieve the tension. Colling obliged by saying, "Mr. Biedermann, what business are you in?"

"Why furs, of course, my boy! Albert here was kind enough to buy my firm in Frankfurt so that I could go to the United States."

Colling had not recognized "Biedermann" as one of the names that Veronika had mentioned to him, but with this revelation, he put two and two together, "Oh, yes. Veronika has told me about this."

"Then you know that the Nazis would have stolen everything if it had not been for Albert. The money we had to accept for the purchase price was useless, worth nothing. But Albert and his sons saw to it that we received payment anyway."

"Yes," said Colling, "I heard that they used Sweden and Switzerland to transfer funds to you. I was told that *Herr* Schönenberg was told by the Nazis to buy four Jewish companies. How have the others fared?"

"As well as my own," said Biedermann, "It was difficult at first, but we had some Canadian contacts, and we have got into these Chinchilla pelts from South America. Very expensive, and very popular with wealthy ladies in New York and Hollywood. Yes, with Albert's help, we all did well. All of our children were able to finish their university studies. But when we learned that Albert had paid such a dear price, it was unbearable, and at the time, there was nothing that we could do. Now things have changed, and it is time for us to repay our debt to you."

Colling was surprised when Albert Schönenberg spoke English, "Max, I doing this for myself, for mine own conscience. In truth, I can do no other."

That a devout Catholic should quote Martin Luther struck Colling as ironic, and he wondered whether Veronika's father knew the source of the phrase, or if he would have recognized it and chosen another if he had spoken it in German.

Biedermann raised his hand, "No, Albert, we must repay what you have given us, as much as we are able. In truth, we owe you our lives. Without you, we might have resisted selling, and if we had remained in Germany even another year, we would never have been permitted to leave."

Frau Schönenberg was now openly weeping, and Veronika was sitting beside her, her arms around her mother, her own eyes red with tears.

Colling was trying to think of something else to say when Biedermann said, "My friends, you must be happy! Things are better now, and they will get even better. I have come as a...how do you say it, Colling?...a deputy from all of us. We wish to provide financing so that you might resume your business, and provide anything that you may need," and glancing from Colling to Veronika, he smiled and added, "And perhaps a nice wedding dress from New York?"

This comment took Colling off guard, given that he had never discussed marriage with Veronika, but on a moment's reflection, he realized that it was not altogether far-fetched. His thoughts on the subject were interrupted by *Herr* Schönenberg saying, "Until Wilhelm and Friedrich come home, to start the firm again is not possible. And we have everything we need. As for a wedding dress, that will be a matter between our daughter and Sergeant Colling. I have not yet heard that a proposal of marriage has been made."

Colling suspected that he was supposed to say something at this point, but he did not, and was relieved to see that Veronika showed no sign of disappointment in his silence.

Max Biedermann spoke soon enough so that a lack of a reply on Colling's part did not become awkward, "Well, you have our offer, Albert. All that is left is for you to say the word. I truly believe that your sons will be home soon."

Veronika asked if Biedermann would join them for dinner, and he responded by inviting all of them to a restaurant. When Albert protested that his wheelchair would make it impossible to accept, both Biedermann and Colling assured him that they would manage everything. Colling recommended the *Apfelbaum*, and after explaining to Biedermann that the streetcar would be more practical than summoning a taxi, they set out.

Herr Schönenberg had not been on the streets of Munich since coming home from his hospitalization three years previously. The districts through which they passed had suffered relatively little bomb damage, and it was a bright fall day, which seemed to invigorate the old man. Colling and Biedermann had little difficulty in lifting his wheelchair onto the streetcar's rear platform, and as they clanged along, he watched the passing scenery with intense interest.

The meal was excellent, as it had been when Colling and Veronika first visited the *Apfelbaum*. Biedermann was obviously impressed, praising the food and atmosphere. Colling noticed that he was eyeing the American military personnel who were the restaurant's primary patrons. Colling had the impression that the man was particularly interested in the ribbons worn by most of them, and was comparing what he saw with what he knew his sons had earned.

When they had been seated, Veronika informed Biedermann that Colling spoke German, and from that point, the table conversation was conducted in that language. Biedermann had a tendency towards speaking loudly, which elicited pained stares in their direction from the Americans seated near them. The New York furrier seemed not to notice, unaware that subdued public behavior was expected of the local population in occupied Germany.

Albert Schönenberg was more animated than Colling had seen him, as he and his old friend exchanged memories of life before Hitler, and compared notes about other acquaintances and business associates. Colling took it all in, glancing occasionally at Veronika, who returned his glances while smiling brightly. The dinner reminded Colling of Thanksgivings in Bel Cors, and he remembered that the holiday would be on them in less than a week.

As soon as they had returned to the Schönenberg home, Biedermann called for a taxi. A half-hour later, the cab had arrived, and he was taking his leave. Colonel Barrowsmith appeared as Biedermann was at the front door, and was introduced by Veronika. Biedermann thanked the colonel for his courtesy in permitting the use of the library. The two men continued to chat as they walked to the waiting taxi. Colling wondered what they might have had to say to one another.

Veronika took Colling's hand and pulled him toward the kitchen. He anticipated that she had arranged for Hilde and Annelise to leave them alone, so that they could neck, but instead, she drew him through the rear door and to the carriage house. Colling began to think that she might have some less routine activity in mind, and once they were inside the deserted building, he drew her into his arms. After one short but eager kiss, she pulled away, "Jim, you remember that I have told you when you first came here that all the motorcars have been taken by the *Wehrmacht?*"

Colling recalled the conversation, and said so.

"Well, this is not *exactly* so. There is a motorcar here," she said.

Colling quickly surveyed their surroundings, "Where? I don't see one."

"Here," said Veronika, leading him to the far end of the room. He followed her as she negotiated a narrow opening behind a rough wall of cinder blocks that partitioned off a section of the carriage house. Inside the space was something covered by a tarpaulin. Veronika swept off the cover, revealing one of the little cars that had been trumpeted by Hitler during the early days of his dictatorship. It was black in color, and under the coat of dust, the paint appeared to still be glossy. Colling walked around the vehicle, peering into the dust-covered windows, "I saw in *Stars and Stripes* a couple of months ago, that the British have resumed building these up in their zone. They're used by the German police up there."

"It is a *KdF Wagen*. This one was my brother's," said Veronika, "Little Albert. He was able to buy the stamps all at once to get one, because he was a Party member, and a member of a Hitler Youth flying club."

"Did he have a chance to drive it?" asked Colling, immediately regretting the manner in which he had posed the question.

His concern turned out to be misplaced, as Veronika seemed not to be troubled, "A few times. He taught me to drive it when he was home on leave. He spoke of driving it to France, but that never happened."

Colling saw that the car's wheels had been removed, and it was resting on blocks. He asked her where the tires were, and she pulled covers off five of them hanging on the wall. Colling examined them, and they seemed to be in surprisingly serviceable condition. Without his asking, Veronika said, "Albert brought me some fluid that the *Luftwaffe* used to preserve tires, and told me to rub some on every month or so. It looks as if it helped."

"How do we get it out of here?"

"Knock down the wall. It seemed the best way to hide it. Friedrich put it up when he was home on leave."

"When was that?" asked Colling.

"In the last part of 1941."

"So it hasn't been driven in six years?"

"Yes," said Veronika, "But for some time, I started the engine every two weeks. But then the other motorcars are requisitioned, and petrol became impossible to get. It has been since 1944 that it was run last."

Colling was calculating which of his fellow soldiers could put the car back in working order when Veronika said, "I know of a man who is a mechanic who can have it running again, if you can obtain petrol and lubricants. He lost an arm in the war, and would be happy with the work."

"Is he hampered, having only one arm?"

Veronika stared at him, puzzled, and he realized she did not know what "hampered" meant. He explained that he was asking if the man could perform the work without difficulty, and she assured him that he was capable of doing so.

With the prospect of having a vehicle to drive that was not painted olive-drab, Colling turned his attention to the challenge of obtaining engine oil, grease and gasoline. In addition to being heavily taxed, the quantity of these commodities available on the open market was primarily reserved for taxis and motor transport companies. Fuel for private automobiles could be obtained, but was expensive, and subject to a monthly maximum. Government officials and those with influence suffered less restriction. The black market in purloined American fuel supplies continued to flourish for those with the ability to pay, especially in hard currency. American officers were allotted a ration of gasoline for their private vehicles, if authorization had been granted for their possession. If the ration proved too little to last out the month, an additional few gallons could be purchased from an "unofficial" source at less per gallon than would have to be paid at a local gasoline station.

Colling was certain that American dollars in the right hands in the hospital motor pool would bring him an adequate supply of the lubricants; with the recent crackdown on gasoline diversion from the hospital, it appeared prudent to purchase fuel from legitimate sources. Colling suspected that finding spare parts might prove troublesome, but Veronika assured him that the mechanic she had engaged would know where they could be obtained.

There was also motor vehicle regulation to consider. Veronika, of course, would be able to register the car, but Colling feared that the fee would be astronomical. In addition, he doubted that she possessed a driver's license, which he suspected would be a mandatory pre-requisite to licensing the vehicle. Colling had been issued a U.S. military driver's license soon after arriving in Germany, but he believed that authority for an enlisted man to own a private vehicle was virtually impossible to obtain. He had heard gossip about some senior NCOs keeping cars off-base, but doing so seemed fairly risky.

The first task was to see to the renovation of the car. Obtaining needed supplies was easy, falling as it did within Colling's area of expertise. A ten-dollar bill to Prentice, and he had six quarts of oil, a two-pound can of grease, and an empty five-gallon jerry can to store extra gasoline.

The one-armed mechanic, who introduced himself as Fritz Lengger, helped him knock down enough of the block wall to be able to remount the little cars wheels and push it out of its hiding place, then back it into one of the stalls in the carriage house. Lengger began renovating the automobile, informing Colling that they were fortunate that while the battery required charging, it still functioned, although he could not say how much longer it would do so. The mechanic called the car a *Volkswagen*. Colling liked the sound of it, but doubted that the name that Hitler had given the automobile would catch on with Americans, if the Germans were ever able to manufacture them for export. Besides, it was small, the engine was in the back, and it was air-cooled; all of which would be hard to sell to American drivers.

Colling decided that the first approach to the license issues would be for Veronika to obtain a driver's permit. They found the bureau responsible for such things tucked away in a side street off the Bahnhofplatz in central Munich. The bespectacled clerk, whom Colling would have guessed had served as a functionary in the same department under the previous regime, comported himself with a mixture of arrogance and boredom. The man exerted himself enough to hand Veronika a pamphlet to study, and an application form.

During the week, Colling asked Sergeant Gayle whether enlisted personnel could have personally-owned vehicles, and the master sergeant informed him that the United States Army in Europe regulations applicable to officers' operation of POVs were expected to be extended to everyone very soon. He added that, as far as he was concerned, if Colling wanted to have a car, he could do so without worrying about any disciplinary action. Gayle warned that Colling should make sure that he had insurance, and as soon as the USA-REUR rules changed, he would have to register it with the hospital headquarters. The sergeant's final caution was to steer clear of the German police and the MP's by not having any accidents, and obeying the traffic laws.

Once Lengger pronounced the little automobile ready to drive, Colling asked Veronika to start it and use the carriage house driveway to test its operation, while Colling watched. She made three or four wide circles before Colling was satisfied that the auto was running properly. It was also clear that she was able to steer, shift gears and brake, and when she came to a stop, he climbed in beside her, and they drove up and down the short stretch of Kleberstrasse in front of the Schönenberg home. Her brother had taught her well, and she handled the little vehicle with ease. When Colling took a turn in the driver's seat, he found that the shift pattern was shorter than he was used to, but he quickly adjusted to the feel of the little car, and was impressed with how well it drove.

In order to accompany Veronika to her driving examination, Colling had to ask Major Elliott for time off during the week. Veronika easily passed the written test, but then Colling was amazed to discover that instead of her having to actually drive a vehicle with an examiner, she was put through a series of trials of her eyesight, hearing and reflexes.

The final portion of the test consisted of her operating a device equipped with a steering wheel, dashboard, floor pedals and gearshift that looked like something Colling had seen in an amusement arcade in Chicago. A rolling belt replicated a roadway, using painted scenery, and Veronika had to react to curves, road signs, speed limits, other vehicles and obstacles. She negotiated the twisting course of the highway, braked at the right times, and managed to stop for a tree that had fallen across the road.

The clerk, who did not disguise his disdain for a female being entrusted with a complex piece of machinery like a motorcar, briskly applied a series of rubber-stamped official seals and approvals to Veronika's application, and then typed out a license. Before handing it over, he asked Veronika for the snapshot of herself that was required, afterwards gluing the portrait to the permit.

The registration of the little car was somewhat easier, but more expensive. Colling had previously located an insurance company that was happy to take his money for coverage. But when the woman in charge of the motor vehicle office informed Veronika that the registration fee was 500 marks, Veronika was not shy about expressing her ire, prompting Colling to step in, counting out the sum in occupation currency and thanking the clerk for her assistance. They received a motor fuel allotment card with the registration. The registration certificate issued to Veronika carried the same combination of numbers that appeared on the license plate for the car which Albert Junior had had made in a local auto shop back in 1939.

With the bureaucratic details completed, Veronika drove Colling to the hospital, and she was laughing with exhilaration when they reached an open stretch of city street that permitted her to press the accelerator. She dropped Colling at the main gate, and as he climbed out of the passenger seat, she eagerly agreed with his suggestion that they might drive into the countryside on the weekend. He watched her drive off, praying silently that she would arrive home safely. One of the MPs on duty at the entrance asked what kind of car Colling's girlfriend was driving as he walked past. Colling told him it was called a *Volkswagen*.

CHAPTER 16

NOVEMBER – DECEMBER, 1947

Thanksgiving Day came before Colling's planned weekend in the country arrived. He ate the mid-day meal in the hospital mess hall, where the kitchen staff had prepared a traditional turkey dinner with all the trimmings. Colling had to admit that the Army always seemed to excel when it came to feeding the troops on the holidays.

Later that afternoon, Colling went to 42 Kleberstrasse to see Veronika, and found her, her parents and the two women servants seated at the big kitchen table around a Thanksgiving dinner similar to the one Colling had finished about an hour earlier. Veronika happily explained that Colonel Barrowsmith and his wife were dining elsewhere with a group of officers and their wives, but had made the turkey and other holiday food from the commissary available for the Schönenberg household. Colling declined to eat, explaining that he had already done so, and contented himself with answering questions about America, while sipping a cup of coffee and watching the others dine.

Afterwards, with Veronika at the wheel of her car, the two of them went for a drive, confining their route to the outskirts of Munich. When they were ready to go back to the Schönenberg house, they exchanged places, giving Colling the opportunity to further familiarize himself with the little vehicle. He pulled into the carriage house on their return, and they tested the suitability of the car as a place to neck. Colling found it less comfortable than the bench in the kitchen, but possessing the benefit of increased privacy.

Over the next two weekends, as the winter weather permitted, they continued to use their new motorized freedom to explore the roads around the city.

Veronika took him to Chiemsee to visit Willi's wife, Elise, and their children. Willi had purchased a small villa near the lake as a refuge from the war, and like most other places that had been a favorite resort of the Nazis, Chiemsee appeared untouched. When Colling and Veronika paid their call, they discovered that Elise was working as a waitress at one of the local restaurants, which were now patronized almost exclusively by American troops. Elise's mother, bombed out of her home in Frankfurt, and Elise's brother, returned from the *Wehrmacht* and working as a bell boy in one of the U.S. Army hotels, were living with her. Veronika fawned over her young nephew and niece, in the usual way aunts do, as they waited for Elise to come home from work.

Colling found Elise's mother reminded him of his grandmother, and he was happy to spend his time answering her stream of questions about life in the United States. The old lady was openly impressed with his ability to speak German.

The reunion between Elise and Veronika was tearful, as the two women shared their fears about the fate of Willi and Friedrich. When they left to return to Munich, Elise's mother insisted they take two pieces of a cake that she had baked the day before.

In the middle of December, Colling announced that he wanted to drive to Grabensheim and Kummersfeld to show Veronika where he had been stationed when he first arrived in Germany. A light snow began to fall when they were thirty kilometers or so outside Munich, and Colling suggested that he take over the driving. When the snowfall became heavier, he decided that they should head back to the city before conditions became difficult.

Serious discussions with women seemed to occur when Colling was at the wheel of an automobile, and this was no exception. There was something that he had been considering for some time, and it suddenly seemed that it was time to reveal his thoughts to Veronika, "Sweetheart, if you could make more money with another job, would you want to?"

"It depends," she said, smiling, "Are you thinking of going into business and making me your secretary...your *private secretary*, as you say it in America?"

"No, although that is an interesting thought. You could sit on my lap and take dictation."

Veronika laughed, "We would never get any work done."

Colling smiled at the thought, but returned to his original train of thought, "True, Sweetheart, but I was thinking of something else. I know someone who might be interested in hiring you as a Russian translator. It would be confidential work, if you know what I mean."

"And who is this person?"

"Someone I know in the Army. I haven't spoken to him yet, but I think he could use someone who's fluent in Russian."

"The last time I used my Russian was when I worked for the *Wehrmacht*, reading Soviet magazines and newspapers and writing out what they said in German."

"But you do have a command of the language, don't you?" asked Colling.

"Yes, I suppose so. But will the U.S. Army want a German doing this kind of work, if it is 'confidential,' as you say?"

"In your case, I don't see that as a problem," said Colling.

"In that case, I would be interested," she replied.

That evening, Colling wrote a letter to Quarles, using the APO address for Corporal Joseph Appleby that the intelligence officer had given him.

Dear Joe –

Hope you are doing well. Work at the hospital goes from light to heavy at the drop of a hat. I've run into someone who might share your interest in Russian literature. Let me know if you want to swap copies of some books.

Hope your family is okay. How much time do you have before you rotate home?

Sincerely,
Jim

Eight days later, Colling received a reply.

Dear Jim –

Nice to hear from you. My mom and dad are doing fine. I'll be seeing them in a few months.

I'd be real interested in swapping some paperbacks with your friend.

I've got a three-day next week, and plan on spending it at that hotel we both stayed at when we got back from the course in Morocco. If you can get some time off, you could bring the books. I've got a couple of extra copies of Tolstoy and Dostoyevsky that your friend might be interested in.

See you then.

Your friend,
Joe

After Colling had read the letter, he tried to recall the route that had been taken when he was driven from Quarles' villa to the Munich railway station. He had been in the rear of the truck, with a limited view. His mind could not picture the exact roads that had been taken, but he knew that Quarles' Bavarian outpost was north of the city. He believed that if he were able to return to the area, he would recognize how to get there.

Colling obtained a weekend pass from Major Elliott, and early on Saturday morning, he and Veronika climbed into her car and took to the roads leading northward from Munich. He was surprised at how easily he was able to find his way to the place. Landmarks that he could not consciously recall took on a familiarity once he actually encountered them. He wondered if the experience gained in his travels behind the Iron Curtain had sharpened his ability to subconsciously memorize a route that he had taken in the past.

When he spied the house where they were to meet with Quarles, Colling directed Veronika to pull off the road in front of the wrought-iron gate set in the stone wall surrounding it. A helmeted military policeman tapped on the driver's side glass, startling both of them.

As Veronika rolled down the window, Colling, leaned forward so that he could see the man's face, "Sergeant, Colonel Quarles is expecting us. If you would tell him 'Jan' is here, I would appreciate it."

The guard looked both of them over carefully before walking away towards a passageway through the wall to the left of the main entrance. Colling and Veronika waited for a few minutes before the MP reappeared and pulled the gate aside. As they rolled through the stone archway, Colling noticed two other soldiers on their right, carbines slung on their shoulders, watching the little automobile drive by.

Colling pointed to a place under some trees where Veronika could park. Before either of them were able to open their doors, two more MPs were alongside the vehicle. The one nearer to Veronika, a sergeant, opened and held the door for her. The other soldier simply stood and eyed Colling alertly, his hand resting on the flap of his pistol holster, as Colling stepped out of his side. With the sergeant leading the way, and the other MP behind them, they went into the mansion and proceeded up the wide staircase to the second floor.

Quarles stepped out of his office to greet them, smiling, and his eyes lighting up, as Colling introduced Veronika. The guards were dismissed, and the intelligence officer invited them to make use of the leather-upholstered chairs in front of his desk.

"Well, Jim, I had no idea your Russian interpreter would be so attractive," said Quarles, seeming to be unable to keep his eyes off Veronika.

Before Colling could comment, Veronika said, "Thank you, Colonel, but I think you flatter me."

"Ah!" said Quarles, "Fluent in English?"

"Yes," replied Veronika, "Jim has been instructing me in your language."

Switching without hesitation to German, Quarles continued, "Wonderful! I am certain that Colling is an adept teacher. And for certain, you are pretty, my dear. My words intended no false flattery."

Veronika responded in German, "You honor me, sir. You will cause me to blush."

Quarles laughed and said to Colling, "You've got a good one here, Jim. She speaks English well enough, but how about Russian?"

"I'm no judge of that, sir," said Colling, "But her family spent half the year in the Soviet Union from the time she was a little girl."

Veronika said something that Colling could not understand, but recognized as Russian. Quarles responded in kind, but awkwardly, obviously having only a rudimentary grasp of the language. The officer looked in Colling's direction and said, "I'll have one of my men see if she's fluent in Russian. It sounds like it to me, but I can't tell for sure."

A moment later, a man wearing an American uniform devoid of insignia joined them, and Colling surmised that Quarles had done something to summon him, probably pushing a button under the rim of his desktop. The new arrival was thin, with dark, deep-set eyes and a morose air about him. Quarles introduced him as "Savron," and told the man to take Veronika into the next room, and that he was to evaluate her ability to speak Russian.

Quarles was the first to speak when he and Colling were alone, "If she's any good, I can sure use her. We have to be very careful about our Red defectors, or anyone else who speaks Russian like a native. Never can tell when they're plants."

"What about this Savron fellow?" asked Colling.

"Fairly safe, I think. He's Ukrainian, served as an auxiliary in a German infantry outfit. No family left alive. When he was captured by our guys, he tried to pretend he was a Kraut, but somebody picked up on the fact that he spoke German with an accent. They figured him for one of those Baltic-State camp guards, and held him for over a year. A friend of mine let me know they had him, and his real background. From everything I can gather, he hates the Reds, and his work so far has been excellent."

"I think you'll find Veronika to be excellent, as well, sir," said Colling, "She did translation work for the *Wehrmacht* towards the end of the war, but it was mostly printed material."

"I know," replied Quarles, "Her family was considered 'unreliable'."

Colling had not expected the intelligence officer to know Veronika's family history, "How do you know that?"

Quarles smiled, "I keep tabs on you, my boy. It didn't take much to figure out that Miss Schönenberg was your Russian language expert."

Colling felt uncomfortable about the prospect of his being watched by the lieutenant colonel's men, and he said, "Sir, I don't appreciate being tailed, by you or anyone else. As far as I'm concerned, I'm not working for you anymore, and I think you know me well enough to know I'm not a security risk."

Assuming a fatherly tone, Quarles said, "Don't forget, Jim, you were the one who contacted me about Veronika. I was just doing what I do. I know all about Veronika Schönenberg and her family, even that her brother was Hitler Youth and a Nazi."

"Then you also must know what her father did."

"Absolutely. And how the Gestapo put him in a wheelchair. That's the main reason I was willing to meet her. There aren't many Germans still alive who did anything to oppose the regime."

There was a knock on the door, and Savron and Veronika returned. The Ukrainian asked to speak with Quarles privately, and the two of them stepped outside. Veronika said, "His test was not so much. We spoke for awhile, and he asked me to read from *Izvestia*. His Russian is that of a foreigner, not an American, but one of the Eastern countries."

"He's Ukrainian," said Colling.

Veronika had just remarked, "Ah, that explains things," when Quarles rejoined them.

"Savron says you will be satisfactory," said the intelligence officer. "If you want to work for me, it will have to be in Heidelberg. Any problem with that?"

Veronika glanced across at Colling, and then answered, "No. That will be fine. Are you able to supply a place for me to be housed?"

"Yes," said Quarles, "I had a WAC officer who just returned to the States, and you can have her place, no charge. The job pays 1200 marks a month."

Veronika stood and facing Quarles, said, "It would be better if I were paid in dollars, like American soldiers. The money to go into an account on which I could draw marks as I needed. Also, I would wish to have a card so that I might be able to buy things in the PX and commissary. For those, I could draw the military payment currency."

Quarles' eyes widened and his brows raised as Veronika outlined her demands. From the expression on the officer's face, Colling was unsure what his reaction was going to be. Before Quarles could respond, Veronika added, "It is clear that this work is important, and secret. You will be paying me less than an American soldier who is able to do this for you. You will not regret granting my wishes."

Quarles said, "You've been around Jim Colling too much, young lady. Okay, I can arrange for what you want. Be in Heidelberg next Monday at eight in the morning. I'll give you the address of your quarters. I'll let the landlady know so that you can move in on the weekend before you'll be starting work."

On the drive back to Munich, Veronika was ecstatic about the prospect of living in Heidelberg and earning American dollars in the bargain. When Colling informed her that she would be making five dollars a month more than himself, she suddenly became serious and told him that the difference would make up for her not having mess hall privileges. Her response was so obviously aimed at assuaging his masculine ego that he had to suppress a laugh. He teased her by speculating that with her new Army identity card, she would undoubtedly have access to the same dining facility used by the Army personnel with whom she would be working.

The elder Schönenbergs took the news of Veronika's new employment with a mixture of emotions. While they expressed their pleasure at her having found a position where she might do well financially, it was clear from their faces and tone of voice that they would miss their daughter.

Veronika had made it clear that she wanted her automobile with her in Heidelberg. Most of the German roadways had been restored to some semblance of serviceability, but Colling did not want her making the journey on her own. He was able to find one of the other medics willing to cover his responsibilities in the clinic in exchange for four cartons of cigarettes and five dollars, and Major Elliott approved a three-day pass.

Colling and Veronika alternated driving her little car the nearly 400 kilometers to Heidelberg. The roads were much better than those that Colling had experienced in traveling from Grabensheim to Frankfurt-Am-Main by truck in the fall of 1945. Most bridges had been fully repaired or replaced, and there were long stretches of the Autobahn where the little *KdF Wagen* performed better than the Buick that Colling's father owned. Colling had brought a jerrycan of gasoline in anticipation that fuel might be scarce, but they were able to refill the car's 25-liter tank outside Stuttgart at an old Leuna station that now bore a Shell sign.

They had to use a GI-tourist street map to find Veronika's new living quarters. The address was a house near the university. They were greeted at the door by a middle-aged woman who frowned at Colling's uniform, and then led them up to the second floor. Colling spoke German when he asked how many rooms the place had, which seemed to improve the landlady's mood, and she responded that the U.S. Army had paid to have the house divided into four flats, leaving her with her own rooms at the rear of the ground floor.

The apartment was luxurious by post-war German standards. What had apparently been a large bedroom had been partitioned so that there was a tiny kitchen, which included a small Swedish refrigerator as well as a gas stove and sink. The remainder of the room was divided by a curtain into a sleeping area and a sitting room. An old but serviceable sofa and easy chair were in the latter half, in front of windows looking out over the street. A double bed nearly filled the other side of the room. There was a small table and two chairs at which to eat under the windows. A mahogany wardrobe was next to a door leading to a bathroom and, from the sparse amount of square-footage remaining, Colling guessed that it had been a larger bath that had been divided between the apartment and the one adjoining. There was a sink, a cramped shower, and a gas hot-water heater mounted on the wall. Seeing Colling eyeing the device, the landlady remarked that if it were lit about a half-hour before warm water were needed, that it would provide it. She added that tokens would have to be fed into the meter in one corner of the kitchen to pay for the gas, and that Veronika could buy them from her, two for five marks. A pay telephone was in the front hallway, the tokens for it were also available from her, one mark each. Veronika remarked that pay phones customarily required fifty pfennings, and was brusquely informed that if Veronika wanted to obtain telephone tokens from the Post Office, she was free to do so.

All of Veronika's belongings were in two large suitcases that Colling had carried up the stairs when they first arrived. He sat in the easy chair and watched her as she unpacked and put things away. When she was done, he pointed out that she would not receive her commissary card until Monday, making it necessary for them to dine out. In addition, he would have to find a place to stay until Sunday, when he would take the train back to Munich.

The tourist map showed the locations of not only the U.S. military facilities, but local hotels and restaurants authorized for use by American personnel. Colling and Veronika used the streetcar, in the interest of conserving gasoline, and with some walking, were able to find a restaurant that provided an inexpensive but ample meal of pasta and meatballs. The waiter informed them that the owner had spent three years in Italy with the German Navy, and had developed his culinary skills there.

After dinner, Colling was able to register at one of the Army hostels in the city. For three dollars in military scrip, he had a place to stay for the weekend, although he would have to share his room with another soldier.

Despite the December chill, they spent Saturday exploring Heidelberg. Veronika had visited the place once or twice while growing up, and she was amazed to find that it had changed so little from the remembrance of it, and had come through the war more or less unharmed. Colling took her to the PX cafeteria for breakfast each day, but for other meals, they chose a different place every time, one of which in particular, they vowed never to re-visit.

Without her saying so, Colling sensed that Veronika was hesitant about their using their time to engage in love-making. He surmised that her restraint was connected with the novelty of her being on her own, and the disturbing reality of the freedom that came from the situation.

As a result, aside from hand-holding, gentle embraces and some brief kisses, they abstained from intimate physical contact.

When Colling kissed Veronika good-bye at the Heidelberg *Hauptbahnhof* on Sunday morning, he gave her fifty dollars in military currency, which she tried to refuse, but then accepted with a promise to repay as soon as she had received her salary. He told her he would try to visit every weekend if he were able, and returned her wave as the train pulled away from the platform.

While performing his duties in the clinic on Monday, Major Elliott asked Colling about his time in Heidelberg, and he told her that Veronika was now employed by the Army there. He avoided disclosing the nature of the work that she would be doing, opting instead to characterize it as a secretarial position. He did describe Veronika's apartment, and the major asked if he would be requesting weekend passes or a furlough to allow him to visit her. When Colling replied that he would, in fact, be asking for time off, Major Elliott told him that the substitutes he had found to take his place had not proven to be up to his caliber. She informed him that the best that she could do would be to allow him a pass every other Saturday and Sunday.

At mid-week, Colling received a letter from Veronika. She had written in German, indicating that things were going well, and that there were two American women with whom she was working. Both of them were WAC officers who did English translations of Veronika's renderings of Russian documents into German. Veronika had been given an APO address for Colling to use, but he was to use the name "PFC Colleen Warden" on the envelope instead of her own. She closed the letter with *"Immer Deine Liebchen."*

Colling wrote a reply, giving Veronika the news that he would be able to travel to Heidelberg only on alternate weekends, and promising that he would be there the weekend before Christmas. He added that he was assuming that she would be given leave to come home for the holiday. With Christmas Day falling on Thursday, they might be able to be together for four or five days.

Colling was pleasantly surprised when he began to receive a daily letter from Veronika. It was strange to have mail every day. While he had weekly missives from his mother, and occasional letters from his sisters, correspondence from Elizabeth had been sporadic at best. He made a pledge to reciprocate with his own daily correspondence to Veronika. It was also refreshing to read something more substantive than the latest society and fashion news that had been the staple of Elizabeth's letters.

Veronika was waiting on the railway platform when Colling stepped off the train on the afternoon of the Saturday before Christmas. She embraced him warmly, and their kiss drew stares from the German passersby unaccustomed to such public displays. Colling was carrying a parcel that her parents had given him to deliver to her. Because of the security concerns that required Veronika to use a pseudonym for her APO address, Colling had also had been acting as the go-between for the Schönenberg's correspondence, enclosing the letters that they gave to him in the envelopes that contained his own, and seeing that they received those that Veronika sent in her letters to him.

She had driven her car to the station, and on the drive to her apartment, she told him that she normally walked the short distance to the building where the Russian translation section was housed. She had not used the *KdF Wagen* since arriving in Heidelberg. Until today, the vehicle had been housed in a garage that Quarles had recommended to her.

After Colling's luggage and the package had been deposited in Veronika's flat, he suggested that they go to supper at a restaurant that they had both enjoyed when Colling was last in Heidelberg. Afterwards, Veronika drove to an Army theater where a John Garfield film was playing. As they bought their tickets, Colling recalled her mentioning in one of her letters that she had gone to the movies with the two American women with whom she worked. As if reading his mind, Veronika repeated what she had written, seeming to want to stress that her only companions on those occasions had been female.

After the picture, Veronika expressed her opinion that Biedermann had been right, that Colling did bear an uncanny resemblance to John Garfield. Colling emphatically disagreed with her assessment, but she persisted, clearly aware that despite his protests, he was flattered by the comparison, however erroneous he thought it might be.

The garage where Veronika left the car was a few blocks from her apartment, and as they walked the distance, she clung tightly to his side, as much as to stave off the cold as from affection, mused Colling.

There was some vestige of warmth in the flat, but Veronika nevertheless turned on the gas hearth as soon as she had shed her coat. Colling had picked up his overnight bag and was bidding her good night before beginning his search for a room when she said, "Oh, no, Jim. I would not send you out at this hour and in the cold. You may sleep on the sofa. I have bought an extra blanket."

He protested, "What will your landlady say?" he searched for an applicable word, "It would not be...seemly...."

"Do not worry. She is asleep by now, as I do not hear the radio playing. Once it is off, she is in bed."

"What about the other tenants? What will they think?"

Veronika laughed, "The other flats are occupied by my WAC friends and another lady who is the receptionist for Lieutenant Colonel Quarles. I know for sure that one of the WACs is in Garmisch with her boyfriend, and the other probably has her own boyfriend in her flat as we talk. The old lady who is a receptionist is on leave to Paris. So there is no reason to worry. Besides, all we are going to do is sleep, is that not right?"

Colling agreed. He really had no desire to traipse around Heidelberg looking for quarters at this hour. Veronika closed the curtain that screened off her bedroom, but an open gap was left so that, a few minutes later, he saw her tiptoe into the bathroom, wrapped in a woolen robe. When she emerged and he heard the rustling of the bedclothes, indicating that she was under the covers, he used the bathroom himself. Veronika had lit the water heater, and he decided to use the hot water to shave.

The gas hearth had gone off while Colling was in the bathroom, and he hurried to arrange the pillow and blanket that Veronika had left on the sofa and then climb into the makeshift bed. He tried to sleep, but the chill in the room was slowly becoming greater without the fire. He whispered to see if Veronika was awake, and she answered. He asked where the gas tokens were, and she apologized, saying she had used the last one that afternoon.

Colling cursed under his breath at this information. Veronika must have heard him, because she said, "Jim, come in bed with me. You must be freezing." He protested, but the thought of a warm bed overcame his resistance, especially when Veronika invited him a second time.

He was shivering when he slipped in beside her, but within moments, he felt warmth begin to return to his feet and legs. In another moment, Veronika's arms were around him, and his lips were on hers. He realized that she was wearing only a thin shift, and he could feel her breasts pressing against him. She moaned, and then it was as if he had been engulfed by her. Her response was so intense and so unexpected that he felt as if his head were spinning. She was moving under him, and he could no longer contain himself. He was afraid that he had left her unsatisfied, but when he looked into her face, he saw that she was smiling.

They were murmuring their love for one another when he realized that he had not used a prophylactic. When he withdrew and expressed his concern that she might become pregnant, she whispered in German, "Good Catholic girls know the right time of the month to make love," and she rolled over and went to sleep.

When Colling awoke to faint sunlight streaming into the room, he was cautious about pulling back the covers, knowing that the apartment had become very cold overnight. He finally steeled himself and jumped from bed, pulling on his clothes as rapidly as possible. Veronika had not shown any inclination to follow suit, even when Colling left to find the landlady and buy some gas tokens. The woman acted as if his knocking on her door in the early morning in search of them was nothing out of the ordinary.

The gas hearth did an efficient job of heating the apartment, and within a half-hour, Colling felt he could remove his topcoat. He heard Veronika stirring on the other side of the curtain, before she said brightly, "Jim, good morning! Do you feel as good as I do?"

"Better," was his response, "Get dressed and we'll go get some breakfast."

"We do not need to do that," she replied, "There is food here. From the commissary."

Colling enjoyed watching the movement of her body as she emerged from behind the curtain. She had put on her robe, her feet in plush slippers. When he glanced down at them, she said, "I buy these in the PX. Better than wearing old ski stockings to keep my feet warm."

She had fresh eggs which she fried, and bacon, toast and jam. Colling was so used to powdered mess-hall eggs that he relished every bite. She seemed to match his appetite, even using a piece of toast to mop up the last mouthful of her eggs. Colling leaned back in his chair and said, "I don't have much time. I have to catch the train to Munich by 11:00."

"Then we should make good use of our time, yes?" said Veronica, smiling.

This time, Colling made sure things lasted longer than they had the night before, and he used a prophylactic. Good Catholic girls might be knowledgeable, but good Catholic boys knew enough to be cautious, despite what Church dogma might say. Veronika made no comment about the use of contraception, but when they were dressed and ready to go to the station, she hugged him and said, "You know, *Liebchen*, you are very good at what you do." Even though he did not respond, he had to silently agree that he probably was.

As Colling had expected, Quarles gave Veronika leave over the Christmas holiday. He met her at the main Munich railway station at noon on Christmas Eve, using a jeep that Colonel Barrowsmith had approved for the purpose of transporting his landlords' daughter home.

In anticipation of being able to resume their love-making, Colling had booked a room in a small but tidy *Gästhaus* near the hospital. His plans were assisted greatly by the generosity of the Colonel's vehicle authorization, which permitted Colling to use the jeep until Sunday night. His plans were set aback somewhat when Veronika told him she would be staying with her parents.

When Colling had reported for duty after returning from Heidelberg, Major Elliott had declared the clinic would be closed on Christmas Day and the Friday and Saturday following, and that any sick call patients were to be referred to the hospital casualty ward. The nurse let slip that she and Major Kinney would be spending the holiday weekend in Garmisch.

Christmas Day was spent in celebration at the Schönenberg house. Shortly after Colling arrived, there was an exchange of presents among the Schönenberg household and himself. Before Thanksgiving, Colling had purchased a scarf and sweater in the PX for Veronika, and through some skillful trading in cigarettes, was able to give coffee, chocolates and Cognac to her parents and the two servants.

The Barrowsmiths had invited everyone, including Colling, to join them for dinner. The Colonel's wife had managed to procure a large standing rib roast, and she insisted, over Hilde's protests, in supervising the cook in the preparation of the meal. The result was a superb table that lent itself to over-eating. Colling tried to take only small portions, but even at that, came away feeling uncomfortably full.

Veronika had been unwilling to leave her family on Christmas Eve, and when the Christmas Day feast and exchange of presents had concluded, she again told Colling that the lateness of the hour required her to remain at home. She did agree to meet him on Friday morning, and Colling promised that he would arrive early and take her to breakfast.

Colling's breakfast plans were frustrated when they discovered that the hospital PX and its snack bar were closed on the day following Christmas. As he had no desire to drive around, looking for someplace that was open, their only option was the hospital mess hall. To add to the let-down, there was only a skeleton staff on duty, and the selection on the tray-line was limited. Veronika assured Colling that she preferred a German-style breakfast at any rate, and she ate a roll and drank coffee while he consumed reconstituted eggs and Spam.

The remainder of the day made up for its disappointing beginning. He took her to the hotel, and they spent the better part of the day making love and sleeping in each others' arms. There was a decent café just down the street where they were able to take their meals. They were holding hands across the table after dinner when Veronika asked, "Jim, are we serious enough about this to think what the future might bring?"

Colling was not surprised that she was obliquely asking him if he intended marriage. While he had certainly considered asking Veronika to become his wife, his experience with Elizabeth made him cautious. He had rashly broached the subject of marriage with Elizabeth, naively believing that she would welcome his proposal. When she did not reciprocate, he had made a decision, almost subconsciously, that he would not open himself to such painful rejection again.

All these thoughts were flowing through Colling's brain as he lamely responded, "What do you think the future should bring?"

Veronika said, "No one knows what the future will bring," clearly having misunderstood his question, so that he repeated it, emphasizing that he was asking for her opinion of what *should* happen. To his chagrin, she suddenly withdrew her hand from his, looking as if she were on the verge of tears.

There was a touch of anger behind the moisture flooding her eyes as she said, "I will not be the one to ask you to do something that you do not wish to do."

At that moment, Colling was overwhelmed by the realization that he would not be able to bear losing Veronika, that he wanted to be with her forever, and that he dare not hesitate to repair the damage that his words had caused.

He reached out and grasped the hand that she had pulled from his, and softly speaking German, said, "Veronika, my love, my treasure. Please grant me your forgiveness. I would do nothing to cause you sorrow. I love you, more than anything. Would you do me the honor to marry me?"

Veronika brushed away tears, not raising her head for a moment, and then she looked up into his eyes, and said, "Jim, is it certain that this is what you want? If it is not, be so kind as to say so."

"I speak true and from my heart, *Liebchen*. I wish you to be my wife. I wish that you will come with me to the United States, and live there with me all our lives."

There was more of a pause than Colling would have liked before Veronika replied, "It would be my honor to be your wife."

At this, Colling smiled, and seeing his expression, Veronika's face broke into a smile as well. She squeezed his hand and said in English, "We have an hour, almost, before you must take me home."

On Sunday morning, Colling put Veronika on the train. Their goodbye was warm, and he repeated his promise that he would come to Heidelberg as often as he was able. Colling was filled with a sense of emptiness for the remainder of the day. He found himself looking forward to immersing himself in the work that taking Monday sick call in the clinic would entail.

CHAPTER 17

JANUARY – FEBRUARY, 1948

Colling was able to obtain a pass for the New Year weekend, and he and Veronika spent most of their time in her apartment. In between love-making and making plans for their marriage, Colling discussed his speculation about what campus married life would be like when he returned to the university to finish his degree. The GI Bill would provide steady income, and with the cash that he had managed to accumulate, he was confident that their life would be somewhat above average.

When Colling was in Heidelberg again two weeks later, he took Veronika a copy of *Life* that contained an article about GI's returning to college, intending that she would learn what to expect as a student-veteran's wife. She leafed through the magazine, and asked him to translate portions of the text and captions on the photographs. Her only comment was, "It seems that American university students live quite well."

Colling's term of service would expire in June, and both Colonel Barrowsmith and Major Elliott tried to convince him that he should re-enlist. He politely declined, explaining that he would be marrying Veronika and completing his education. The Colonel suggested he seek a Reserve commission when he graduated, and Colling told him that he would think about it.

The paperwork necessary to gain approval for his marriage to a German national was extensive. There were vestiges of the "non-fraternization" attitude that remained in existence, and when Colling was handed the stack of forms that would have to be completed, he felt overwhelmed. It seemed that it would be impossible to provide the extensive documentation and obtain approvals from all the levels of bureaucracy that were required. His first step was to obtain the permission of his commanding officer, which he believed would be the easiest stage of the process. He gave the completed authorization form to Master Sergeant Gayle with a request that he give it to Colonel Barrowsmith for his signature.

The response was unexpected. Major Elliott told him he was to report to the CO immediately, and when he asked, she said that no explanation had been given as to why Barrowsmith wanted to see him. Minutes later, Colling was standing at attention in front of the colonel's desk, wondering what blank it was on the request form that he had failed to complete.

Colonel Barrowsmith returned his salute, then leaned back in his swivel chair, "I got your request form, Colling."

"Yessir," said Colling, hesitant to inquire about the reason for the summons.

"You know, higher echelon is very concerned about GI's marrying German girls who might have Nazi connections in the past?"

"Yessir," said Colling, suddenly recalling with a sinking heart, that Veronika's youngest brother had belonged to the Hitler Youth and had been a Party member.

"I think you can eliminate any concerns by our higher-ups on that score," said Barrowsmith, as he handed Colling a sheet of paper that had been lying on his desk.

It was a carbon copy of a letter to the Director of the Civil Affairs Section of the American Representative, Allied Control Commission, on the letterhead of *Biedermann and Sons*, with a New York City address. It had been signed by Max Biedermann and the others whom Albert Schönenberg had helped escape from Nazi Germany. The letter outlined how *Herr* Schönenberg had risked his own well-being to see that they were compensated for property that the Nazis had stolen from them, closing with their vouching for his honesty and integrity, and that of his family.

When Colling finished reading, Barrowsmith said, "When I met that Biedermann fellow and he told me what Albert had done for him and his friends, I suggested he write that letter. I figured it would come in handy, once I heard that you and Veronika were going to tie the knot."

Given the fact that Biedermann's visit had preceded Colling's proposal of marriage by weeks, Colling was left with the impression that the gossip about him in the Schönenberg household must have been widespread. These thoughts were interrupted by Barrowsmith offering to provide him with a photostat of the letter to attach to the personal and family history form that would have to be completed. Colling thanked him, grateful for the Colonel's prescience. The officer told him he would have Gayle obtain the photographic copy of the letter in a day or two, and before Colling left the office, handed him the signed authorization for the marriage.

The Schönenbergs assisted him with locating birth and marriage records, and Colling plowed ahead on the applications. Two weeks went by before he was able to obtain a weekend pass from Major Elliott, and only after he had convinced her that Tech-four Henshaw, one of the more experienced medics, would take his place in the clinic on Saturday morning. Henshaw's price was high: Ten dollars and Colling's cigarette ration for the rest of the month.

Colling had taken the late afternoon train from Munich, and had managed a series of connections that brought him to the Heidelberg *Hauptbahnhof* just before midnight on Friday. He was anticipating surprising Veronika at her apartment when Colling was startled to see Quarles coming in his direction as he walked through the gate leading from the platform. The lieutenant colonel waved to draw Colling's attention, and when they met, Quarles said, "Jim, I have bad news. The Reds have snatched Veronika."

Momentarily speechless, Colling finally said, "What the hell do you mean, sir?"

"Come with me, Jim," said Quarles, placing his hand on Colling's arm, and urging him towards the street exit, "I tried to reach you by phone as soon as I found out, but that nurse you work with said you'd already left. I figured you took the night train, and that it would be best to meet you here."

Colling was trying to absorb what was happening, "Sir, what do you mean, the 'Reds snatched Veronica'? Did they just grab her off the street, or what?" he asked as they climbed into the back of Quarles' staff car.

The driver had pulled away from the curb and was taking advantage of the late hour to drive through the deserted streets at a faster pace than was normally possible.

Quarles explained as he gazed out his window, "She apparently got word that her brother, Friedrich, was being released by the Reds. In Berlin."

"As a POW, you mean?" asked Colling.

"Right. The Russians have been sending back German prisoners in dribs and drabs. She showed Savron a published notice from some detention center in the Soviet Sector, announcing that Friedrich would be released this week...today, actually. Veronika must have decided to go meet him."

"Where the hell did she get the notice?"

Quarles hesitated for a moment, "It showed up in her APO post office box."

"Addressed to her in her own name?"

"No, they used the Colleen Warden pseudonym," answered Quarles.

"For criminie's sake, sir, didn't that seem a little suspicious?" exclaimed Colling, "So much for the security of your mail."

"Hold on, Jim. I didn't know anything about it until after I found out she'd left for Berlin."

Colling was becoming angrier by the moment, his emotions fueled by his growing fear about Veronika, "This Savron guy knew about it. What's he got to say? Son-of-a-bitch is probably a Red agent."

"He claims she asked him to not say anything. She figured I wouldn't give her time off to go get her brother, on account of she'd gotten leave over Christmas, after only starting working here."

"And now she's been kidnapped," said Colling.

"They grabbed her as soon as she arrived in Berlin and crossed into the Soviet Sector. Jim, none of my people goes to Berlin alone. Some of them, I *never* allow there, but those that I do, always have someone along as an escort."

"How'd she get to Berlin? Did she take her car?"

"No. She went by train. They probably would have grabbed her as soon as she crossed into the Soviet Zone, but apparently there was a group of Army nurses and doctors on the same train, headed for Berlin, and she was with them. If the Reds had tried anything, it would have made a stink. So, they just tailed her and when she was in their Sector of the city, they had her."

"Do you know if she's okay?"

"I think so. One of my sources gave me the news about her being kidnapped, and claims she's being held in an apartment building on Zellenstrasse, even down to the apartment number, which makes me suspicious."

Colling's eyes narrowed as he said, "That's *all* that makes you suspicious about this?"

"Not all.., of course. But it's all too pat. I think it's a set-up."

"A set-up for what?" asked Colling.

Quarles leaned back in his seat, and half-turned towards Colling, "They want you to try and get her out, and they want to catch *you*."

Colling gave a snort of disbelief, "Catch *me*? What on earth for?"

"You've become number one on their hit parade, Brother. I don't think they've figured out who you are. Word is, they call you 'The Pole.' They think you're Polish, and that we trained you in the U.S. to speak English and act like an American. They're on to the Woznica and Krazinsky aliases. I'd guess they're on to the German POW act, as well, but the jury's still out on that one."

Colling could feel a pressure in his chest, and he said nothing, unable to forgive himself for placing Veronika in danger. Finally, he asked, "Did they pick Veronika because they know who I really am, and she's the logical choice to get my attention?"

"I don't think so. She's one of my people, and she had a vulnerability...her brother. My guess is, they knew grabbing her would get *my* attention, and I'd call in my top guy to try and get her out."

"Well, they were right about that part, anyway," said Colling.

"Hey, Jim, I can't let you go in on this one. I just wanted to be the one to tell you what happened."

"Wrong, sir. She's in this because of me, and I *am* in on this one."

They had pulled up to a pair of heavy wooden gates. An MP appeared and checked their credentials before signaling that they should be allowed to pass. They alighted from the staff car in a courtyard surrounded on all sides by a three-story building. Quarles led Colling through a door and up a flight of steps. When they were in the intelligence officer's familiar office, Colling realized that they must have come by way of the rear entrance to the place.

Colling's mind had been working from the moment that Quarles had first informed him about Veronika. He asked, "Sir, was Veronika's brother really due for release?"

"Yes. I checked on that as soon as I heard. It was legit," was Quarles' reply.

"If he was released today, where is he?"

"I'm ahead of you on that one. I sent someone to pick him up as soon as he walked out of the place. We have him in solitary in the Berlin stockade. Still locked up, but the food and accommodations are better."

Colling expressed his main concern by posing a question, "What do you think the chances are that Veronika is still okay?"

"Pretty good, I think. I have a hunch that their plan is, after they nab you, they'll make an offer to exchange her for a couple of their guys that we got on ice. If they knew that she was your gal, the tip about where she is would have included something about having the Pole's girl-friend. I think that all they know is, she's one of my translators in the analysis branch, new to the job, and not a major player. I don't even think they'll try and squeeze her. They picked her because it was easy to get her to come to Berlin."

"I wish I could be as confident," said Colling. "Can you get me some orders so I can get away from the hospital for a couple of weeks?"

"Yeah, but are you sure you want to do this?"

"Absolutely sure. Now I have to try and figure out how I'm going to get into Berlin, and fast."

Quarles promised that he would set the wheels in motion to initiate the mission. He showed Colling a room with a cot where he could stay until everything was arranged. Colling's mind was racing so that he could not sleep, but by the time it was light outside, he had a mental outline of what he intended to do.

The orders relieving Colling of duty at the 511th for two weeks were based on his mother being seriously injured in an auto accident. A bogus message from the Red Cross about her was grounds for an automatic emergency furlough, issued through the Army housing office in Heidelberg, which, in turn, allowed Colling to be absent from duty, all the while eliminating the need for him to return to Munich. Colling hoped that no one at the hospital would think it necessary to send his mother best wishes for a speedy recovery. She would undoubtedly be surprised.

To provide a cover identity, Colling requested that Quarles have travel orders issued to a private soldier, fresh from the States, on his way to join his outfit in Berlin. He also asked for a uniform and an ID card, as well as a wallet-full of personal items to round out the false persona. Once he had these, Colling would make his own way into the city. One of Quarles' men took his photo, asking that he wear a pair of non-refractive eyeglasses as an added touch to his disguise.

The following day, Colling received a new buck private's uniform, an identity card with his likeness on it, wearing the glasses, together with a manila envelope containing the eyeglasses themselves and other items he had requested. Included were thirty dollars in Military Payment Certificates and over a hundred occupation marks. The card said he was Private William Carter Brown. Other documents asserted that he was from Milwaukee, had the same birthday as himself, and that Brown's mother and father happened to have the same first names as his own.

He remained uncertain about what he would do when he managed to arrive in Berlin, but accepted the fact that his actions would depend on whether Quarles could find out precisely where Veronika was being held.

Quarles insisted that he not work alone. Colling was hesitant, wary of the risks posed by involving anyone whom he did not know.

After considerable debate, the intelligence officer convinced him that it would do no harm if two of his men were made available, should Colling need them. Colling insisted that they be Russian speakers, speculating that that skill could prove useful as events unfolded. Quarles immediately recommended a pair whose names were Yakov and Malik. Both of them had served in the Red Army, with front-line experience. Their histories differed, but both hated the Communists as much as they hated Nazis. They would be waiting in a Berlin DP facility, supposedly Latvian refugees, just in case Colling should require their services.

Colling also wanted to secure Friedrich's release from the stockade, and Quarles obliged by providing orders for his release. Colling intended to use his identity as Private Brown to effect that part of his scheme.

The new private's uniform was loose on Colling, but then he recalled that the weight loss that occurred in basic training normally meant that newly-minted soldiers' uniforms tended to fit poorly. The quartermaster for the intelligence section had issued extra sets of GI underwear, socks, and shirts to him, as well as a canvas zipper bag in which to put them. Colling dutifully stenciled the last four digits of Brown's Army serial number on it, and packed it, shoving in a couple of paperbacks and a copy of *Life Magazine* dated in December. If questioned, he would say that his other duffel was still on board the transport that had brought him to Wilhelmshaven.

Quarles gave him the name of a Signal Corps major named Wilkins who was stationed in Berlin, telling Colling that the officer could be trusted, and that he would serve as his contact. Major Wilkins would see that air transportation to Rhein-Main was provided at the conclusion of the mission.

When Colling said goodbye to Quarles, the officer shook his hand and wished him luck, and in parting, advised him that there were a thousand dollars in U.S. currency sewn into the lining of the canvas carry-all.

Colling decided that for the first part of his foray into Berlin, he should travel in the back of a U.S. Army truck to Frankfurt. He did not want to go by train, assuming that the Soviets would have all the terminals in the U.S. Zone under surveillance, as well as those in Berlin. With most inter-city road traffic consisting of military vehicles, one more deuce-and-a-half would not engender any particular interest.

Both Quarles and Colling had agreed early on that a diversion would be of immense help, so the intelligence officer had arranged for a heightened level of radio traffic into Poland, at times using a code that he suspected had been broken by the Soviets. The messages created the illusion that Quarles was contacting "The Pole," and fomenting an attempt to extract Quarles' female data analyst from Soviet custody. At the same time, an extremely courageous Polish operative was directed to arrange to be observed in various places in Poland, as if seeking to throw off pursuit while heading towards Germany, deliberately drawing attention to himself until he was able to drop out of sight. If successful, this ploy would divert the MVD's vigilance eastward, to the border with Poland, for awhile at least. Colling said a silent prayer for the man's safety while giving thanks for his willingness to risk his life to create the deception.

One aspect of Colling's plan was dependent upon the vagaries of the U.S. military. Quarles informed him that there was no direct American military road traffic permitted across the Soviet Zone to Berlin. Instead, all truck convoys were required by the Russians to be carried on flat-bed rail cars. Consequently, when Colling was dropped off from the deuce-and-a-half that Quarles had arranged to deliver him to the outskirts of Frankfurt, Colling walked to the railway yards, seeking a convoy train that would be crossing the Soviet Zone into Berlin.

There had been many changes since his last visit in the fall of 1945. The warehouses and other buildings that had been bomb-damaged had been demolished, repaired or replaced. He had difficulty in recognizing the warehouse where had met his first Negro soldier, and when he did find it, he noted that its doors were closed and pad-locked. He wondered what had happened to Sergeant Woodrow Blackshear in the intervening years.

The January cold was piercing, causing Colling to pull his overcoat tightly to his neck as he wandered across the tracks. It was fully dark before Colling spied an engine slowly pulling a line of flat-bed cars that held a collection of 2½- and ¾-ton trucks. He was certain that they were not replacement vehicles by the number of American soldiers sitting in and on them. The train rolled to a stop, and a first lieutenant, accompanied by a first sergeant, dropped down from a passenger car behind the engine, and began walking its length, the NCO calling out names and numbers from his clipboard.

Colling watched from a distance, trying to remain inconspicuous, until he saw the officer say something to the NCO and stride towards the front of the line of cars. The first sergeant remained behind, using a pencil to make notes on his travel documentation. When the NCO finished and followed the lieutenant, Colling approached a group of five men who were beside a deuce-and-a-half on one of the flatbeds in the center of the train.

A PFC appeared to be the highest-ranking among them, and Colling addressed him, "Hi. You guys headed for Berlin?"

Two of the privates simultaneously said, "Yeah," and Colling asked the PFC, "Any chance I can catch a lift with you guys."

The PFC said, "Why the hell don't you just use your travel voucher and take the passenger train? It'd be a damn sight warmer than ridin' with us."

Colling had made sure his tie was pulled to one side, and he had a suitable disheveled appearance. He said, "I got into kind of a jam with some Kraut cops in the train station. If I go back, they'll catch me. All's I want is to get the hell out of here."

"What's your name?" asked the PFC.

"Bill Brown...Private Bill Brown," said Colling.

"You got orders for Berlin?"

"Sure," said Colling, reaching into his overcoat pocket and pulling out the papers that Quarles had provided, assigning him to a signal company in the city's garrison.

The PFC perused the documents that Colling had handed him, then asked, "You really have a run-in with the *Polizei*?"

"I never heard of no "po-leets-eye," replied Colling, "But I do know the Kraut cops are looking for me."

The PFC laughed and made some comment to the other soldiers about "Fresh Meat," and then invited Colling to climb aboard. The timing was fortunate, because the train began rolling just as Colling pulled himself up onto the flatbed. A moment later, Colling had climbed into the bed of one of the big trucks with the other soldiers. He found himself sitting on a stack of cartons containing canned goods. One of the other men said, "Rations. We take 'em in every week. Russians don't let us buy food from their zone."

During their journey across the American Zone, Colling was asked why the German police were after him, and he spun a tale of having had some kind of misunderstanding with a woman on the railway platform. He thought she was a prostitute, and he must have said something she did not like, because she started screaming. The policemen who responded to her cries tried to take him into custody, and he resisted. One of the officers was knocked down, whereupon he decided not to wait around to see what would happen next. He ran out of the station and out onto the tracks, where he evaded them until they finally stopped chasing him. A little while later, he saw the train with the U.S. vehicles, and decided to try and hitch a ride.

The PFC's name was Hazeltine, and he was amused by the ignorance that Colling was displaying. He began trying to teach Colling some German phrases, which Colling dutifully mispronounced; ultimately declaring that he did not care to learn how to talk to a bunch of "damned Nazis," after which he said he was going to sleep the rest of the way to Berlin. He rolled over and wrapped himself in his overcoat

The train jolting to a stop woke Colling. The track was lit by floodlights, and when Colling peeked out from under the canvas cover, he saw groups of Russian soldiers on either side, most of them carrying their round-drummed submachine guns. An American captain, with the first lieutenant and first sergeant whom Colling had watched earlier at his side, was talking to a Russian officer. It appeared to Colling that the conversation was growing heated.

Hazeltine said, "Fucking Commies. The bastards do everything they can to keep us from going through their territory, even though we got the God-damned right to do it!"

One of the other soldiers commented, "Word is, they want to isolate Berlin so's we'll have to get out."

"Well," said Hazeltine, "If they do, we'll kick their asses. Truman ain't gonna let them get away with it."

Colling was about to voice his doubts that the American occupation forces, which were sorely depleted in both manpower and equipment, could kick as much ass as Hazeltine thought, but he checked himself. Instead, he mumbled his agreement with the PFC's opinion.

The argument between the American officers and the Russians was ultimately won by the Soviets, and the first sergeant began barking orders for all the American personnel to leave the train and form up in ranks. Colling left his canvas bag in the truck and took a place behind Hazeltine in the formation.

Two Russian officers strode arrogantly down the ranks of Americans, scowling darkly. They refrained from confronting anyone individually or touching them, but it was clear to Colling that it would not take much for the situation to escalate into a physical confrontation. Colling's palms were moist, and his insides were churning with tension, so that he breathed a silent sigh of relief when the pair of Russians completed their quasi-inspection of the U.S. troops, and they were ordered to re-board the train.

He had his foot on the railway car's step when he felt a hand on his shoulder. He turned to find the first sergeant behind him. "Who the hell are you, soldier?" the sergeant asked.

"Brown, Sergeant. William Brown."

Hazeltine was beside the sergeant, "He's a new guy, Sarge. I checked his orders, and he's on his way to Berlin."

"Hazeltine," said the sergeant, "It is no God-damned wonder that you are a PFC with six years in the service. This man should *not* be on this convoy."

"Yeah, Sarge. But he got into a fray with the *Polizei*, and they would have picked him up if he'd tried to get on a passenger train. Besides, what are we gonna do, leave him here in the middle of Commie-land?"

The sergeant growled with frustration at what Hazeltine had done, then looked at Colling and said, "Get your ass up on that train."

Colling put on a suitably chastised expression and said, "Right, First Sergeant."

The convoy train was stopped twice more before they reached their destination. Each time, all the U.S. troops were forced to de-train and form up to be glared at by Russian officers. None of the Soviets asked Colling for identification, so that he was confident that his passage was probably going un-noticed. As the sun was com-ing up, Hazeltine woke him from a deep sleep and handed him a sandwich and a bottle of Coca Cola. When Colling offered to pay, the PFC was overjoyed when Colling pulled out U.S. dollars and gave him two singles.

Their final stop was a rail terminal in the British Sector of Berlin. As an added form of harassment, the Soviets were forcing American rail traffic to detour northward and link with the line running from the British Zone into Berlin, alleging that the tracks directly into the American Sector were still in the process of being repaired, after two years of occupation. At the British railway yard, the trucks were unloaded from the flatcars and the convoy drove into the American Sector of the city.

Colling asked Hazeltine to let him know when they were close to where his new unit was quartered, and the PFC banged on the back of the truck's cab to signal the driver that they should stop at a particular intersection, then nudged Colling's shoulder and told him he was there. Hazeltine pointed across the street as he handed him his canvas bag and wished him well.

As soon as the convoy was out of sight, Colling strolled until he saw a post office. He asked the clerk whether there was a telephone directory available, and was directed to a counter on the other side of the room. What served as a directory was a battered stack of mimeographed pages that had been bound together with string. It was secured by a wire fixed to the counter, undoubtedly in order to keep the makeshift volume from being purloined.

Colling began leafing through the pages, and was pleased when he saw that there were a few pages devoted to an index of businesses. He located the category for taxicabs, then ran his finger down the list, looking for the name Breitmann. There was no listing, but there was one for "Taxi Service H.B.," and Colling decided to take a chance that the listed number was the one he was looking for. He wrote it down and then bought some tokens from the post office clerk. He was directed to a booth, where he placed the call.

The telephone was answered by Helga Breitmann, whom Colling had last spoken to in Lübeck, eight months' previously. He had been willing to wager that she would not recognize his voice, but the woman fairly chirped with pleasure when he said, "Helga, this is Jerry."

"Ah, Jerry! It is wonderful to hear your voice!"

"How goes it with Hermann?" asked Colling.

"Good, very good. Where are you? Are you in Berlin?"

"For sure. Give me the address where you are."

"I can have Hermann come and fetch you," said Helga.

"Neh," said Colling. "I will find you."

Helga gave him the address, pointing out that it was a garage. Colling asked the post office clerk for directions, and then set out on foot. Nearly an hour later, he had turned into a narrow street of older buildings that seemed to have escaped serious war damage, and saw the sign, "Garage H.B." hanging over the street.

When he walked through the open double doors, he saw Helga seated at a desk towards the rear of the place. She was speaking on the telephone and writing on a note-pad, and Colling gathered that she was acting as a dispatcher for their taxi business. The garage contained four automobiles parked side-by-side, one of which had its hood up. A man in coveralls was leaning into its engine compartment, engrossed in something, and paid no attention to Colling's arrival.

Helga, however, seemed to be waiting for him. She jumped up from her chair as he approached and took Colling's hands in hers. She looked him up and down, and her first words were, "You have been reduced in rank?"

Colling laughed, "You may say so. Do you have somewhere that I may wash?"

She directed him up a flight of stairs behind her desk, explaining that he should help himself, that she could not leave the telephone unattended.

The Breitmanns' apartment took up more than half the upper floor of the garage, providing a spacious accommodation in the ruins of Berlin. The furniture was worn, but looked expensive, and Colling guessed that the various pieces had been salvaged or purchased from their prior owners at distress prices. Colling found the bathroom and used a wet washcloth to scrub off the grime that had accumulated during his journey. He brushed off his uniform, which had remained fairly clean under his overcoat. There were empty coat hangers on a hook behind one of the doors, and he hung the coat and uniform jacket on them.

Colling intended to ask Helga if she had any civilian clothes that would fit him, and was debating whether to return to the garage to pose the question, when Hermann came through the door and grabbed him in a bear hug. The German was shorter than Colling, but heavier, and the wind was momentarily squeezed out of Colling's lungs before he was released and Hermann stepped back, and greeted him, "My friend! It is so good to see you once again!"

"It has been a long time," said Colling, adding, "It seems it goes good with you."

"Very good," said Hermann. "The taxi business is good. I have six autos now. Sadly, I have only two drivers other than myself. Helga handles the calls."

"And your own mechanic, I see," said Colling.

"Ach, yes. He is very competent. But I have to pay him a fortune," replied Hermann, then after a pause, "What brings you to Berlin? I see you are yet a soldier."

"Yes. I come for the same reason I came to Poland, to save a young woman from the hands of the Reds."

The revelation of Colling's mission sobered Hermann, and the German asked, "She is this Elizabeth woman that was in Poland?"

"Neh," said Colling, "Another, a German woman. Elizabeth

has gone to the States many months ago, and I have no word from her."

Hermann frowned, "So sad. She was a great beauty."

"Yes," replied Colling, "She is a great beauty, but this German woman I have come for, whose name is Veronika, is herself a beauty."

Hermann smiled and nudged Colling's shoulder, "Ach, you can find them, my friend. What is it that you are called now?"

"You may, for now, use the name 'Bill Brown,' a private soldier newly-come to Berlin."

This elicited a sly grin from the German, who said, "No longer 'Jerry' then?"

"No," said Colling, "And if I may borrow some civilian clothes, I may be someone else. Perhaps someone of your creation."

"Pole or German?"

"German, not a Pole," replied Colling.

"It can be done," said Hermann. "Papers are easily manufactured these days, but the Russkies are hard to fool."

Colling explained that he had information that the woman he was seeking was being held in an apartment house at the address that Quarles had provided. He added that the MVD was thought to have given false intelligence, and it would be necessary to attempt to verify whether Veronika was, in fact, at that location.

Hermann surprised him when he declared that he was familiar with the place, which was in one of the few intact blocks of structures in the city. A German bureaucrat with the city utility department lived in the building immediately adjacent. Three days a week, the man was required to go to Spandau, and he was regularly scheduled with Taxi Service H.B. for a cab to pick him up in the mornings and bring him home at night on those days.

Of greater interest, Hermann said that the man had once revealed that he had hidden his wife and two daughters from the Russians when the city fell to the Russians. He had used an underground passageway connecting the cellars of the two apartment houses. The tunnel had been built after Berlin began to be bombed, both as an escape route and a shelter. Hermann's passenger had found a way to block it up so that when the Red Army came, their soldiers had not discovered it was there. The man found it amusing that the connection still existed, unknown to the Russians who were using the building next door to house their officers.

The next day, Colling, in German clothes, and wearing a cap marking him as a taxi driver, had Hermann drive him around the streets in the vicinity of his objective. If stopped, their story would be that Hermann was training him to drive the cab. There were few people seeking transportation in the Russian Sector, but one Russian officer did wave them down, and they delivered him to an address that had been written on a scrap of paper. The Russian attempted no conversation, and Colling was convinced that the man did not speak German. Despite this, Hermann and Colling refrained from conversation during the drive.

When they arrived at the Soviet officer's destination, he gave Hermann twice too many occupation marks, and strolled off. Hermann remarked that the Red Army men had pockets-full of the currency, and Colling told him that Roosevelt's government, ideologically captivated by "Uncle Joe" Stalin, had made a gift of the printing plates for the occupation money to the USSR, which had proceeded to run its presses day and night to make the stuff. If it were not for the U.S. treasury propping up their value, the bills would be worthless.

They made three passages down the street on which the apartment house where Veronika was supposed to be was located. To Colling's eye, the entire area seemed to be under surveillance by men posted at strategic but inconspicuous locations. A large furniture truck with an enclosed rear compartment had been parked in the same place, across from the building, every time they drove by. On their third trip, Colling took a closer look at the lettering on the side of the truck, and saw that the center of the "O" in *"Grostler und Vecht, Möbelhändleren"* was actually a peep-hole.

It was clear that the address was being watched, and that a trap had been laid, but Colling still did not know whether Veronika was actually being used as bait. He asked Hermann how difficult it would be to cross into the Soviet Sector at night, and the German informed him that the Russians had a curfew, and any civilian motor traffic would be immediately stopped. But then Hermann smiled and said, "Of course, a motorcar full of Russkies could pass without interference."

"Where would one find Red Army uniforms," asked Colling.

"They are available," said Hermann. "You would be surprised at what the Russkies will trade for American cigarettes and home-made vodka."

"And have you made such trades?" asked Colling.

"A few times," said Hermann, another sly smile on his face. "American soldiers use cigarettes to pay for cab rides, especially in the week before they are paid. I, not a smoker, have used the cigarettes to obtain many things from Red Army men, including their clothing. And, in the cellar of the ruined building behind my garage, there is an alcohol still in which potato peels and other things are made into something like vodka."

Colling smiled, "You will be known as the Al Capone of Berlin."

"Ach, so," replied Hermann, "I have heard of this man. Was he not the subject of a film?"

"Many films," said Colling. "Where do you get the potato peels? I would think they would cost dearly in this city."

"The Amis," replied Hermann, and then catching himself, he continued, "Beg pardon, Jerry...that is, Bill, I sometimes forget that you are American."

"It matters not. So the U.S. Army sells you their kitchen waste?"

"True," said Hermann. "When I arrived last year, I found that the Americans were not receiving a fair price, and I offered more. I must also make a gift of a bottle of French Cognac to a certain NCO each month, but I have the contract. It has been beneficial to all concerned."

Colling returned to Hermann's original statement regarding Russian uniforms, "And so you have obtained Red Army dress in these trades?"

"For sure. It comes in handy when some friends of mine wish to conduct business at night in the Eastern Sector. I, of course, charge a rental fee for this clothing."

"Might I borrow such a uniform?" asked Colling.

"For you, Bill, anything. Myself and Helga will always be in your debt for bringing us out of Poland."

While it would be extremely dangerous to do so, Colling wanted to make an attempt to verify that Veronika was being held where Quarles' source had said she was. He gambled that if he were to enter the apartment house next door in the early hours of the morning, it would be more likely that any MVD personnel on duty would be less alert.

His inability to speak Russian was his greatest weakness, but Hermann insisted in accompanying him, and advised that if they both spoke Polish, and used a few words of Russian, that they could pass as conscripted "volunteer" Poles. In Hermann's earlier late-night forays into the Soviet Sector he had been taught or picked up a few basic Russian phrases. He proceeded to teach these to Colling. Helga turned out to be Hermann's resident forger. First she used a camera to photograph Colling and Hermann in uniform, and then she typed out two Red Army identity cards, to which she stapled their likenesses. She admitted that the result was crude, but felt it might pass muster if examined at night by flashlight.

Hermann suggested they use a motorcycle and sidecar as their transportation. When Colling inquired where they would find one, the German led Colling to a dark corner of his garage and pulled a tarpaulin off a DKW *Wehrmacht* model that had been repainted Red Army brown. Hermann remarked that its markings were facsimiles of the real thing. Several large baskets were nearby, filled with bottles which Hermann indicated were vodka that they would take with them. They would be simulating a pair of soldiers out to sell some bootleg liquor they had managed to bring in from their Polish homeland. Colling recognized the labels as a popular brand in Poland, and Hermann said he had them made up by a printer friend. He added that there would be no moon in two nights, and that they would go at that time.

CHAPTER 18

FEBRUARY, 1948

Colling was on edge, bundled into the sidecar beside Hermann, who was speeding through the deserted streets at two in the morning. Whether it was his friend's driving or the nature of their mission was open to debate. He was supposed to use the name "Casimir" which was the one on his identity card, and Hermann was to be called "Gregor" they were both Polish conscripts, privates in a Red Army engineering outfit. Colling kept mentally repeating the information on the ID card, hoping that he would not forget it, or the elementary Russian on which Hermann had drilled him that afternoon.

As it was, they encountered only a single Russian military truck, and waved a greeting to the men in its cab. Later, they went by a duo of Russian MPs riding in an American jeep that now displayed red stars and Russian lettering. The military policemen paid them no heed, and Colling and Hermann stared straight ahead as they passed.

Hermann cut the engine on the motorcycle and they pushed it into an alley between the skeletal remains of some buildings two blocks from their destination. The German suggested they each carry two bottles of the vodka inside their coats. When Colling noted that one of Hermann's was only partially full, the German replied that it might be useful if it looked as if he had been drinking his own wares.

They quietly approached the apartment house adjacent to the address that Quarles had provided, and Hermann led Colling through a narrow alley and down a short flight of steps to a door leading to its basement. The German slipped a pry bar from inside his overcoat and used it to force the lock. A moment later, they were inside the cellar. Colling immediately realized that he had no idea how to find his way to the tunnel that Hermann's acquaintance had spoken of, when the German whispered at him. In the light of a small flashlight, Hermann was examining a crudely-drawn diagram of the cellar.

Colling asked, "Where have you gotten this?"

"One of my associates in the vodka business was kind enough to buy it from the man who lives in this place."

"Yes, but what excuse did your friend give for wanting such a map?" asked Colling, concerned that someone making such an inquiry might have been compromised them.

"Do not be concerned," said Hermann, "My associate said he wished to store liquor there, and gave the man a couple of bottles of this so-called vodka, as well as some money."

They followed the floor plan until they arrived at the place where the tunnel was supposed to be. All that Colling saw was a brick wall, but he followed Hermann to a corner where a large boiler appeared to have been installed flush against the cellar's wall. The pipes running out of it into the ceiling had been disconnected, and there was a crude sign hanging over the firebox door that said, "*Nicht in Ordnung*," Hermann pushed aside the sign and opened the firebox. After poking his head inside and scanning the interior, he crawled through. Colling followed, and saw that there was an opening in the boiler's plate-iron side which provided an entrance into a tunnel high enough for Colling to stand upright.

Using Hermann's flashlight, they walked along the passageway until they reached another similar opening. When they crawled through, they found that they were in another boiler situated like the first. They crawled out of its firebox door, and were in the cellar of the apartment building where Veronika was said to be held.

From this point, they had no diagram to guide them, but as they made their way through the underground corridors, Hermann seemed to make the right choices when they came to intersections, and it did not take long before they saw steps leading upward. Hermann went first, and when he reached a door at the top of the stairs, he motioned for Colling to stop, then to follow cautiously. A second or two later, the two of them were in a hallway that Colling surmised was at the rear of the building. Hermann pointed towards a staircase, and they tiptoed forward. As they were about to round the banister and begin climbing, they heard a snort, and turned to see a man next to the front door, sleeping in a chair that he had tipped back onto the wall behind him. He had been half-hidden in the shadows.

Hermann held his finger to his lips, and they quietly continued upwards. Quarles' information was that Veronika was a prisoner in apartment number six, on the second floor. When they reached the landing, they were both crouching, and Hermann quickly glanced around the corner into the corridor. When the German turned back towards Colling, he was holding his hand up, gesturing for silence. He leaned close to Colling's ear and whispered that there was a guard outside number six. Colling crept forward to see for himself. There was a soldier in a blue-trimmed MVD uniform seated in a chair, his head lolling back, a cigarette dangling from his hand.

Colling was startled when Hermann stood up. The German tiptoed into the hall, and Colling decided he had no choice but to follow. When they were a few feet from the MVD man, Hermann coughed, awakening him. The soldier had half-drawn his pistol when he saw that Hermann was smiling and holding up a bottle of vodka. Hermann began speaking slurred Polish, using a few Russian words, acting as if he had had too much to drink himself. Colling gathered that Hermann was explaining that they had been admitted to the building by the guard downstairs, who had suggested that his comrade on the upper floor might want to purchase some bootleg alcohol. The MVD man stood and pulled out a roll of military currency, and peeled off several bills, which he exchanged for the bottle Hermann was holding.

Smiling and nodding his head, Hermann pointed to the door of the apartment and in a combination of Polish and pidgin Russian, asked if anyone inside might want a drink. After taking a swig of vodka, the Russian sneered and speaking Polish told him that there was no one there. He thought it foolish that they should be guarding an empty room, but orders were orders. The MVD man took another long swallow before adding that the higher-ups had some idea that the Americans might come and try to free the imaginary person who was supposed to be in the room. If they did so, he was looking forward to shooting them.

Hermann and Colling played the part of foreign draftees into the Red Army, displaying just the right amount of subservience, wishing the soldier a pleasant night, thanking him profusely, as they backed away towards the stairs. The sleeping guard on the ground floor was still leaning back in his chair and snoring. Colling held his breath when Hermann crept close to the man and set his partially-empty bottle of vodka next to him.

Once they were in the tunnel, Hermann laughed and said that if the two MVD soldiers bothered to have a discussion in the morning, with any luck, they would wonder whether their recollections of how they obtained the vodka were accurate.

Now that he knew where Veronica was not, Colling began pondering how he could find out where she was. He voiced his frustration to the Breitmanns over breakfast the following morning, and Helga mentioned the name "Melchner" to Hermann, who nodded his head in agreement, then promised Colling he would attempt to discover Veronika's location.

Colling had delayed retrieving Friedrich from the stockade since his arrival in Berlin. He put on his private's uniform and false eyeglasses, and with the documents that Quarles had prepared, had one of Hermann's drivers take him to the American military prison facility for Berlin. Assuming the self-important air of a low-ranking soldier sent to run an errand for his superiors, he strolled into the reception area and handed the release orders to the sergeant manning the desk. Colling was surprised when he had to wait less than ten minutes before an MP came out leading a tall, thin man by the arm. He was wearing a threadbare gray German Army overcoat and carrying a bundle of his belongings. The MP pointed in Colling's direction, and when the man approached, Colling pretended to consult a notepad before brusquely asking, "You Fryed-rich...uh... Shon-berg?"

The man said that he was, correctly pronouncing his name, Colling ordered, "Come with me," before striding away. Friedrich followed, and once they were outside, Colling motioned towards the waiting taxi. He allowed Friedrich to climb in first, and then slid into the rear seat beside him. In the confines of the automobile, Colling experienced the odor emanating from the man. A mixture of unwashed woolen clothing, sweat, dirt and other unpleasant substances; Colling had smelled it on German POW's he had once had to interview. And on more than one occasion, he had to admit that it would have come from his own person.

Colling spoke German when he said, "I am a friend of your sister, Veronika,"

Friedrich stared wide-eyed for a moment, no believing what he was hearing, and then he said, "My sister? For truth, you know Veronika?"

"Yes," said Colling, deciding that he would leave the news of their betrothal for later. "She was at the home of your parents, in Munich, when we met."

"My father and mother, how are they?" asked Friedrich.

"Well enough," said Colling. "They have been concerned about you, but now that you are safe, they will have less worry. Do you have any news of Willi?"

"Sadly, no. I last saw him just before I was captured. But he was in good health then."

"And you?" asked Colling.

"Better than many others," replied Friedrich. "Because I could speak Russian, I was spared much of the hard labor and was put to work as an interpreter. The Russians even wanted me to become a Communist."

"Did you?" asked Colling.

"I went to their indoctrinations, and I spouted the words that they wanted to hear, but no, I did not become one of them. Your German is excellent, you know."

"Thank you. Do you know why you were released?"

"No. It came suddenly. I think it was somewhere in the Urals, but the camp could have been anywhere. About two weeks ago, I was told I was going home. They put me on a train, and here I am."

"Did others come with you?" asked Colling.

"No. But...somewhere along the way, six more of my kind were loaded into the boxcar. They were all full of Red slogans, saying that they had seen the light, and were going home to work for a Socialist Fatherland," said Friedrich. He had been looking out the window of the taxi, taking in the city's devastated landscape, and he added, "It seems there will be more than enough to do to rebuild any sort of Fatherland."

Friedrich had confirmed what Colling had been led to suspect. Veronika's brother had been repatriated specifically in order to draw her into Berlin and the hands of the MVD. Quarles' speculation that the kidnapping was part of a scheme to catch "The Pole" seemed to be accurate. It was comforting to know that the Soviets had laid their trap, and that he knew enough to avoid being caught, but the knowledge did nothing to allay his anxiety about Veronika.

Helga made a face when Colling introduced Friedrich, and ordered *Herr* Schönenberg to go upstairs and get out of his filthy clothes and bathe. When he was done, he was to bring his rags down so that she might burn them. Colling followed Friedrich as he climbed to the apartment, and as soon as the German had gone into the bathroom, Colling changed out of Brown's uniform and into civilian clothes. Just as he finished, Helga arrived and flurried around until she had laid out a clean set of clothes on a chair in the living room. She left mumbling that she had not expected so tall a man, hoping that the trousers were not too short.

Colling found food in the kitchen and prepared a meal for himself and Friedrich. As the German wolfed down everything Colling offered him, punctuating each mouthful with sighs of pleasure, Colling told him that he was to be known to Friedrich as "Bill Brown." The Breitmanns, who owned the garage, were old friends. He then explained how Veronika had been taken by the Soviets. At this, Friedrich stopped eating, and Colling sought to assure him by saying that he did not believe his sister would be mistreated, and that he was there to free her, if possible.

Friedrich's ability to speak Russian would be of great value, but first they had to find out where Veronika was being held. Hermann Breitmann had contacts in the city that had proven useful, and

Colling hoped that he might be able to use them to shed some light on Veronika's location.

Much to Colling's disappointment, that evening Hermann informed them that he had been unable to learn anything about the abduction of a dark-haired German girl by the Reds. As Colling and Friedrich sat at the dinner table with the Breitmanns, Hermann was apologetic, pointing out that he had had to be extremely cautious in even making such inquiries, fearing that exhibiting an interest would garner unwanted attention.

Working outside Quarles' circle had been Colling's preference from the time that he had come to suspect that the intelligence officer's operations were subject to being compromised. But his situation seemed desperate, and that after considering his options, Colling decided that it was time to see if Quarles had any contacts that could help find Veronika.

As Private William Brown, Colling visited the Signal Corps detachment and said that he had a dispatch for Major Wilkins from Lieutenant Colonel Quarles. Wilkins turned out to be a thin man, graying at the temples. His demeanor spelled "Regular Army." When the NCO who had ushered Colling into his office had left them alone, he immediately asked Colling, a hint of suspicion in his voice, "What does Colonel Quarles have for me?"

"I'm working for Colonel Quarles, sir. He said you were to be my contact in Berlin. I was wondering whether he had sent any messages for "Private William Brown," or "Jan," or some other name?"

Wilkins unlocked a drawer in his desk and brought out a small envelope of the kind used to hold wedding invitations or cards of condolence. The major glanced at it, and then said, "This one's for 'J.C.' I thought it might be for Jesus Christ, but Quarles knows He's not at this address. Might you be 'J.C.' by any chance?"

"Yessir. Sorry, but I can't say what the initials stand for."

"I understand," said Wilkins, handing over the envelope. "The code for the pick-up was 'Bill Brown,' who would fit your description. Good luck."

"Thank you, sir. I hope to be in touch again in a few days for a ride out of here."

"I'll be saying a prayer that I'll hear from you," said Wilkins, standing and stretching out his hand to Colling.

The message from Quarles was handwritten and said simply, "Treffigshof Müggelsee." Colling guessed that a lake was involved because of the use of *See* in the second word. When he showed the note to Helga, he was proven correct. She informed him that the message must refer to one of the villa's on the north shore of the Gross Müggelsee, a large lake southeast of the city.

Friedrich was familiar by reputation with the Müggelsee, but admitted he had little knowledge about the large estates that lined its northern shore. When Hermann arrived home, he was able to be of somewhat greater help. He said he had had occasion to take passengers to the Müggelsee district, almost all of them Russian officers who were using the area's large houses, at least those that had escaped bomb and shell damage, as recreational facilities. Hermann also believed that there were some high-ranking Soviets quartered in a few of the mansions. He promised that the following day, he would make a trip to the lake and find out which of them was the Treffigshof. In the meantime, suggested Hermann, Colling might wish to have a look at the pre-war street map of Berlin and its suburbs that was in his desk downstairs. When Hermann identified the Treffigshof, they could mark its location.

While waiting for Hermann to return, Colling perused the map that Helga had pulled from the desk in the garage, but thoughts of a plan of action to free Veronika kept him from concentrating. He was pleased when Friedrich went off to take a long nap, seeming to sense that Colling wanted to be left to himself. By late afternoon, Colling had decided that the first step he would have to take would be to conduct a reconnaissance of the Treffigshof.

Hermann used a pencil to make an "X" at the spot where he believed that the former mansion of the Treffig family was located. When Colling asked him how he could be certain, the German smiled and said, "All of these places have Russkie sentries at their gates. It was necessary only to say that I had been summoned to provide a ride to an officer at the Treffigshof in order to receive directions to the place."

Colling announced that it would be necessary for him to look over the estate himself, and that he must go alone. He asked Hermann if he could spare one of his taxis, and the garage owner said that he would not advise it, recommending instead that he give Colling the use of the DKW motorcycle. Hermann explained that the cycle would be easier to hide if Colling had to go on foot to explore the grounds surrounding the house.

When Colling protested that his inability to speak Russian would be fatal if he were stopped wearing a Soviet uniform and riding a Red Army motorcycle, Hermann laughed and said that all that would be necessary was to paint over the military brown and attach new license tags.

The task of using a brush to apply a coat of dull black paint to the DKW fell to Colling, while Friedrich put his hand to changing the numbers on a civilian motorcycle tag that Hermann produced from somewhere. By morning, the vehicle had a suitably shabby appearance, calculated to reduce the chance that some Russian soldier would decide to confiscate it. Helga gave him a Berlin driver's license and other identity papers that she said would appear to be more genuine than the Red Army documents she had manufactured two nights previously.

Hermann loaded two wicker baskets into the sidecar. One was full of bottles of home-made vodka with fancy Polish labels, the other had two bottles of real French Cognac from Hermann's storeroom, along with more vodka. Colling's story would be that he was delivering the liquor to a Soviet officer's hostel on the lakeshore. Hermann assured him that it was considered one of the costs of doing business for boot-legers to use a bottle of vodka here and there as a bribe, but that he should not be too generous. A full bottle to an officer or NCO, and another for private soldiers to share was the going rate.

When Hermann finished his instructions, Colling gently reminded him that he had also been in the Mercedes when they had crossed Poland together a year before, and he had not forgotten how they had facilitated their journey with gifts of liquor at Red Army checkpoints.

It had been a year since Colling had ridden a motorcycle, an old Zündapp which had served its purpose in Poland, but he quickly adapted to the handling characteristics of the DKW. He found it to have more power than either the Zündapp or the little Indian motorcycle on which he had learned to ride as a teenager in Wisconsin.

The lake district was on the far outskirts of Berlin, at a distance greater than Colling had visualized. Once he was beyond the city proper, he found himself riding through stretches of woodland where patches of snow remained on the ground. He was sharing the road exclusively with Russian military traffic, and he waved and smiled at the occupants of the trucks.

Colling encountered his first checkpoint at a place that seemed to have been selected at random. The bored guards looked at his papers, and asked where he was going. Using the pidgin Russian that Hermann had taught him, along with a lot of gestures, Colling got it across that he was taking a delivery of vodka to one of the officer's hostels on the lake. When one of the soldiers asked, "Which one?" Colling shook his head and used a phrase Herman had told him to memorize, "Your honor, I am not permitted to say." When the man smiled, Colling reached under the blanket covering the baskets and pulled out a bottle of vodka, which he held up before handing over. He was told to go about his business, and when he rounded the next curve, he discovered the reason for the roadblock: An entire town that appeared to have been converted into some sort of Red Army headquarters. Its streets were packed with military vehicles and men in uniform. Colling did not pass un-noticed by the occupants of the place, many of whom stared at the civilian motorcycle in their midst, but no one made any move to stop him.

There was another checkpoint on the way out, and he had to repeat the process of bribing the soldiers who were manning it. He was not stopped again, and when he turned east to skirt the lake on its northern side, he began to notice that there were gates and gatehouses every few hundred meters, clearly marking the entrances to the lakeside estates. Most had one or two armed Russian sentries who watched him as he rode past. Following Hermann's directions, it was easy to pick out the gatehouse belonging to the Treffigshof. There were two Red Army men in front of a closed iron gate, and as Colling went by, the fact that they were not MVD troops surprised him.

The guards watched him until he was around a slight curve in the road, and when Colling was confident that they could no longer see him, he found a place that was bare of snow, so as to leave no tire tracks, and pulled the motorcycle off into the trees. He had placed himself on the side of the highway opposite to that of the Treffigshof estate. While he would have to run across the highway, he would avoid being observed bringing the DKW out of the forest bordering the estate.

He waited behind a tree for a few moments, listening for the sound of engines, and when he heard nothing, he dashed, crouching, across the road and into the tangled brown underbrush on its other side. A few meters into the woods, he encountered a high stone wall. Colling walked parallel to the wall until he found a place where a sapling provided a way for him to climb over. Before doing so, he stood perfectly still for a minute or two, listening intently. When he heard nothing but wind blowing through the bare branches above his head, he scaled the wall.

The stand of trees and undergrowth on the other side extended for a depth of forty or fifty meters until they gave way to what had once been a broad lawn surrounding the mansion. The grass was now brown with the winter's cold. Colling spotted a fallen tree on its edge, and crawled until he was hidden behind it. For awhile, there was no movement, and then two soldiers appeared, walking side-by-side about fifty meters from Colling, rifles slung over their shoulders. They were talking, paying no attention to where Colling was hidden, and Colling had the impression that they were walking a perimeter, perhaps because of laziness, keeping somewhat closer to the house than they were supposed to.

Colling continued to observe the mansion for over an hour,

during which he saw movement at the windows, and watched as Red Army men came and went. At one point, a man whom Colling guessed was an NCO, came out into the gravel driveway in front of the house and started shouting, at which twenty men, at Colling's count, rushed from the house and fell into formation. The NCO appeared to call roll, which he then followed with a harangue that lasted for several minutes, after which he dismissed the soldiers, who all trotted back into the house.

There was no sign of the blue piping that the MVD used to trim their uniforms, and Colling was beginning to have serious doubts that Quarles' information was accurate, when he saw a familiar pale face framed by dark tresses appear at one of the windows on the third floor. Even at a distance, he recognized Veronika. Satisfied with the results of his reconnaissance, he crept back the way he had come, searching mentally for the means by which he might get inside the Treffigshof.

In addition to the two road blocks, Colling was also stopped by a pair of Russians riding in a Soviet-style jeep. Whether these particular Red Army men pulled him over at random, or whether they were charged with checking the papers of all civilians, Colling did not know. What he quickly realized was that they were as susceptible to being bribed with vodka as the others he had encountered.

The guards at the checkpoints expected to receive a second bribe when he passed through on his return, so that he had had to expend six bottles of vodka as the price of his expedition. He noticed that while he had been stopped at one of the checkpoints, two Red Army vehicles were allowed to drive through unmolested.

When he sat down with his companions that evening, Colling had not fully formulated his plan of action. He had decided that an approach to the estate in Russian uniform perhaps held the greatest promise of success, but he was not sure what further ruse might be most likely to be accepted by the Soviets guarding the place. He toyed with the idea of making it look like a delivery of supplies was being made, but it was probable that those were scheduled, and arrival of an unexpected load of rations would trigger a response that could prove fatal for himself and anyone with him, as well as for Veronika.

Whatever course of action he settled on, it was becoming clear to Colling that he would need more manpower. He decided that he would have to retrieve Yakov and Malik from their sojourn at the displaced persons camp.

That process proved to be easier than Colling would have predicted. Hermann drove him to the DP facility in his cab late in the afternoon, when it was more likely that the inmates would have returned from work. The place consisted of rows of Quonset-hut style barracks inside a barbed-wire fence. There were no guards or towers, leading Colling to believe that the barrier was intended more to protect its residents than to confine them.

Dressed like a German bureaucrat in a suit and tie, and carrying a briefcase, Colling simply walked into the building with the "Administration" sign and asked the receptionist if he could speak to Yakov Cohen and Malik Kunstler. Colling was questioned as to the purpose of his visit, and he informed the clerk that they were to be offered employment by his company. He was led by a member of the camp's staff to one of the barracks, where the man shouted for Yakov and Malik, who stepped forward from among the rows of bunks that filled the room.

Yakov was about Colling's height, thin and Semitic in appearance, but despite his slight frame, he looked as if he would be formidable in a fight. Malik was big, over six feet and muscular. His blue-eyes suggested that if his head had not been shaven, he would have had blonde hair. Both of them had the hard look about them that Colling had noticed was possessed by some of the SS men at *Stalag S-1*.

Colling motioned for the men to join him outside, where he introduced himself as a friend of Quarles. The two of them acknowledged that they had been sent to Berlin by the intelligence officer, and Colling told them to gather their belongings. In a few minutes, Yakov and Malik returned, each of them burdened down by two bulging U.S. Army duffel bags. With Colling in the lead, they returned to the administrative center, where they were all required to sign documents to verify that the two DPs would be moving to Munich, where they would be employed by a construction company called "Holzbauer, A.G."

In the taxi, Colling asked if they had brought weapons, and Yakov informed him that they were in the duffel bags. During the remainder of their ride to Garage H.B., Colling asked enough questions to determine that Yakov was reasonably fluent in German, while Malik's command of the language was minimal. He also discovered that both of the Russians had more facility with English than with German. The two men openly discussed their service in the Red Army, omitting anything about their personal lives. There was no question in Colling's mind that "Cohen" and "Kunstler" were pseudonyms. He surmised that Yakov was Jewish, so that "Cohen" might be apropos, but he was certain that Malik had not been born with a German surname, like Kunstler.

Colling was unsure how Yakov and Malik would react to Friedrich and Hermann, so he spoke English when he asked their opinion of Germans. The question caused both of them to become wooden-faced, and it was clear to Colling that their war-time experience had left them with little, if any, tolerance for their former enemies. Friedrich's role in the rescue would be crucial, and Colling was determined that the members of his team be able to set aside any grudges if they were to function effectively. He asked, "Did Colonel Quarles tell you what this mission is about?"

Yakov answered, "The Colonel has told us we are to come to Berlin to help someone escape from the Bolsheviks. He does not say who this is."

"It's a woman, a German woman, who is employed by the Colonel. Will you be able to help me to free a German woman, or does the fact that she is German keep you from doing your job?"

The two Russians looked at one another for a moment, then Yakov said, "We are here to serve Colonel Quarles. He has promised to us that if we work for him for two years, that we can go to the States. We will do what you ask us to do."

"You will have to work with the woman's brother, who was in the *Wehrmacht*. He speaks Russian, so it is possible that he interrogated

Russian POWs. Will you be able to work with him?"

Malik spoke, "Vas he in de SS?"

"No," said Colling. "The army. He was a supply sergeant. Even though he was educated and from the upper class, the Nazis would not make him an officer. They considered him politically unreliable because his father helped some Jews escape from Germany before the war."

At this, Yakov exclaimed, "Is this so? Are you speaking the truth? This German you speak of helps Jews?"

"Yes," said Colling, "All true. And this man driving this taxi, who is also a friend, spent the war in Poland, not serving either Germany or Russia."

"I vill be able to serve as you ask," replied Malik, and Yakov nodded his head and agreed that he could do so as well.

Despite their stated willingness to work with Friedrich, both the Russians warily eyed Veronika's brother when Colling introduced them to him. Colling asked Friedrich to converse with Yakov and Malik in Russian, and that afterwards, he would want each of them to comment about their respective linguistic abilities.

Surprisingly, all three men were in accord that Friedrich's Russian was most like that of an educated Muscovite, while Malik sounded like a farmer, and Yakov, of course, had a Jewish accent. Based on this, Colling decided that Friedrich would be disguised as a Soviet officer and do most of the talking in whatever scenario Colling managed to organize.

His inability to come up with a plausible excuse that would induce the guards at Treffighof to grant access to the mansion prompted Colling to ask Yakov and Malik, who had first-hand experience with the manner in which the Red Army functioned, for their thoughts about a solution to his problem. Yakov pondered for awhile before shrugging his shoulders and admitting that he could think of nothing that had not already been put forward.

Malik was reclining on the couch, listening to Colling as he outlined the situation at the estate, and remained silent while Yakov and Friedrich both interrupted with questions and comments. When there was a pause in the conversation, Malik unexpectedly spoke, "Films."

Everyone looked in Malik's direction and Colling said, "Films?"

"*Da*. Films. Every-ting stop when cinema unit come to show films to soldiers. Iv you go to this place as cinema unit, you get in, and vhen film is showing, you find lady and get avay."

Yakov excitedly concurred, "This is true. In Red Army, showing films is important. Political officers always are showing movies when troops are not in front lines. Everyone has to watch."

Colling was intrigued by the idea, but he could not imagine where they might find Soviet motion pictures, and he said so out loud.

Hermann and Helga had been sitting quietly to one side, watching whoever was speaking, and Colling had assumed that they were unable to understand what was being said, when Hermann interrupted, speaking German, "I know of a place. There is a place where the Soviets show cinema. A club for officers."

The garage owner's intervention made it clear that the man possessed some knowledge of the English language. With greater respect for the man's talents, and his ability to conceal them, Colling asked, "How would we get the films?"

"To steal them would be possible," replied Hermann. He went on to describe where the Russian officer's club was located, and how he knew the Berliner who had been press-ganged into serving as a projectionist for the place. Hermann's friend was unhappy with the arrangement because he was often insulted and ordered about, and paid only a pittance. He was not even allowed to filch any leftovers from the kitchen, or to take home bottles that still had liquor remaining in them.

"We will need a Russian military vehicle," said Colling.

"Easy enough," said Hermann, "My friends in the vodka business have a small truck that has been made to look like a Red Army vehicle that would suit perfectly."

"We cannot guarantee its safe return," said Colling, recalling the various modes of transportation that he had been forced to abandon in Poland.

"If it is purchased, that will not be a problem," replied Hermann, as if he were relying on Colling having the cash to do so, and somehow aware that there was a thousand U.S. dollars sewn into the lining of Colling's canvas bag.

"How much will do?" asked Colling.

"If it is American dollars, two or three hundred, I would say," replied Hermann, "Best to start low, and not to pay too dearly, or it may arouse the interest of the wrong people. I can say that I wish to send a cargo of stolen American coffee and canned meat out of the city, perhaps to Frankfurt an der Oder. It is near the Polish border. Such a journey would carry such risk that it would be necessary to pay a great deal, in case the truck is confiscated."

"So it shall be done," said Colling. "Tomorrow, I shall have the money. For now, Hermann, you shall talk to your projectionist friend and discover all you are able about this officer's club, and where the films and equipment are stored. We shall require not only a projector, but a sound amplifier and loudspeakers."

While the conversation was going on, Colling had noticed that Friedrich was whispering a translation of the German for the benefit of Yakov and Malik. Switching to English, Colling asked, "Anyone here know how to operate a movie projector?"

The blank looks and shrugs told Colling that as far as Friedrich and the two Russians were concerned, the answer was negative. He repeated the question in German, and both Helga and Hermann shook their heads. Colling said, "Well, I guess that leaves me, if the equipment is American."

Friedrich responded, "That is good. If you are the projectionist, you can seem so engrossed in your work that you will not be expected to converse."

"That is true," added Yakov, "In the Red Army, anyone who has technical skills is above common soldiers. You may ignore anyone except officers. 'Look down your nose,' is what you Americans say, is it not?"

Responding to Colling's primary concern, Malik said, "All film machines that I haff seen are from U.S. of A. All to do is to steal from Bolshevik officer club."

The plan had begun to come together in his mind, and Colling outlined how it would be carried out. Hermann would purchase the truck and elicit some precise intelligence regarding the officer's club. Helga would put together four Red Army uniforms. At this, Yakov and Malik informed him that they had uniforms in their luggage, and that the weapons they had brought with them were three PPSh submachine guns, two M44 MN carbines, and several pistols; as well as a supply of ammunition. Yakov volunteered to assist Helga in forging documents and a document that would authorize the cinema unit to visit Treffigshof. As soon as they knew more about the Red Army club, he would figure out a way to purloin some films and projection apparatus.

The purchase of their transportation was arranged for three hundred American dollars. It was after midnight when Hermann drove the truck into his garage and it was hidden under a tarpaulin. The garage owner also had a diagram of the layout of the officer's club, and his friend had assured him that the motion picture equipment and the films were stored in its cellar. The projectionist was not required to work on Mondays, meaning they would have to make their move that night.

There was, however, a serious problem. The place was locked tight, and the streets on all sides of the building were patrolled regularly by armed guards. The schematic drawing of the building included the location of utility lines, which Hermann had thought might be important. When Colling learned that the kitchen was supplied with Berlin municipal gas, he told Hermann that they would have to repaint his oldest taxi with Berlin gas company markings, and obtain some badges or other identification as employees of the *Berliner Gasdienst.*

With four men applying themselves to the task, the transformation of an old Horch taxi into what they hoped would pass as an official city vehicle was rapidly accomplished before Hermann returned from his rounds as a cab driver. When he did, he brought three sets of well-worn blue German workman's uniforms, and after they had eaten supper, he, Colling and Friedrich changed into them. Malik had some experience in working metals, and he had hammered out three shiny metal discs that he had embossed with numbers and the words "Berlin Gas." No one was certain whether the city's gas company employees even used badges, or what they looked like, but Colling hoped that they would not have to undergo much scrutiny. To increase trust, Helga sewed small red stars to the front of the uniforms' slouch caps.

They threw some bags of tools into the trunk of the Horch. Colling kept his left arm inside his jacket, so that the sleeve was hanging empty. Friedrich had tied a stick of wood like a splint to his own right knee, so that he would have to walk with a stiff leg. Suitably disguised as disabled war veterans who had been fortunate enough to regain their pre-war employment, they drove to the officers' club. Hermann was at the wheel, and at Colling's instructions, he accelerated the final two blocks to their destination, so that they arrived with a screeching of brakes.

Brushing past the guard who had come to the curb, Colling dashed up the steps, and pounded on the door, shouting, "Gas leak! Gas leak!" in German at the top of his lungs. Friedrich and Hermann added to the charade by hurriedly retrieving the satchels of tools, and rushing to join him. The door was opened by a Russian soldier wearing a white mess jacket, and when he did not move aside, Friedrich shouted something at him in Russian. This caused the man to turn and retreat rapidly, and Friedrich was holding up his badge and continuing to shout. This resulted in a noisy storm of activity, as uniformed men seemed to come from all directions in a mad rush to find the exit.

Friedrich kept on shouting in Russian, pointing towards the door, directing the crowd outside, while Colling and Hermann located the entrance to the cellar and clambered down the steps. There were two extra canvas tool bags folded inside the one that Hermann was carrying. The projector was in plain sight on a table, and Colling was relieved to see that it had the Bell and Howell label on its case. The amplifier and speakers were not immediately in evidence, but Colling finally spotted them on a lower shelf, and he shoved them into one of the bags.

Hermann had been pulling canisters of film from a shelf and dropping them into the satchel containing the projector. Colling asked if he were done, and the German reached over and pulled the coil of an electrical extension cord from where it was hanging and added it to the stack of round film cans. Each of them carrying two bags, they hurried back to the ground floor, where they found Friedrich standing in the doorway and continuing to give orders alternately in Russian and German. Colling could see into the street, and it was clear that the occupants of the club were all at a distance, most of them continuing to back away.

Colling put his bags on the floor next to Friedrich, and ran into the cellar. He easily located one of the gas lines, and followed it until he found a joint in the pipe. He used the wrench he had been carrying in his belt to loosen the connection until there was a pronounced hissing noise. He backed slowly away and up the steps. At the top of the landing, Colling stopped to light a cigar that Helga had given him from Hermann's humidor. When its tip was glowing brightly, he tossed the cigar half-way down the cellar stairs, and shouting "Fire," at the top of his lungs, he ran towards the building's front door. Hermann and Friedrich beat him out into the street, even though they were burdened with the tool bags, but he was close behind.

The blast threw Colling forward, causing him to stumble as he reached the side of the Horch. Hermann was already at the wheel, and Friedrich was in the front seat with him when Colling threw himself into the back seat. There was a second explosion as they raced away into the night, causing Colling to look back, where he could see figures running in all directions, illuminated by the flames that were pouring from the burning Red Army officers' club.

CHAPTER 19

MARCH, 1948

Curious as to how the explosion and fire might be reported, Colling asked Helga whether there was a newspaper that would carry a story about the event. She suggested instead that he listen to the Berlin station of the American Armed Forces Radio, which usually covered news coming from the Soviet Sector.

According to the AFR announcer, Russian authorities had reported that there had been an attack by reactionary, die-hard Nazi terrorists on a Red Army billet the previous night. Soviet forces had successfully fought off the assassins, killing more than a dozen of them. There had been no casualties among the defending troops, but the billet had been totally destroyed by explosive charges that the attackers had managed to place before being driven off. The explosion had severed gas lines in the area, but Red Army engineers had quickly responded and repaired the damage.

Colling said a silent prayer for the poor souls who would be rounded up and punished for the destruction of the officers' club. He wondered how intensive the investigation would be regarding the three employees of the Berlin gas company who disappeared in the wake of the disaster. If all went well, before the Soviets figured out that piece of the puzzle, Veronika would have been freed, and the team would all be back in American territory. As that thought crossed his mind, however, he remembered that the Breitmanns would be remaining behind in Berlin, subject to retaliation by the MVD if their involvement became known.

At the first opportunity, Colling expressed his concerns to Hermann about his safety and that of his wife. Both the Breitmanns acknowledged that the danger did exist, but Hermann simply said that he would refrain from entering the Soviet Sector, and his drivers would do the same. Hermann explained that for a variety of reasons, they kept pistols in the garage and the apartment, in spite of the American ban on Germans owning firearms. He added that he had hoped that Colling would see that some of the weapons that had been brought in by Yakov and Malik would be left in his care when everyone departed.

Colling had to refer to a calendar to calculate that it had been twenty-four days since Veronika had been kidnapped. In his mind, one day was too long to be in the hands of the Soviets, let alone, more than three weeks.

With everyone gathered around the Breitmann's dining room table, Colling outlined what they would do the following night. He, Friedrich, Yakov and Malik would attempt to gain entrance to Treffigshof as the Red Army cinema unit, timing their arrival for 2000, when it would be fully dark. Friedrich would be an officer, and both of the Russians agreed that he should be wearing the shoulder boards of a senior lieutenant, the highest of the three lieutenant grades in the Soviet forces. They agreed to show Helga how to create a proper set of officer's insignia for him. Colling would pose as a sergeant, fitting for his status as a technician; while Yakov and Malik would be corporals, and would carry the submachine guns.

Malik would have the task of remaining with their truck while the others were occupied inside the mansion. Colling would set up and operate the projector, if they were granted entry, so that the soldiers billeted in the mansion would be giving their attention to the movie screen while Friedrich and Yakov searched the upper floors for Veronika. When they had located her and brought her downstairs, one or the other of them would let Colling know, and he would leave the projector running and get back to the truck.

They would then use the truck to transport the five of them away from the estate. They would be required to pass the two checkpoints, but based on Colling's observation that military vehicles were not stopped, they should be able to drive through without any trouble. Once past the second roadblock, Hermann would be waiting with a car, and they would hide the truck and transfer to the automobile so that the six of them could drive back to the American Sector.

After reviewing everything that *should* happen, Colling began discussing what would have to be done if things did not go as planned. If they were stopped at the gatehouse, they would attempt to overpower the guards there. If that were the case, someone, Yakov or Malik, would be required to remain at the entrance. If they got past the soldiers at the gate, but were stopped when they arrived at the mansion, they must attempt to overpower whoever was barring their way. If there were too many soldiers opposing them, they would be forced to either shoot their way in or retreat. If they were admitted to the house, but then discovered to be imposters, they would have to use whatever force was necessary to effect their escape.

Colling pointed out that anything could go wrong at any time. If the rescue turned into a fiasco, he suggested that everyone run for the woods that bordered the estate and try to get outside the wall. It might be possible to evade capture, but he expressed his belief that the probability of escape in such circumstances would be virtually nil. For Hermann's benefit, he emphasized his strict instruction that the garage owner not wait past 2230. If they had not arrived by then, he was to return immediately to Berlin and save his own skin.

Colling asked if there were any questions, and when no one spoke, he asked if anyone had any doubts or wanted to back out. The answer to his question was written on their faces. Everyone was nodding their assent, and it dawned on Colling that his five companions actually had enough faith in him to believe that they would succeed, and at that moment, he had no doubt that they were ready to risk their lives to follow him.

The motion picture equipment had been loaded into the rear of the truck, and Yakov was conducting a last-minute inspection of everyone's uniforms, when Hermann appeared at Colling's side, a film canister in his hand. He handed it to Colling and suggested that he run it after the first movie that Colling planned to show, a short documentary that Malik had informed Colling was titled *Tank Battle Victory at Kursk*. Colling put Hermann's offering in line as the second reel in his collection of films.

Colling had brought along two other movies which they had

appropriated from the officers' club. According to Malik, the first was about the joy of collective agriculture in the U.S.S.R.; and the second was a long epic about the fall of Berlin. The Russian admitted that number two was a fine color film, but that it glorified Stalin considerably. The one about farming was, in his opinion, extremely boring, except for the scenes where girls dressed in peasant costume were performing dances that required them to swirl their skirts almost to their waists.

With Colling at the wheel of the Red Army truck, they followed Hermann out of Berlin. The garage owner was driving a large touring car that Friedrich informed Colling was called an Audi, and Colling admitted that he had never seen nor heard of that particular make of automobile.

At a suitable clump of trees close to the highway on its right side, Hermann pulled off. Colling watched in the rear-view mirror and saw the Audi's headlights disappear as they were switched off.

As Colling had anticipated, they were waved through both roadblocks without being stopped. Colling smiled, confirmed in his belief that official vehicles and uniforms constituted a passport in totalitarian regimes, always eliciting a certain level of deference and respect, seasoned with a slight amount of fear.

Colling was counting on this when he pulled off the road onto the gravel drive and stopped beside the Treffigshof gatehouse. One of the guards leaned over on Colling's side and said something. Colling nodded in Friedrich's direction, and the German took out a portfolio in which the cinema unit's supposed schedule was contained, and began reading from it. Friedrich's shoulder-boards, and his assertive demeanor, seemed to carry weight with the guards, and one of them went into the gatehouse, where Colling could see he was using a telephone. Just as the soldier finished talking and hung up, Colling was alarmed to see Malik jump down from the rear of the truck, and making a gruff comment, walk off into the bushes behind the gatehouse. A few moments later, he re-emerged, buttoning up his fly, and climbed back into the vehicle. The guard who had made the call waited until Malik was back on board before making a comment to Friedrich, after which he stepped aside and motioned for them to pass.

As soon as they were clear of the entrance, Colling turned to Friedrich and speaking German, said, "What is that fool doing? Stopping to take a piss at such a time!"

Friedrich looked over and replied, "He was cutting the telephone wire. If we are fortunate, there will be no need for someone to use the telephone before we are finished our business."

Colling was chagrined that he had not thought of severing the line, but he admitted, "That is good. I was in error not to think of it."

Friedrich was smiling at him when he said, "You cannot think of everything, my friend. It was Malik who suggested it, just before we began this journey. Perhaps because it is I who am wearing officer's shoulder-boards, he forgets that I am not in charge."

The call from the gatehouse had apparently alerted everyone in the mansion that they were going to be able to view a motion picture, and Colling had to fend off all the hands reaching for the projection equipment. As it was, he had only to carry the projector itself into the house, everything else was being handled by others. Malik took up a position near the truck, his submachine gun slung so that he was holding it across his abdomen, ready for use.

What must have been a ballroom when the Treffigshof had been occupied by its wealthy German owners had been rapidly set up as a makeshift theater, using chairs of all descriptions, and the soldiers were milling about impatiently. Friedrich had apparently called for a bed sheet for use as a screen, and as Colling was unpacking the projector and placing it on a table that had been provided for it, he saw the German standing and directing two Russians as to how it was to be hung.

Some of the Red Army men kept coming over to Colling and speaking to him, and he went about his work, ignoring them with an air of self-importance, occasionally saying, "*Da*" or using a phrase that Friedrich had taught him, "*Odya moment, Tovarich.*" As he was arranging the speakers and stringing the wires to them from the amplifier, he noticed Yakov huddling with some of the men, then leading them outside. In a minute or two, they returned, and Colling could see that the soldiers seemed to be concealing bottles under their uniform blouses. Colling quickly deduced that Yakov was selling some of Hermann's vodka out of the back of the truck.

When he had threaded the Kursk documentary, and was ready, he signaled to Friedrich, who shouted something that caused everyone to look for a place to sit, resulting in what Colling could only describe as a massive game of musical chairs. Friedrich shouted again, and everything became quiet. Someone turned off the lights, and the picture began.

Colling was pleased when nothing went wrong. He stayed close to the projector, watching as Friedrich and Yakov unobtrusively slipped from the room. The movie consisted of multiple shots of T-34 Russian tanks rolling forward or firing, with an occasional grainy scene showing German men and equipment on the march. The musical score was triumphant and inspiring, and the narration, of which Colling could understand not a word, sounded the same way.

That the film was reaching its final minutes was evident to Colling when the screen was filled with pictures of destroyed German Panzers, and the music and the narrator's voice were growing louder and more forceful. The audience of soldiers had been cheering for the Red Army units when they appeared on the screen, and booing when the *Wehrmacht* was on stage, especially whenever a Swastika was shown. As the film progressed, the signs of alcohol consumption had increased, and when the last few feet of film ran through the projector, there was a great deal of boisterous shouting and clapping.

Colling had been holding Hermann's canister in his hand, ready to thread it the moment the first picture ended. Fortunately, someone thought to turn on the lights, and he worked quickly to insert the strip of film through the labyrinth of wheels and sprockets. He finished, but without Friedrich to bring order, all he could do was raise his hand as a signal to extinguish the lights. The motion picture had begun to run before the room was completely dark.

Hermann had provided what was known in the U.S. as a "stag

movie." Two women were slowly removing their clothing as a pair of men clad only in their underwear ogled them. There was a moment of silence from the audience of Red Army men, and then a collective sigh before the catcalls began. Colling's was the only set of eyes that left the screen as the womens' breasts were bared. He was watching the door behind him, anxiously waiting for Friedrich or Yakov to look in.

There was a roar of approval regarding something else that was happening, and Colling guessed that the women must have removed the last of their garments, revealing all. Just as the noise became loudest, the door to the ballroom opened a crack, and Yakov's face appeared. He paused for an instant when he saw what was being shown, but then motioned for Colling to join him. No one seemed to notice as the projectionist left the room.

Friedrich had Veronika bundled into a blanket, and she pulled out of his arms and ran to embrace Colling. He briefly reciprocated, then took her by the hand, hurrying her to the truck. Veronika climbed into the vehicle's rear, followed by Yakov and Malik. Colling slipped behind the wheel, Friedrich into the passenger seat. The truck's engine started immediately, and Colling drove, as quickly as he dared, down the gravel drive leading to the highway.

When they reached the gatehouse, Colling came to a stop, and Friedrich said something to the guards. There seemed to be some controversy, and Friedrich motioned to Colling to go.

There were shouts behind them as Colling pushed the accelerator to the floor, but no gunshots, which Colling took as a good omen.

It seemed like a prudent idea to slow when they reached the first roadblock. Colling was relieved when the guards stood aside and waved to them as they passed. The same thing happened at the second checkpoint, and Colling relaxed, thinking they might actually have succeeded.

Colling found the place where Hermann was waiting, and they transferred to the car. Hermann was driving, Friedrich beside him, Yakov and Malik were in jump seats that had been hidden in the floor, and Colling and Veronika were together in the rear seat.

Malik began to laugh when Hermann pulled the car onto the road. The garage owner drove slowly and carefully, and Colling pulled Veronika into his arms and whispered to her how happy he was to be able to hold her again. He saw that she was crying, and he pressed his hand tighter on her shoulder to calm the shaking that was overtaking her.

Colling was telling Veronika that everything would be fine when Hermann shouted that there was someone behind them. An instant later, Colling heard the popping of a weapon being fired, and there was a "thwock" as something slammed into the back of the Audi. Malik was the first to move. He jumped between Colling and Veronika and used the butt of his PPSh to smash the rear window, and then shoved the muzzle of the gun out and began firing. The vehicle behind them returned fire, and Colling heard more metallic clanks as bullets penetrated the trunk lid.

When the magazine on Malik's submachine gun was empty, he turned and held it up, and Yakov handed over his. There were more shots from the car behind them as Malik re-loaded, and then began a new round of firing. Colling and Veronika were crouched low on either side of the Russian, and when he was hit, drops of his blood splattered over both of them. The big man gave a loud sigh and slumped down between them onto the floor.

Colling picked up the PPSh and took Malik's place. He was certain his shots were going home, but they seemed to have no effect on the vehicle behind them, which had come close enough several times so that he could make out the three-pointed star of a Mercedes hood ornament.

Hermann was screaming something over the blast of frigid air roaring through the shattered windows of the Audi, and it sounded to Colling as if he were saying something about armor-plating. As Colling squeezed off the last rounds from the submachine gun's magazine, it registered that the Mercedes behind them must have been one of the Nazi Party official's cars that were fitted with steel plates and bullet-proof glass.

Colling looked expectantly at Yakov, who was trying to staunch Malik's wound, and the Russian shook his head and said, "We left the extra ammunition in the truck. There is no more. Use this," before tugging a pistol from his holster and handing it to Colling.

The gunfire from the Mercedes was flying through the rear window of the Audi and out through its windshield. Hermann was twisting the steering wheel, so that the Audi was going from one side of the road to another, and he and Friedrich were half-crouched in their seats, reflexively bobbing their heads as the bullets whined by. Colling pushed Veronika down as far as he could, then snapped off two shots at the car behind them.

He knew it would only be minutes before they found their way blocked by Red Army or MVD troops that had been alerted by their pursuer. There was no chance that they could run a roadblock, and he toyed with the idea of using the pistol to shoot Veronika and then himself. He had seen what the MVD could do to those in its custody, and he was convinced that death was preferable.

Angry and frustrated, Colling grabbed both of the useless PPSh submachine guns, wrapping them together with their slings to make a larger missile, and tossed them out the window in one final act of defiance. He watched the guns bounce along the surface of the road, and under the Mercedes, ducking as more bullets whined around and through the Audi.

There was an abrupt change in the sounds coming from behind them, and Colling risked peering above the seat to see what was happening. The Mercedes had fallen back, and was skidding back and forth, seemingly out of control. Whoever was driving was having a difficult time controlling the vehicle, and seemed to be accelerating, rather than slowing. The car left the road and when its front wheel went over the edge of the pavement, it tipped sharply, then rolled over. To Colling it seemed as if the spiraling of the Mercedes went on for a long time. The only reason that Colling could think of that would have caused what he had just witnessed was that the guns he had thrown from the Audi had somehow gone under the other automobile, and damaged its steering or something else that caused it to spin out of control.

With the car no longer following them, Hermann slowed and suddenly turned left into a dirt track leading off the main road, where they bounced along for some time through what Colling guessed was a pasture. When a stand of trees loomed out of the darkness ahead of them, Hermann steered for it, and once hidden among the shadows, he switched off the lights and cut the engine. The only sound was Malik softly groaning. Colling asked Hermann if he had a flashlight. The garage owner responded that he did not, but offered a cigarette lighter.

By the flickering light, Colling did his best to examine Malik. The man was still conscious, which was a good sign, but he had lost blood, even though Yakov had managed to stop the worst of the flow. Friedrich stepped out of the Audi and removed his overcoat and jacket. He then took off his shirt and tore it so that it would readily fold into a compress. When Veronika saw what her brother was doing, she joined him and began to make strips out of the remains of his shirt which could be used to tie the pad in place.

Colling applied the makeshift bandage, and Malik insisted he wanted to leave the car. Colling tried to convince him that he might have internal injuries that would hemorrhage if he moved, but Malik replied that if he stayed where he was, the Bolsheviks would kill him anyway.

Colling asked Hermann how far they were from the American Sector.

"Twenty or twenty-five kilometers if we were to return to the city center," said Hermann.

"And if we do not return to the city center?" asked Colling.

Pointing to the west, Hermann said, "Another road lies there. There are houses, and the outskirts of the city begin. If we are willing to move between the houses, through people's gardens and over their fences, it is ten or fifteen kilometers. There are also drainage ditches and other obstacles, and we are sure to be seen. But the American Sector lies there."

It was 10:45, according to Hermann's wristwatch, and Colling estimated that they had about six to seven hours before the sun would start to come up. He decided that if they were going to move, it would be best to do so immediately. Telling everyone to gather their things, he asked Hermann to guide them, while he and Yakov took Malik's arms and held him between them.

Colling noticed that when Friedrich had donned his overcoat once more, he tore off his Soviet shoulder boards, and left the belt with his pistol holster on the ground where he had dropped it while removing his shirt. He did keep his Tokarev pistol, thrusting it into his outside coat pocket. Yakov noticed what Friedrich was doing, and did the same thing, afterwards discarding the belt holding his empty holster as well.

Colling followed suit, ripping the insignia from Malik's jacket and unbuckled the equipment belt from around the man's waist. When he had finished with Malik, Colling reached up to his own shoulders and pulled off his sergeant's shoulder boards. Like the others, he retained his Russian handgun.

Except for Veronika, who had only a blanket on which to rely, they all were wearing overcoats, but the heavy Russian wool could not completely keep out the penetrating cold. Even with the physical exertion involved in their flight, and in lifting Malik from the car, it seemed like only minutes before Colling began shivering, and felt his fingers going numb. Veronika was standing close beside him, her blanket held tightly around her, and Colling could imagine the misery she must be feeling. He took off his heavy coat and helped her into it, then wrapped her blanket around himself.

He wanted to do more for her, but he had to take turns with Yakov and Friedrich carrying Malik, and when Colling was replaced at the wounded Russian's side, he was too tired to do more than put his arm around Veronika to bring her some warmth, and support her so that she would not fall.

They followed Hermann westward, stumbling from time to time over the rough ground, until they reached the first row of cottages. There were no lights showing in any windows, but they crept by as quietly as possible. The first road was where Hermann had said it was, deserted and without traffic of any kind. They crossed and were among another row of houses like the first. More time went by as they traveled in this fashion. Sometimes they were able to follow streets heading in their direction, but just as frequently, they had to climb over backyard fences or push through hedges. They got soaked when they had to cross drainage ditches, and emerged cold and smelling bad.

Veronika lost her shoes while wading through one of the water courses, and Colling could do nothing but hold her close to him when he had the chance. There were some areas where it was obvious from the ruined houses and landscape that battles had been fought there during the Red Army's drive on the city, so that they had to pick their way across broken masonry and through old trenches and shell holes.

If they had been on a straight course, Colling would have thought that walking nearly nine miles, burdened as they were with a wounded man, would take three or four hours, but they had been traveling in a twisted path necessary to overcome the obstacles that they had encountered during the night, and Colling realized with dismay that it was likely to be daylight before they reached the American Sector. To further slow their progress, at about 0100, the first mists of ground fog began to appear, and became more dense as the last hours of the night went by. As their surroundings began to grow lighter with the dawn, they were engulfed in a heavy morning fog, limiting their visibility to no more than a few meters.

Colling was doing his best to keep moving, supporting Malik's weight, when he heard a whispered warning from Hermann that they should stop. A moment later, the German garage owner appeared out of the fog and informed them that there was another road ahead, and that it could be the one that marked the line between the Soviet and American Sectors. Colling had to force himself to ask Hermann how sure the man was that they had reached the demarcation line, and was disappointed when his response was that he could not be sure, and moreover, it would be foolish to try to continue on when there was no way to see where they were going.

Trying to find a positive side to things, Colling comforted himself with the idea that they were safe from being seen by any airplanes that the Soviets might send to find them. They had stopped in a place where the ground seemed to be relatively flat, and there was grass underfoot. At least Hermann had chosen a good place to rest, thought Colling.

Colling was exhausted, and nearly lost his grip on Malik when he and Yakov lowered the wounded Russian to the ground. Veronika dropped into a fetal position, pulling her bare feet under the overcoat that Colling had given her. Friedrich had been keeping his sister on her feet while Colling was with Malik, and he was stretched out beside her.

Colling fell face-down next to Malik, unable to move, conscious that Yakov was on Malik's other side. After waiting for a few minutes to regain some of his strength, Colling rolled over, hoping to crawl to Veronika's side. When he did so, he felt something in the small of his back, and heard a "click" that caused him to freeze.

He recalled being instructed in basic training that some models of landmines did not detonate until the firing switch was released, so that if one were to realize that he had stepped on a mine, and it did not explode, that it was best to continue to hold down the pressure plate until the mine could be disarmed. With this in mind, Colling whispered urgently across Malik, "Yakov, I think I just triggered a landmine."

There was a pause as the Russian seemed to be digesting what Colling had said, then he replied, "Why is it, Bill, that you think you have done this?"

"Don't move without checking around you to see if there's any by you," instructed Colling.

The exchange had roused Friedrich, and he sat up and asked in German what was happening. Colling told him, and saw from the corner of his eye that he was carefully searching in the grass next to him. Friedrich repeated Colling's warning to Veronika and Hermann, who also sat upright and surveyed the ground around them.

Hermann exclaimed, "*Mein Gott! Wir sind in Minenfeld!*" and started to rise to his feet.

"*Stillstehen!*" hissed Colling, "Don't move! You'll kill all of us!"

Friedrich seconded Colling's advice, then picked his way through the grass to Colling's side. An instant later, Veronika, obviously controlling her panic, said, "There is, I think, one of these next to me."

"Do not move, sweet sister," said Friedrich, "I will be there soon."

After sliding his hand under Colling, and then withdrawing it, Friedrich asked, "Has anyone a knife or bayonet?"

Colling heard the sound of a blade being withdrawn from a scabbard, and Yakov handed Friedrich a trench knife.

"Do not be alarmed," said Friedrich, "When I was captured by the Reds, they put me to clearing mines. I was either skillful or lucky, perhaps both, because I did that sort of work for a year, and I am still here."

"Can it be disarmed?" asked Colling.

Friedrich smiled as he began digging away the earth under Colling, "If not, my friend, it will all be over quickly."

A few minutes later, after scooping out many handfuls of dirt, Friedrich peered into the excavation and said, "Ach, not so bad. It is a *Wehrmacht* thing. Anti-tank. I have some familiarity with this one. Stay still, my friend. If you hear a loud noise, I will see you in heaven."

The German continued to remove soil from around the mine, and then began using the knife to work on the device. Colling could see sweat beading on the man's forehead, and Colling closed his eyes, silently praying.

"You may move now, but slowly," said Friedrich, and as Colling rolled to one side, Friedrich pulled the mine out. It was larger than Colling had expected, and he saw that Friedrich was holding the detonator down with his hand, before beginning to twist it. When it was free, he gingerly lifted it out, and unscrewed the primary charge. When they were separated, he released the switch, which clicked loudly. "So," said Friedrich, "There is one. Let us see what else we have."

A cautious search of their area that they had chosen to rest turned up four more mines, all large anti-tank types. Friedrich speculated that the field had been laid by *Volksturm* or Hitler Youth defenders, because two of the devices had not been properly armed before being buried.

The fog was beginning to dissipate, and Friedrich suggested that he would go first, searching the ground for more mines. He warned everyone to use extreme care in choosing where to put their feet. Hermann took over Friedrich's place at Malik's side, and with Colling supporting Veronika, they pushed slowly on.

At least an hour went by and it seemed to Colling that they had not moved more than a hundred meters. Visibility was rapidly improving, and Colling saw that there were ruined buildings all around them. The remains of a church loomed a few dozen meters to his left, and there were mounds of masonry on all sides.

They came to a trench that Colling guessed had been a defensive position covering the minefield. Friedrich had begun moving with less caution, and they quickly climbed past the earthworks and were walking rapidly across a grassy field when Colling spotted the fence.

It consisted of only five strands of plain wire set on wooden posts. Colling surmised that the demarcation line followed a street or other thoroughfare, because the barrier seemed to have been placed in its middle. A dirt track remained on either side; no doubt, thought Colling, to permit vehicle patrols.

The Russians had demolished houses on their side to create an open space that would discourage anyone who wanted to cross without being noticed. Colling looked in both directions and saw no guard towers. Apparently the Soviet government's construction of a stronger barrier to isolate its sector had been delayed.

Friedrich had brought them to a halt in a waist-high stand of grass where there was more cover, and Colling was able to observe that there were houses closer to the fence on its other side, but while some of them looked like they might be occupied, many were in ruins. Colling noticed a lazy stream of smoke rising from the chimney of one, and his stomach growled, causing him to remember that he had had nothing to eat for over twelve hours.

There seemed to be no one in sight, and Colling urged Veronika to the front of their little column, and after handing her over to Friedrich, said that he would now go first. He crept forward in a crouch, looking left and right, until he was on the verge of the road. When he was certain that they were alone, he returned to where the others were waiting and said, "Let's go. Before we're spotted."

It was relatively easy to climb through the fence, although they had to drag Malik under the bottom wire. Once on the other side, it looked like they had escaped, and were safely in the American Sector. It seemed too good to be true, and all that Colling could think about was why they had experienced no further pursuit. Had they gained time after the Mercedes crashed because its occupants had no way to signal ahead? Would not the Soviets have sent their own patrols to meet the Mercedes and cut off the Audi's retreat? Were the Russians still scouring the road, expecting them to try and reach the city center? Why was there no general alarm, and guards on every inch of the line where the American and Soviet Sectors met?

Colling could think of no answers to his questions, and he was too tired, too cold and his muscles were aching too much to effectively concentrate his mental processes. He was helping Hermann boost Malik to his feet between them when he heard Friedrich shout something, and saw a weapons carrier coming rapidly in their direction. A machine gun was mounted above its cab, and it was being aimed at them. Colling had a sinking feeling that the vehicle was actually a Red Army truck, and that they must have lost their way in the fog, and somehow were still in Soviet territory.

With his hand closed on the Russian pistol in his coat pocket, Colling caught Yakov's attention and warned him to arm himself. At this, Yakov reached into his own overcoat, but did not withdraw his hand, following Colling's lead in concealing the fact that he was prepared to open fire.

Friedrich was with Veronika, and the German had stopped in his tracks, holding his sister so close to him that her feet were actually off the ground. Colling was confident that if shooting were to start, that Friedrich would run for cover, carrying Veronika with him. Colling pulled the Tokarev partially out of his pocket, freeing it for use.

The carrier was slowing, and Colling began gauging how long he should wait before opening fire. He had decided to aim for the machine gunner, and hope that he could at least prevent the weapon from being fired, or distract the man sufficiently to spoil his aim.

The passenger side door opened, and a man in uniform stood

on the vehicle's running board, holding the open door in front of him and began shouting. Fortunately, he did so loudly.

"You! Yeah, I mean you! You Goddamned Russkies, stay right where you are!"

Colling had not expected the command to be in English, and he was momentarily confused, and had to check the urge to reflexively take out the pistol and start shooting. His hesitation permitted the truck to close the distance, so that he was able to see that the soldier doing the shouting was an American staff sergeant. Colling relaxed his grip on the gun and told Yakov not to shoot.

The sergeant's confusion was understandable, given that Colling and his companions were wearing Red Army dress. Before the weapons carrier had come to a full stop, Colling did some shouting of his own, "Hey! We're not Russians! Don't shoot!" while holding his arms high above his head. Colling glanced back to see that Yakov also had his hands raised, although Hermann and Friedrich were able only to put their free arms up.

The Americans were cautious, uncertain what to make of four men in Russian uniform, a German male civilian, and a girl with bloody feet wearing a Red Army overcoat. It took some minutes before Colling convinced them that they were refugees from the Soviet Sector. He knew he had succeeded when the gunner suddenly swung his .50 caliber so that it pointed over the wire. At the place where he was aiming, another vehicle had appeared, a deuce-and-a-half with red stars on its doors, which disgorged a squad of MVD troops that scattered out, taking up firing positions.

The driver of the weapons carrier had a microphone in his hand, urgently placing a radio call for assistance. The staff sergeant ordered Colling and the others to move so that the American truck was between them and the Russians. Friedrich pushed Veronika down behind one of its wheels, at the same time drawing his own pistol. Colling and Yakov were aiming their guns at the MVD detachment, and Colling had selected one of the men sprawled in the grass as his first target, once the firing started. Out of the corner of his eye, Colling was surprised to see Hermann crouched at the front of the weapons carrier, a Luger in his hand. The staff sergeant had retrieved a Thompson submachine gun from the vehicle's cab, and he noisily pulled back the slide, cocking the weapon.

It seemed like a long time went by before an MVD officer stood up, waving a white piece of cloth tied to a stick. He stopped close to the fence, as if waiting for someone to approach. When the staff sergeant stayed where he was, the man shouted, "You, American! Listen me! Deese peoples must come back to Soviet land! Dey are criminals. You send back, we not shoot."

The American staff sergeant propped his Tommy gun on his hip and shouted back, "These folks are in the American Sector. You shoot, we shoot," and cocking his thumb at the heavy machine gun, he continued, "And I got a bigger gun to shoot with. Now, why don't you all just move out, and we'll all go home. You first."

The MVD officer turned and walked back to where his men were hidden. He stood talking to someone on the ground in front of him before returning to the wire. He had almost reached the fence when they all heard the sound of more vehicles coming from the American Sector. As the M-8 armored car and two truckloads of troops came to a stop behind the weapons carrier, the MVD officer shouted an order, and his detachment left their positions and clambered into their truck.

Colling watched as the vehicle disappeared in a cloud of dust.

A lieutenant colonel was in command of the reinforcements. Colling repeated all that he had explained to the staff sergeant, and he was told to get his companions into the weapons carrier to be taken into the city. Colling requested that they go to the Signal Corps unit where Wilkins was located, as the most likely place where medical attention could be obtained for Malik. The Russian had not completely lost consciousness, but his head was lolling as he leaned against Yakov.

It took about thirty minutes to arrive at the Signal Corps barracks. As Colling and the others clambered out of the rear of the carrier and lifted Malik to the ground, the American soldiers coming and going from the headquarters building stopped and stared. A technical sergeant was the first to react, walking to where they were waiting and confronting the staff sergeant who had brought them. "Hey, Sarge, deese guys can't come here. This ain't no hospital. They got to go somewheres else," and then as he caught a whiff of the odor coming from the group, he exclaimed, "Jeez! Get them the hell out of here."

Colling stepped close to the man and said, "I'm an American, and I'm here to see Major Wilkins. I don't want to stink up the place too bad, so if you would, Sergeant, I'd appreciate it if you would go tell him I'm here. Tell him "J.C." has risen."

The technical sergeant's mouth gaped open, and then, seeing that he was having no impression on the crew of the weapons carrier, and noting Colling's expression, he turned and did as Colling had requested.

A few minutes later, Major Wilkins came striding out of the headquarters. He recognized Colling, in spite of the fact that he no longer was wearing glasses, and was clad in a filthy Red Army uniform. The major first thanked the men who had delivered Colling and his friends, and after dismissing them, he said, "I see you are indeed risen, J.C." He noticing Malik lying on the ground, and added, "Looks like you need a medic. Sergeant, call for an ambulance. We got a wounded man here."

Colling said, "Sir, we've been walking all night, and we know we're a mess. Is there any chance we can borrow a shower? And the lady will need some privacy, if possible."

"I can accommodate, J.C. We have WAC's quarters where she can freshen up."

Colling would not have characterized what was needed as "freshen up," but he declined to argue. Almost as if by magic, a pretty WAC corporal appeared and asked Veronika to follow her. As they walked away, Colling heard the WAC say, "Honey, what *have* you done with your shoes?"

Another NCO appeared to take Colling and the other men to clean up, but Colling asked to stay with Malik until the medics arrived. He did not have to wait long, and as the two medical corpsmen put the Russian on a stretcher and loaded him into the ambulance, Colling explained what had happened, and as much as he could about Malik's condition, adding that he was a medic himself.

The hot shower went beyond welcome, and Colling stayed under the spray for longer than usual after he had scrubbed himself. He came out of the stall to find the other four men already dressed in American khakis, and a pile of clothes waiting for his own use.

Hermann had telephoned Helga to tell her he was safe, saying that the flight from Amsterdam had been delayed because of the weather. When he hung up, the garage owner said to Colling, "It is rumored that the Reds listen in to all the American Army telephones."

CHAPTER 20

MARCH - MAY, 1948

Wilkins put everyone except Hermann and Malik on a C-47 out of Tempelhoff that afternoon. When Colling inquired, he was informed that the Russian had suffered a wound that would have killed anyone else. Surgery had been performed, and he was expected to have to recuperate for a few weeks, but full recovery was expected. Hermann had returned to his garage, and had accepted Wilkins' offer to have some discreet surveillance watching over him for a few weeks.

The plane took them to the Air Force terminal at Rhein-Main, where they were to lay over for a connecting flight to Heidelberg. While waiting, they learned that Quarles had arranged for civilian clothes to be brought to the air port, and they were able to change out of the borrowed khakis and into warmer attire. Veronika was pleased with the navy blue, light-weight woolen suit that Quarles had chosen for her, but she told Colling she was embarrassed that she had to wear it with the fluffy bedroom slippers that one of the WACs had loaned her. Colling informed her that she was still beautiful, whispering endearments into her ear that included some promises of what he was going to do to her when he could arrange for them to be alone, and to which she replied, "Oh, is that so?"

Quarles met them at a small air strip outside Heidelberg, and Colling, Veronika and her brother were driven to his headquarters in the University district. Another car picked up Yakov, and they all exchanged farewells. Colling was surprised to see the Russian's eyes welling with tears when he stepped away from the final bear hug Yakov gave him.

Colling and Friedrich were billeted in a small bachelor officers' quarters near Quarles' office. Colling questioned whether the lieutenants and captains living there would object to having a mere tech-four and a former German army NCO in their midst, but the lieutenant colonel replied that they would both be wearing civilian clothes, meaning no one would know who or what they were.

Veronika was to stay at an apartment occupied by one of Quarles' WAC officers. The place was big enough for the two women to share for a short period of time. Quarles did not want anyone knowing Veronika had returned to Heidelberg, and informed her that she would be transferred to his operation outside Munich, where she would be translating intercepted Russian transmissions. The villa where the facility was located was large enough that housing was provided on site, and she could have a small apartment of her own if she did not wish to live with her parents until she and Colling were married.

It took most of a morning for Colling to be debriefed. He provided as much information as he could, leaving out the details concerning anything that would compromise Hermann's business dealings. At the end, Colling told Quarles that he had informed Hermann that he would find some American cash in the lining of his bag, and that the garage owner could keep it in partial compensation for the loss of his Audi. Quarles replied that the payment was probably less than fair, and that his budget could stand it, although any further payment was out of the question.

Colling asked to be present when Friedrich was interrogated, but Quarles refused. After the session, Friedrich told Colling that Quarles was very interested in his Russian language skills, and hinted at an offer of employment. Friedrich said that he had declined with the excuse that he wanted nothing more than to go back to Munich and attempt to rebuild the family firm.

For the first time, Friedrich mentioned his wife and children, confiding in Colling that he had been told that they had perished in Dresden, and that he had to believe that if that were not true, that they would have found some way to rejoin his parents and Veronika in Munich. With Dresden in the Soviet Zone, there was no way that Friedrich could conduct a personal search for his family, but he was determined to seek help in learning their fate from whatever social agencies might be available.

Before they were taken to the airstrip for the flight to Munich, Quarles had Colling's tech-four uniform delivered to Colling's room in the BOQ. He wore it out the door, causing the orderly on duty to give him a quizzical look as he walked by the front desk.

The flight to Munich was more luxurious than what Colling was used to. The C-47 had been refurbished like a commercial air liner, with comfortable upholstered chairs instead of hard benches. There were no passengers other than the three of them, and Friedrich took a seat at the rear of the cabin. Colling and Veronika seated themselves a few rows away, and spent much of their time necking.

Friedrich wanted his arrival at 43 Kleberstrasse to be unannounced. Consequently, they asked that the taxi from the airport drop them on Nymphenburgerstrasse, and they walked to the house. When Annelise answered their knock at the front door, Veronika whispered to the maid that she remain quiet while the three of them slipped up the stairs to the elder Schönenbergs' room.

Friedrich's father and mother were so shocked at their son's sudden appearance that Colling feared that one or the other of them might collapse, and was relieved when it did not happen. Colling, the outsider, watched as tears were shed, and was embarrassed when he saw Friedrich fighting to keep from breaking down himself.

The bittersweet joy of the reunion was enhanced when *Frau* Schönenberg announced that packages addressed to Veronika had arrived from New York, sent by Max Biedermann. They had not been opened, and Veronika's mother brought the parcels out of a cupboard and everyone urged Veronika to see what was inside. Veronika instructed Colling to leave the room, in case one of the cartons contained a wedding dress, which he was forbidden to see before they were at the altar. Colling dutifully waited in the hall until Friedrich said it was permissible for him to return.

Colling learned that Veronika's guess about the wedding gown had been correct, but it had been replaced in its box, hidden from view. There was an assortment of other articles of clothing, many of which bore Saks Fifth Avenue labels. Veronika let Colling know that she was familiar with the famous New York store, and asked if he had ever purchased anything there. He replied that he preferred shopping at Saks' closest competitor, J.C. Penney.

Colling decided to take the streetcar to the 511th. He reported to the hospital administration office, where Sergeant Gayle asked him about his mother's condition. Colling assured him she was doing well, and went to his quarters to put on a white lab jacket before going to the dispensary.

Major Elliott also asked him about his mother, and Colling lied artfully, describing the various fractures that she had endured when his father's Buick had skidded on an icy highway. He ended his tale by saying how grateful he was to the orthopedists who brought about the near-perfect mending of his mother's bones. Major Elliott waited until he was finished, and then said, "You know, Jim, I sent a get-well card to your mom, and guess what? I got a letter back telling me I must have sent it to the wrong Mrs. Colling."

All Colling could do was grin sheepishly and say, "You got me, Major. Veronika and I went to Paris for three weeks. It's real cheap there, this time of year."

The nurse shook her head, a disgusted look on her face, "I should turn you in to the Colonel and let them pack you off to the stockade."

"Ma'am," said Colling, trying to appear duly chastised, "I'm very sorry about taking off, and if you were left in the lurch, I'll try and make it up to you by working my rear-end off. I'm sorry."

"I swear, Tech-four Colling, you are the most untrustworthy individual I've ever encountered, and also one of the most charming," said Major Elliott, unable to suppress a smile.

Colling decided to risk taking advantage of her good nature, and asked, "Ma'am, speaking of charming, how's Major Kinney?"

The question brought a wider smile to the nurse's face, and she held up her hand so that Colling could see the engagement ring that was on her finger.

"Congratulations, Major! When's the wedding?" said Colling.

"Couple of months, when Frank's tour is up. He's been accepted for a detective's spot with the Omaha police department, and I don't imagine I'll have much trouble finding a job with a doctor's office or a hospital."

Colling smiled, "I'll be sure to behave myself if I'm ever in Omaha."

"I hope you can control yourself long enough to come by and look us up after you're out of the Army," said the major, "And by the way, when's the big day for you and Veronika?"

"Middle of May," answered Colling, "Just before I ship home. I'm hoping we can sail together. If not, she'll fly and meet me in New York after I'm discharged. Eight June, '48, is the date, for which I wait."

"The Colonel talked to you about OCS? You'd make a fine pharmacy officer."

"No, Ma'am. Even if I wanted to make the Army my career, I'd have to finish college."

EPILOGUE

MARCH – MAY, 1948

Colonel Barrowsmith did give him a speech about officer's candidate school, and when Colling protested that he wanted to complete his pharmacy degree, Barrowsmith tried to convince him that he should enroll in ROTC at Wisconsin, or apply for a direct commission when he graduated. Colling decided it was best to say he would think about it. After the Colonel's talk, Master Sergeant Gayle called him in and gave him the obligatory lecture regarding re-enlistment, and the benefits of Army life. Colling gave the sergeant the same answer that he had given Colonel Barrowsmith.

The government paperwork necessary for Colling to marry Veronika was completed and sent on its way by March 15th, leaving Colling to worry that there would not be time enough for all the approvals to be final before the wedding, which had been scheduled for the eleven of May.

Veronika began working out of Quarles' Munich facility, and accepted his offer of housing at the villa. Her new apartment was larger than the one in Heidelberg, with a separate bedroom and a larger bath. She was engaged in translating transcripts of Soviet radio interceptions, and as she grew more comfortable with English, she began rendering the final versions into that language directly from Russian, rather than German. On an increasing number of occasions, she was asked to listen to voice transmissions, and simultaneously dictate the messages to a stenographer. When Veronika gave notice to Quarles that she would be terminating her employment, he accepted it, but indicated that she would be contacted once she had re-located to the States, with an offer to continue performing work for the Army.

Colling went by train to retrieve her car from Heidelberg, and drove by himself to Munich. With the *KdF Wagen* available to him for transportation, Colling began spending all his free time with Veronika, frequently spending the night in her quarters. He was apprehensive at first that Quarles would raise objections to the arrangement, but nothing was said, and the other staff members living at the villa gave no indication that there was anything amiss with Colling's frequent overnight stays.

Major Elliott asked Veronika to serve as her maid of honor at her marriage to Major Kinney, and Colonel and Mrs. Barrowsmith insisted that the wedding reception be held at the Schönenberg house. The guest list included all the officers from the 511th, and a few of the enlisted men, and Kinney invited more than two dozen Constabulary officers and NCO's. The proceedings were properly sedate while conducted at the Kleberstrasse address, but later in the evening, when the celebration migrated to a dance hall near the *Hauptbahnhof,* things became decidedly raucous. Colling followed the crowd, promising Veronika he would limit himself to one beer, and then come back to drive her to her apartment. He kept his promise about imbibing, but had to almost physically extricate himself from the others in order to leave.

Major Elliott was replaced by a younger nurse-lieutenant by the name of Jane Maldron. She lacked the major's experience, as well as her medical insight and intuition. She tended to refer most of their sick call cases to the casualty ward, and Colling found his work less challenging and less interesting. He consoled himself that he had only a few weeks left in his tour, and decided he could easily tolerate almost anything for that period of time.

The approvals for Colling's marriage to Veronika all came through at the end of April. The banns had been published, and Colling was feeling a mixture of trepidation and anticipation about the future as he walked back to the outpatient dispensary from lunch, four days before the day of his wedding. Lieutenant Maldron had decided to use the afternoon to play golf with another nurse and two of the hospital physicians, and while Colling liked being on his own for the rest of the day, he was not pleased about having to finish up the nurse's share of the morning's paperwork.

Colling was surprised to find the clinic unlocked, as he remembered locking the door behind him when he left for the mess hall. He cautiously pushed the door open, not sure what to expect. The woman leafing through the papers on the clinic's desk had her back turned to him. She was wearing a stylish navy suit, set off by a smart matching pillbox hat and white gloves. Her blonde hair was pinned up, but he knew who she was before she turned to face him.

"Hi, Jim. Remember me?" said Elizabeth Hamilton, smiling brightly.